SADLIER

VOCABULARY WORKSHOP®

ACHIEVE

Level F

Jerome Shostak

Senior Series Consultant

Vicki A. Jacobs, Ed.D.
Director, Teacher Education Program
Harvard Graduate School of Education
Cambridge, Massachusetts

Series Consultants

Louis P. De Angelo, Ed.D.
Superintendent of Schools
Diocese of Wilmington
Wilmington, Delaware

John Heath, Ph.D.
Professor of Classics
Santa Clara University
Santa Clara, California

**Sarah Ressler Wright,
  M.A. English Ed, NBCT**
Head Librarian
Rutherford B. Hayes High School
Delaware, Ohio

Carolyn E. Waters, J.D., Ed.S.
Georgia Dept. of Education (Ret.)
English Language Arts Consultant
Woodstock, Georgia

Reviewers

The publisher wishes to thank for their comments and suggestions the following teachers and administrators, who read portions of the series prior to publication.

Cover: Concept/Art and Design: MK Advertising, Studio Montage and William H. Sadlier, Inc. Cover pencil: Shutterstock.com/VikaSuh.
Photo Credits: age fotostock/Aleruaro: 213 *top*. akg-images/IAM: 57 *top*. Alamy Stock Photo/Nikreates: 40; David Cole: 220; Jiri Hubatka: 160; B. O'Kane: 148; Stuart Pearce: 84; Chris Pearsall: 57 *bottom right*; Michael Schmeling: 213 *bottom right*; A.F. Archive: 64; Arco Images GmbH/Michael Therin-Weise: 212; Asia Photopress: 157 *top*; ClassicStock: 157 *bottom*; Danita Delimont: 145 *bottom*; DC Premiumstock: 81 *top*; epa european pressphoto agency b.v./Stefan Zaklin: 172; Global Warming Images: 144; Lebrecht Music and Arts Photo Library: 28; Mary Evans Picture Library: 72; Pictorial Press Ltd: 116; robertharding/John Ross: 204; VikingIllustrations: 16; World History Archive: 56; ZUMA Press, Inc.: 76. Ansel Adams Publishing Rights Trust/Ansel Adams: 188. The Art Archive/Chopin Foundation Warsaw/Collection Dagli Orti: 124 *top*; Hans Christian Andersen Birthplace Odense Denmark/Collection Dagli Orti: 125. Art Resource, NY: 152; Werner Forman: 156 *top*; Archaeological Museum, Pireus/Marie Mauzy: 120; Scala: 80 *bottom*. Associated Press/Fabian Bimmer: 68 *bottom*. Bridgeman Images/Portait of a soldier from the 8th NY Heavy Artillery (b/w photo), American Photographer, (19th century)/Private Collection/Photo © Civil War Archive: 12 *right*; Calculating Machine Known as 'The Difference Engine' from 'Cyclopaedia of Useful Arts & Manufactures', edited by Charles Tomlinson, c.1880s (engraving), English School, (19th century)/Private Collection/Ken Welsh: 57 *bottom left*; Centennial Commemoration at Philadelphia, 1876 (colour woodcut), American School, (19th century)/Private Collection/Courtesy of Swann Auction Galleries: 60. Courtesy of The Barnum Museum, Bridgeport, Connecticut: 124 *bottom*. CSA Images: 68 *background*. Digital Stock: 144 *background*, 188 *background*. Digital Vision: 80 *background*. Everett Collection: 196, 208. The Granger Collection: 13 *bottom*, 25 *center*, 25 *bottom right*, 201 *bottom*. Getty Images/Bettmann: 13 *top*, 88, 101 *top*, 132, 176, 189, 216; Gamma-Keystone: 36 *right*; Hulton Deutsch: 12 *left*; Jupiterimages: 80 *top*; Lambert: 128; Library of Congress/London Stereoscopic Company: 101 *bottom*; National Geographic/Louis S. Glanzman: 108; New York Daily News: 37 *bottom*; Universal History archive: 104; Michael Ute Utech: 169 *left*; Phil Walter: 145 *top* WireImage/Jim Spellman: 32. Christophe Gin: 213 *bottom left*. The Image Works, Inc./Daemmrich Photography/Marjorie Kamys Cotera: 24. iStockphoto.com/monkeybusinessimages: 10. LACMA/Bicentennial gift of Mr. and Mrs. J. M. Schaaf, Mr. and Mrs. William D. Witherspoon, Mr. and Mrs. Charles C. Shoemaker, and Jo Ann and Julian Ganz, Jr.: 201 *top*. musicals101.com: 36 *left*. New York Public Library Picture Collection/Print Collection, Miriam and Ira D. Wallach Division of Art, Prints and Photographs: 200. Panos Pictures/G.M.B. Akash: 68 *top*, 69. Photodisc: 36 *background*, 124 *top*, 168 *background*, 200 *inset*, 201 *inset*. PhotoEdit/Jeff Greenberg: 25 *top left*. Shutterstock.com/BuketGvozdey: 124 *background*; Olena Zaskochenko: 12 *background*; Rex/CCI/The Art Archive: 164; Rex/Everett/Paramount: 20; Rex/The Art Archive: 168; Rex/The Picture Archive/Kobal: 169 *right*; Rex/Warner Brothers: 44. Todd-Bingham Picture Collection, Manuscripts and Archives, Yale University: 192. Wikimedia Commons/Amon Carter Museum, Fort Worth/Billy Hathorn: 156 *bottom*. Wikipedia: 37 *top*,100.

Illustration Credits: Sholto Walker: 112, 113.

S® and **VOCABULARY WORKSHOP**® are registered trademarks of William H. Sadlier, Inc.

Printed in the United States of America.
ISBN: 978-1-4217-8511-0
4 5 6 7 8 9 10 BRR 24 23 22 21 20

For additional online resources, go to SadlierConnect.com.

CONTENTS

iWords Audio Program is available at **SadlierConnect.com**.

PROGRAM FEATURES

For more than five decades, VOCABULARY WORKSHOP has proven to be a highly successful tool for vocabulary growth and the development of vocabulary skills. It has also been shown to help students prepare for standardized tests. VOCABULARY WORKSHOP ACHIEVE maintains that tradition in a newly designed format.

Each of VOCABULARY WORKSHOP ACHIEVE's 15 Units introduces 20 words in two 10-word lists—**Set A** and **Set B**. Both Set A and Set B contain exercises to help you develop deeper understanding of the 10 words in each set. Combined Sets A and B then provide practice with all 20 of the words in the Unit. Review and Word Study activities follow Units 3, 6, 9, 12, and 15 and offer practice with the 60 vocabulary words in the preceding three Units.

Each level of VOCABULARY WORKSHOP ACHIEVE introduces and provides practice with 300 vocabulary words and contains features such as reading passages, writing prompts, vocabulary in context, evidence-based questions, and word study that will help you to master these new vocabulary words and succeed in using skills to comprehend unfamiliar words.

Each Unit in VOCABULARY WORKSHOP ACHIEVE consists of the following sections for **Set A** and **Set B**: an introductory **Reading Passage** that shows how vocabulary words are used in context, **Definitions** that include sentences that give examples of how to use the words, **Using Context, Choosing the Right Word**, and **Completing the Sentence**—activities that provide practice with the vocabulary words. Each introductory **Reading Passage** is a nonfiction text that includes most of the vocabulary words from the Unit to which it belongs. In addition, **Synonyms**, **Antonyms**, and **Vocabulary in Context** in combined Sets A and B round out each Unit with practice with all 20 Unit words.

The five Review sections cover all 60 words from their corresponding Units. **Vocabulary for Comprehension** is modeled on the reading sections of college entrance exams. It presents reading comprehension questions, including vocabulary-related items and evidence-based items that are based on the reading passages.

Word Study sections that contain activities on **Idioms**, **Denotation and Connotation**, and **Classical Roots** follow the Review. These sections will help you develop your understanding of figurative language and practice skills that will help you to determine the meaning of new and unfamiliar vocabulary.

The Final Mastery Test assesses a selection of words from the year and allows you to see the growth you have made in acquiring new vocabulary words and in mastering the comprehension skills you need to understand unfamiliar words.

ONLINE RESOURCES

SadlierConnect.com

Go to **SadlierConnect.com** to find iWords, an audio program that provides pronunciations, definitions, and examples of usage for all of the vocabulary words presented in this level of VOCABULARY WORKSHOP ACHIEVE. You can listen to the entire **Reading Passage** and the 20 Unit vocabulary words one word at a time, or download all of the words in any given Unit.

At **SadlierConnect.com** you will also find interactive vocabulary quizzes, flash cards, and interactive games and puzzles that will help reinforce and enrich your understanding of the vocabulary words in this level of VOCABULARY WORKSHOP ACHIEVE.

VOCABULARY IN CONTEXT

The context of a word is the printed text of which that word is part. By studying a word's context, we may find clues to its meaning. We might find a clue in the immediate or adjoining sentence or phrase in which the word appears; in the topic or subject matter of the passage; or in the physical features—such as photographs, illustrations, charts, graphs, captions, and headings—of a page itself.

The **Reading Passages** as well as the **Using Context**, **Choosing the Right Word**, **Vocabulary in Context**, and **Vocabulary for Comprehension** exercises that appear in the Units, the Reviews, and the Final Mastery Test provide practice in using context to decode and to determine the meaning of unfamiliar words.

Three types of context clues appear in the exercises in this book.

A **restatement clue** consists of a synonym for or a definition of the missing word. For example:

> Faithfully reading a weekly newsmagazine not only broadens my knowledge of current events and world or national affairs but also _____ my vocabulary.
>
> **a.** decreases   **b.** fragments   **c.** increases   **d.** contains

In this sentence, *broadens* is a synonym of the missing word, *increases*, and acts as a restatement clue for it.

A **contrast clue** consists of an antonym for or a phase that means the opposite of the missing word. For example:

> "My view of the situation may be far too rosy," I admitted. "On the other hand, yours may be a bit (**optimistic, bleak**)."

In this sentence, *rosy* is an antonym of the missing word, *bleak*. This is confirmed by the presence of the phrase *on the other hand*, which indicates that the answer must be the opposite of *rosy*.

An **inference clue** implies but does not directly state the meaning of the missing word or words. For example:

> "A treat for all ages," the review read, "this wonderful novel combines the _____ of a scholar with the skill and artistry of an expert _____."
>
> **a.** ignorance . . . painter   **c.** wealth . . . surgeon
>
> **b.** wisdom . . . beginner   **d.** knowledge . . . storyteller

In this sentence, there are several inference clues: (a) the word *scholar* suggests knowledge; (b) the words *novel*, *artistry*, and *skill* suggest the word *storyteller*. These words are inference clues because they suggest or imply, but do not directly state, the missing word or words.

VOCABULARY AND READING

There is a strong connection between vocabulary knowledge and reading comprehension. Although comprehension is much more than recognizing words and knowing their meanings, comprehension is nearly impossible if you do not know an adequate number of words in the text you are reading or have the vocabulary skills to figure out their meaning.

The **Reading Passages** in this level provide extra practice with vocabulary words. Vocabulary words are in boldface to draw your attention to their uses and contexts. Context clues embedded in the passages encourage you to figure out the meanings of words before you read the definitions provided on the pages directly following the passages.

Test Prep

Your knowledge of word meanings and your ability to think carefully about what you read will help you succeed in school and on standardized tests, including the SAT® and ACT® exams.

The **Vocabulary for Comprehension** exercises in each Review consist of a reading passage followed by comprehension questions. The passages and questions are similar to those that you are likely to find on standardized tests.

Types of Questions

You are likely to encounter the following types of questions in VOCABULARY WORKSHOP ACHIEVE and on standardized tests.

Main Idea Questions generally ask what the passage as a whole is about. Often, but not always, the main idea is stated in the first paragraph of the passage. You may also be asked the main idea of a specific paragraph. Questions about the main idea may begin like this:

- The primary or main purpose of the passage is . . .

- The author's primary or main purpose in the passage is to . . .

- Which of the following statements most nearly paraphrases the author's main idea in the ninth paragraph (lines 77–88)?

- The main purpose of the fourth paragraph (lines 16–25) is to . . .

Detail Questions focus on important information that is explicitly stated in the passage. Often, however, the correct answer choices do not use the exact language of the passage. They are instead restatements, or paraphrases, of the text.

Vocabulary in Context Questions check your ability to use context to identify a word's meaning. For example:

- As it is used in paragraph 2, "adherents" most nearly means . . .

Use the word's context in a passage to select the best answer, particularly when the vocabulary word has more than one meaning. The answer choices may contain two (or more) correct meanings of the word in question. Choose the meaning that best fits the context.

Inference Questions ask you to make inferences or draw conclusions from the passage. These questions often begin like this:

- It can be most reasonably inferred from the information in the fifth paragraph (lines 53–69) that . . .
- The passage clearly implies that . . .

The inferences you make and the conclusions you draw must be based on the information in the passage. Using the facts you learn from the passage in addition to the knowledge and reasoning you already have helps you understand what is implied and reach conclusions that are logical.

Evidence-Based Questions ask you to provide evidence from the passage that will support the answer you provided to a previous question. These questions often begin like this:

- Which choice provides the best evidence for the answer to the previous question?
- Which statement is the best evidence for the answer to the previous question?

Questions About Tone show your understanding of the author's attitude toward the topic of the passage. To determine the tone, pay attention to the author's word choice. The author's attitude may be positive (respectful), negative (scornful), or neutral (distant). These are typical questions:

- The author's primary purpose in the passage is to . . .
- Which word best describes the author's tone?

Questions About Author's Technique focus on the way a text is organized and the language the author uses. These questions ask you to think about structure and function. For example:

- In the context of the passage, the primary function of the fourth paragraph (lines 30–37) is to . . .
- The organizational structure of the passage is best described as . . .

To answer the questions, you must demonstrate an understanding of the way the author presents information and develops ideas.

VOCABULARY AND WRITING

The **Writing: Words in Action** prompt provides you with an opportunity to practice using text evidence to respond to a prompt about the introductory **Reading Passage**. You will have the opportunity to demonstrate your understanding of the Unit words by incorporating the new vocabulary you have learned into your own writing.

WORD STUDY

Word Study helps build word knowledge with strategies to help you look closely at words for meanings. Word Study instruction and practice include **Idioms**, **Denotation and Connotation**, and **Classical Roots**.

Idioms

Three Word Study sections feature instruction on and practice with idioms. An idiom is an informal expression whose literal meaning does not help the reader or listener understand what the expression means, such as "raining cats and dogs," "the apple of my eye," or "a dark horse." While every language has its own idioms, English is particularly rich in idioms and idiomatic expressions. Developing a clear understanding of idioms will help you better understand the figurative language that authors use in their writing.

Denotation and Connotation

Instruction in **Denotation and Connotation** and practice with connotations is included in two of the Word Study sections. Understanding a word's connotation will develop your skills as a reader, writer, and speaker.

Understanding the difference between denotation and connotation is important to understanding definitions and how concepts are used, as well as in choosing the right word. In these exercises, practice choosing the correct word by determining the emotional association of the word.

Classical Roots

Each Word Study includes a **Classical Roots** exercise that provides instruction in and practice with Greek and Latin roots. Developing a useful, transferable technique to make sense out of unfamiliar words through Greek and Latin roots will help you unlock the meanings of thousands of words. An example word drawn from the vocabulary words in the previous Units is referenced at the top of the page and serves as a guide to help you complete the exercise.

PRONUNCIATION KEY

The pronunciation is indicated for every basic word in this book. The pronunciation symbols used are similar to those used in most recent standard dictionaries. The author has primarily consulted *Webster's Third New International Dictionary* and *The Random House Dictionary of the English Language* (*Unabridged*). Many English words have multiple accepted pronunciations. The author has given one pronunciation when such words occur in this book except when the pronunciation changes according to the part of speech. For example, the verb *project* is pronounced **prə jekt'**, and the noun form is pronounced **präj' ekt**.

Vowels	ā	lake	e	stress	u̇	loot, new
	a	mat	ī	knife	u̇	foot, pull
	â	care	i	sit	ə	jump, broken
	ä	bark, bottle	ō	flow	ər	bird, better
	au̇	doubt	ô	all, cord		
	ē	beat, wordy	oi	oil		

Consonants	ch	child, lecture	s	cellar	wh	what
	g	give	sh	shun	y	yearn
	j	gentle, bridge	th	thank	z	is
	ŋ	sing	t̶h̶	those	zh	measure

All other consonants are sounded as in the alphabet.

Stress   The accent mark follows the syllable receiving the major stress: en rich'.

Abbreviations	*adj.*	adjective	*n.*	noun	*prep.*	preposition
	adv.	adverb	*part.*	participle	*v.*	verb
	int.	interjection	*pl.*	plural		

*Read the following passage, taking note of the **boldface** words and their contexts. These words are among those you will be studying in Unit 1. It may help you to complete the exercises in this Unit if you refer to the way the words are used below.*

The Camera in Wartime
<Textbook Entry>

When crowds gathered at photographer Mathew Brady's New York City studio in late 1862 to gaze at the first images of the Civil War (1861–1865), they became the first witnesses to distant battles. The exhibition did nothing to **assuage** the public's fears about the conflict. Instead, the gruesome, even **lurid**, views of battlefield corpses **elicited** terror and sadness. Photography had brought home the terrible reality of war.

Early Photography

Invented in 1839, the camera played only a minor role in the Mexican-American War (1846–1848) and the Crimean War (1853–1856). Early photographs, called daguerreotypes, were difficult to make; a single exposure took up to 30 minutes and yielded only one low-quality image.

During the **hiatus** between those wars and the American Civil War, photography **transcended** its early limitations. With the new wet plate process, exposures could be made in just a few seconds, and a photographer could mass-produce prints from a single negative. That advance made photography practical—and profitable—and when the Civil War began, a **coalition** of photographers fanned out to cover the action.

Civil War Photography

Most Civil War photographers produced images of individual soldiers. Almost every soldier wanted photos of himself in uniform to send to family and friends. Today, their faces stare out at the viewer from across the centuries: the wide-eyed teen, not yet tested under fire; the **jaded** sergeant, worn-out from the horrors

Civil War portrait of a soldier from the 8th New York Heavy Artillery

Mathew Brady's photographic buggy, circa 1863

he has witnessed; the **unctuous** junior officer, trying hard to appear sincere.

Photography quickly gained the **approbation** of military leaders. Art imitates life, after all, so when officials needed photos of bridges, terrain, and armaments to plan their attacks, a skillful photographer became a valuable asset. Photos of surgical procedures were distributed as well, showing doctors new techniques that saved lives in **provincial** field hospitals.

Few Civil War photographs show a battle in progress; action shots were not yet generally possible. Once the fighting was over, however, it was the photographer's **prerogative** to rush in and record the aftermath. Such graphic results tended to highlight the grim toll of the war, and many people eventually took **umbrage** at this emphasis. The courage of the soldiers was moving, but the unrelenting carnage was difficult to view.

Marines land on the coast of Normandy the day after D-Day: June 7, 1944.

Mathew Brady and Alexander Gardner

A few Civil War photographers should be singled out for their **meritorious** efforts. Mathew Brady (1823–1896) took thousands of photographs of wartime leaders and battle scenes, and his images continue to help historians better understand the Civil War era. Inspired to document the entire war, Brady conducted his photographic work at his own expense. When federal officials refused to buy his prints, Brady **expostulated** with them to no avail, and he died penniless.

Alexander Gardner (1821–1882) was Brady's assistant in Washington, D.C. When the Civil War began, Gardner successfully **interceded** with President Lincoln, getting him to allow photographers to accompany the army.

Gardner himself traveled with Union forces to photograph the battles at Antietam, Gettysburg, and Petersburg. Never **hackneyed** or dull, Gardner's images offered fresh insights into the reality of modern warfare.

Photography in Later Years

In contrast to Civil War photography, the photographic records of the Spanish-American War (1898) and World War I (1914–1918) are relatively limited. Beginning with World War II (1939–1945), however, combat photographers consistently traveled with the troops, risking their lives to capture wartime events. In addition to clarifying the details of every battle, war photographs have depicted the harsh realities endured by ordinary soldiers and helped build support for the war effort on the home front.

Audio

For iWords)) and audio passages, go to SadlierConnect.com.

W. Eugene Smith (1918–1978), American WWII photographer, on the island of Okinawa, 1945

Definitions

Note the spelling, pronunciation, part(s) of speech, and definition(s) of each of the following words. Then write the appropriate form of the word in the blank space in the illustrative sentence(s) following.

1. approbation
(ap rə bā' shən)

(n.) the expression of approval or favorable opinion, praise

My hint that I had paid for the lessons myself brought smiles of _approbation_ from the judges at the recital.

2. coalition
(kō ə lish' ən)

(n.) a combination, union, or merger for some specific purpose

The various community organizations formed a _coalition_ to lobby against parking laws.

3. elicit
(ē lis' it)

(v.) to draw forth, bring out from some source

My attempt to _elicit_ information over the phone was met with a barrage of irrelevant recordings.

4. hackneyed
(hak' nēd)

(adj.) used so often as to lack freshness or originality

The Great Gatsby tells a universal story without being marred by _hackneyed_ prose.

5. innuendo
(in yü en' dō)

(n.) a hint, indirect suggestion, or reference (often derogatory)

Those lacking the facts or afraid of reprisals often tarnish an enemy's reputation by use of _innuendo_ .

6. intercede
(in tər sēd')

(v.) to plead on behalf of someone else; to serve as a third party or go-between in a disagreement

She will _intercede_ in the dispute between the two children, and soon they will be playing happily again.

7. meritorious
(mer i tôr' ē əs)

(adj.) worthy, deserving recognition and praise

He was honored by the committee after thirty years of _meritorious_ service.

8. provincial
(prə vin' shəl)

(adj.) pertaining to an outlying area; local; narrow in mind or outlook; countrified in the sense of being limited and backward; of a simple, plain design that originated in the countryside; (n.) a person with a narrow point of view; a person from an outlying area; a soldier from a province or colony

The banjo, once thought to be a _provincial_ product of the Southern hills, actually came here from Africa.
At first, a _provincial_ may do well in the city using charm alone, but charm, like novelty, wears thin.

9. **transcend**
(tran send′)

(*v.*) to rise above or beyond, exceed
A great work of art may be said to *trandscend*
time, and it is remembered for decades, or even centuries.

10. **unctuous**
(əŋk′ chü əs)

(*adj.*) excessively smooth or smug; trying too hard to give an impression of earnestness, sincerity, or piety; fatty, oily; pliable
Her constant inquiring about the health of my family at first seemed friendly, later merely *Unctuous*.

Using Context

*For each item, determine whether the **boldface** word from pages 14–15 makes sense in the context of the sentence. Circle the item numbers next to the six sentences in which the words are used correctly.*

1. He is so **provincial** that he welcomes today's trends in style and fashion.

2. Although the job applicant never once mentioned the other candidate for the position, she made an **innuendo** about his lack of experience.

3. Some of the local business owners are forming a **coalition** to create a campaign encouraging residents to shop locally.

4. Some think that the story of star-crossed lovers is a **hackneyed** plot in movies, but I enjoy seeing different directors' adaptations of it.

5. My teacher issued me an **approbation** when I arrived late to class, saying that another tardy would result in a detention.

6. Even though I had studied hard, I found myself becoming **unctuous** and nervous as the tests were handed out.

7. We were enjoying a pleasant walk down the street when a panhandler tried to **intercede** in our conversation and asked us for money.

8. She is such a perfectionist that even when she earns an A, she doesn't consider it a **meritorious** achievement but rather exactly what is expected of her.

9. I like to study artists that **transcend** cultural norms in their work and open my eyes to new points of view.

10. The national anthem can **elicit** strong emotions of pride and patriotism in some citizens.

Choosing the Right Word

*Select the **boldface** word that better completes each sentence. You might refer to the passage on pages 12–13 to see how most of these words are used in context. Note that the choices might be related forms of the Unit words.*

1. The American two-party system almost always makes it unnecessary to form a (**provincial, coalition**) of minority parties to carry on the government.

2. How can you accuse me of employing (**approbation, innuendo**) when I am saying in the plainest possible language that I think you're a crook?

3. Apparently mistaking us for the millionaire's children, the hotel manager overwhelmed us with her (**hackneyed, unctuous**) attentions.

4. Popularity polls seem to be based on the mistaken idea that the basic task of a political leader is to win immediate (**approbation, coalition**) from the people.

5. My teacher can (**transcend, elicit**) some degree of interest and attention from even the most withdrawn children.

6. His skillful use of academic jargon and fashionable catchphrases could not conceal the essentially (**hackneyed, meritorious**) quality of his ideas.

7. The magnificence of the scene far (**interceded, transcended**) my ability to describe it in words.

8. We cannot know today what sort of accent Abraham Lincoln had, but it may well be that there was a decidedly (**meritorious, provincial**) twang to his speech.

9. If you try to (**elicit, intercede**) in a friends' quarrel, you will only make things worse.

10. The defense attorney quickly realized that the witness's statement was filled with (**innuendo, coalition**), not facts.

11. The most (**meritorious, unctuous**) form of charity, according to the ancient Hebrew sages, is to help a poor person to become self-supporting.

12. Are the townspeople so (**provincial, hackneyed**) in their thinking that they will object to having the first traffic light installed at this dangerous intersection?

Completing the Sentence

Choose the word from the word bank that best completes each of the following sentences. Write the correct word or form of the word in the space provided.

~~approbation~~   ~~elicit~~   ~~innuendo~~   ~~meritorious~~   ~~transcend~~
~~coalition~~   ~~hackneyed~~   ~~intercede~~   ~~provincial~~   unctuous

1. If you take pride in expressing yourself with force and originality, you should not use so many _hackneyed_ phrases.

2. If you cannot meet the college's entrance requirements, it will be futile to have someone _intercede_ on your behalf.

3. His confidence grew as he received clear signs of the _approbation_ of his superiors.

4. In the question-and-answer session, we tried to _elicit_ from the candidates some definite indication of how they proposed to reduce the national debt.

5. The manager expressed her unfavorable opinion of the job applicant by _innuendo_ rather than by direct statement.

6. In an age when the United States has truly global responsibilities, we cannot afford to have leaders with _provincial_ points of view.

7. The only way to defeat the party in power is for all the reform groups to form a(n) _coalition_ and back a single slate of candidates.

8. The issue of good faith that your conduct raises far _unctuous_ the specific question of whether or not you are responsible for the problem.

9. Forever humbling himself and flattering others, Dickens's Uriah Heep is famously _meritorius_.

10. I certainly appreciate your praise, but I must say that I can see nothing so remarkably _transend_ in having done what any decent person would do.

Definitions

Note the spelling, pronunciation, part(s) of speech, and definition(s) of each of the following words. Then write the appropriate form of the word in the blank space in the illustrative sentence(s) following.

✳ **1. assuage**
(ə swāj′)

(*v.*) to make easier or milder, relieve; to quiet, calm; to put an end to, appease, satisfy, quench

Her eyes told me that more than a few words would be needed to *assuage* her hurt feelings.

✝ **2. decadence**
(de′ kə dəns)

(*n.*) decline, decay, or deterioration; a condition or period of decline or decay; excessive self-indulgence

Some viewed her love of chocolate as *decadence* because she ate two bars a day.

✳ **3. expostulate**
(ik späs′ chə lāt)

(*v.*) to attempt to dissuade someone from some course or decision by earnest reasoning

Hamlet finds it useless to *expostulate* with his mother for siding with his stepfather.

---

4. hiatus
(hī ā′ təs)

(*n.*) a gap, opening, break (in the sense of having an element missing)

I was awakened not by a sudden sound but by a *hiatus* in the din of traffic.

● **5. jaded**
(jā′ did)

(*adj.*) wearied, worn-out, dulled

The wilted handclasp and the fast-melting smile mark the *jaded* refugee from too many parties.

— **6. lurid**
(lür′ əd)

(*adj.*) causing shock, horror, or revulsion; sensational; pale or sallow in color; terrible or passionate in intensity or lack of restraint

Sensational often *lurid*, some old-time movie posters make today's newspaper ads look tame.

✳ **7. petulant**
(pech′ ə lənt)

(*adj.*) peevish, annoyed by trifles, easily irritated and upset

An overworked parent may be unlikely to indulge the complaints of a *petulant* child.

— **8. prerogative**
(prē räg′ ə tiv)

(*n.*) a special right or privilege; a special quality showing excellence

She seemed to feel that a snooze at her desk was not an annoying habit but the *prerogative* of a veteran employee.

---

9. **simulate**
(sim′ yə lāt)

(*v.*) to make a pretense of, imitate; to show the outer signs of
Some skilled actors can ___*simulate*___ emotions they might never have felt in life.

10. **umbrage**
(em′ brəj)

(*n.*) shade cast by trees; foliage giving shade; an overshadowing influence or power; offense, resentment; a vague suspicion
She hesitated to offer her opinion, fearing that they would take ___*umbrage*___ at her criticism.

Using Context

*For each item, determine whether the **boldface** word from pages 18–19 makes sense in the context of the sentence. Circle the item numbers next to the six sentences in which the words are used correctly.*

(1.) While on vacation, I thought I was justified in treating myself, but now I see a week of excessive eating and lack of exercise as unnecessary **decadence**.

(2.) As president of the debate team, I have the **prerogative** to accept or reject any applicant.

(3.) When it is dark out during the winter, it may be useful to have lamps that **simulate** sunlight to help you wake up naturally in the morning.

(4.) I have traveled so much over the past year that, rather than being thrilled by the prospect of seeing new places, I am simply **jaded** from all of the logistics involved.

5. Although he was happy to have won the award, he reacted with such **umbrage** when his name was called that his cheeks reddened and he tried to hide his face as he walked up to the stage.

(6.) The singer decided to take a **hiatus** from touring for a few months to rest her voice and spend more time with her family.

7. The valedictorian plans to **expostulate** about her hopes and dreams for the future of the graduating class during her speech.

8. The customer services representative was known for her ability to **assuage** even the angriest clients.

9. The **lurid** aroma of whatever my mother was cooking for breakfast roused me from a deep sleep and beckoned me to the kitchen.

(10.) Her **petulant** demeanor is incredibly refreshing in a world where people are so fast-paced that they rarely ever stop to say hello.

Choosing the Right Word

*Select the **boldface** word that better completes each sentence. You might refer to the passage on pages 12–13 to see how most of these words are used in context. Note that the choices might be related forms of the Unit words.*

1. I enjoy science-fiction movies, as they provide a short but exciting (**umbrage, hiatus**) from the problems of everyday life.

2. Perhaps it will (**expostulate, assuage**) your fright if I remind you that everyone must try something for the first time at some point in his or her life.

3. On the air the star seemed calm, but he privately sent (**petulant, jaded**) notes to those who gave him bad reviews.

4. At the Senior Prom, my sister and most of her friends were glad that men are no longer expected to take the (**prerogative, hiatus**) in choosing dance partners.

5. To impress her newly made friends, she (**simulated, assuaged**) an interest in modern art, of which she knew nothing.

6. When the (**umbrage, hiatus**) in the conversation became embarrassingly long, I decided that the time had come to serve the sandwiches.

7. After watching four TV football games on New Year's Day, I was (**jaded, petulant**) with the pigskin sport for weeks to come.

8. Who would have thought he would take (**prerogative, umbrage**) at an email from a friend who wanted only to help?

9. I truly dislike the kind of sensational popular biography that focuses solely on the more (**lurid, jaded**) or scandalous aspects of a superstar's career.

10. They try to "prove" the (**umbrage, decadence**) of modern youth by emphasizing everything that is bad and ignoring whatever is good.

11. I see no point in (**expostulating, simulating**) with a person who habitually refuses to listen to reason.

12. Because she had just received a large bonus, Joan felt it was her (**decadence, prerogative**) to purchase a luxury convertible car.

Completing the Sentence

Choose the word from the word bank that best completes each of the following sentences. Write the correct word or form of the word in the space provided.

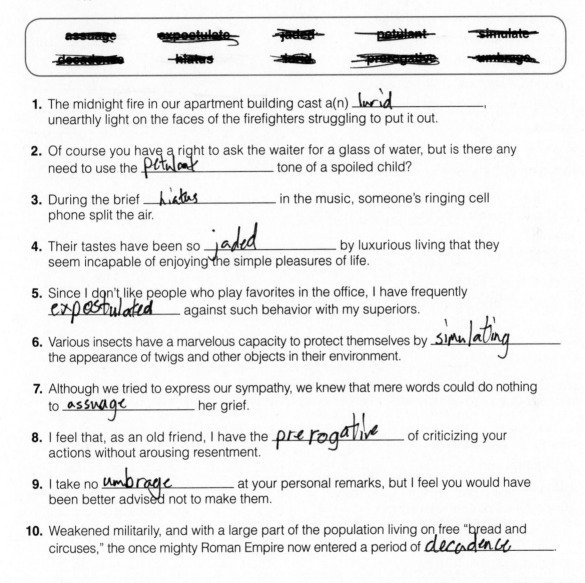

| ~~assuage~~ | ~~expostulate~~ | ~~jaded~~ | ~~petulant~~ | ~~simulate~~ |
| ~~decadence~~ | ~~hiatus~~ | ~~lurid~~ | ~~prerogative~~ | ~~umbrage~~ |

1. The midnight fire in our apartment building cast a(n) __lurid__, unearthly light on the faces of the firefighters struggling to put it out.

2. Of course you have a right to ask the waiter for a glass of water, but is there any need to use the __petulant__ tone of a spoiled child?

3. During the brief __hiatus__ in the music, someone's ringing cell phone split the air.

4. Their tastes have been so __jaded__ by luxurious living that they seem incapable of enjoying the simple pleasures of life.

5. Since I don't like people who play favorites in the office, I have frequently __expostulated__ against such behavior with my superiors.

6. Various insects have a marvelous capacity to protect themselves by __simulating__ the appearance of twigs and other objects in their environment.

7. Although we tried to express our sympathy, we knew that mere words could do nothing to __assuage__ her grief.

8. I feel that, as an old friend, I have the __prerogative__ of criticizing your actions without arousing resentment.

9. I take no __umbrage__ at your personal remarks, but I feel you would have been better advised not to make them.

10. Weakened militarily, and with a large part of the population living on free "bread and circuses," the once mighty Roman Empire now entered a period of __decadence__.

Synonyms

*Choose the word or form of the word from this Unit that is the same or most nearly the same in meaning as the **boldface** word or expression in the phrase. Write that word on the line. Use a dictionary if necessary.*

1. seeking the boss's **commendation** _____
2. exploding in **annoyance** _____
3. **feign** a reconciliation _____
4. a **benefit** of her rank _____
5. **intervened** to stop the argument _____
6. a **naive** point of view _____
7. **depleted** by too much networking _____
8. took a **break** between high school and college _____
9. formed an **alliance** to help feed the homeless _____
10. an **implication** not supported by fact _____
11. **alleviate** his worst fears _____
12. **disagree** with her clothing choices _____
13. unceasing and **servile** modesty _____
14. a lifestyle of **intemperance** _____
15. impolite and **snappish** attitude _____

Antonyms

*Choose the word or form of the word from this Unit that is most nearly opposite in meaning to the **boldface** word or expression in the phrase. Write that word on the line. Use a dictionary if necessary.*

1. a record of **discreditable** actions _____
2. an **original** script _____
3. **surrender to** the conditions of their environment _____
4. **stifled** the crowd's strong response _____
5. heard all the **dull** details _____

Writing: Words in Action

What are the drawbacks to or benefits of having the stark reality of war brought into people's homes? Write an essay in which you support your opinion with your own observations, personal experience, and the reading (refer to pages 12–13). Write at least three paragraphs, and use three or more words from this Unit.

Vocabulary in Context

Some of the words you have studied in this Unit appear in **boldface** *type. Read the passage below, and then circle the letter of the correct answer for each word as it is used in context.*

Martha Ellis Gellhorn (1908–1998) was born in St. Louis, Missouri. She attended Bryn Mawr College but left in 1929 to pursue a writing career. After a few months writing for *New Republic* magazine, she left for France to work as a foreign correspondent. From 1930 to 1934, she wrote on European politics for the *St. Louis Post-Dispatch* and on fashion for *Vogue*, completed her first novel, and traveled in Germany. Convinced that war was inevitable, she returned home to report on the Depression for the Federal Emergency Relief Administration. In 1936, she put her experiences into her second novel, *The Trouble I've Seen,* which established Gellhorn's literary reputation. Her authentic writing did not just **simulate** emotion, and the book's tone of compassion and rage came to characterize her writing, in war and in peace.

Gellhorn traveled to Madrid in 1937 as a foreign correspondent. She did not align herself with any of the conflicting political interests in Spain. It was the same throughout her career; she was committed to reporting the facts of war and poverty—her work was said to **transcend** political allegiances.

Throughout her career, Gellhorn had to struggle against the widespread belief of a **petulant** audience that war correspondent was no job for a woman—but Gellhorn exercised her **prerogative** to be on the battlefield. Gellhorn ignored the smears and **innuendo** about her arrival precipitating the **decadence** of journalism. In 1944, she had to stow away on a hospital ship to report on the D-Day landings, and her coverage of international conflicts after World War II intensified her sympathy with ordinary foot soldiers and civilians—she mistrusted war correspondents who failed to report what they saw. Gellhorn always told the truth as she saw it, and she often suffered for her compulsion to bear witness by being forbidden access to the front lines.

---

1. To **simulate** is to
   a. show emotion
   b. show favoritism
   c. pretend
   d. upset other people

2. If your beliefs **transcend** personal concerns, they
   a. satisfy them
   b. rise above them
   c. deny them
   d. indulge them

3. The word **petulant** most nearly means
   a. peevish
   b. boring
   c. attractive
   d. unreasonable

4. If you assert a **prerogative**, you are claiming
   a. a wish
   b. an opinion
   c. a need
   d. a special right

5. An **innuendo** is a
   a. damaging story
   b. baseless lie
   c. rumor
   d. indirect derogatory suggestion

6. The word **decadence** most nearly means
   a. decline
   b. dishonor
   c. delight
   d. disarray

*Read the following passage, taking note of the **boldface** words and their contexts. These words are among those you will be studying in Unit 2. It may help you to complete the exercises in this Unit if you refer to the way the words are used below.*

Why Vote?

<Persuasive Essay>

saddening

It is dispiriting to acknowledge the lack of interest that citizens of the United States display when it comes to exercising their right to vote. Many eligible voters, nearly 40 percent, in fact, stayed home in the last presidential election, while at the turn of the twentieth century there was an 80 percent turnout rate for presidential elections. Why has such **lassitude permeated** a society that once was vigorous and energetic about voting? *less ppl are voting*

Nonvoters contend that their vote makes little difference and that they cannot vote because candidates are all loud-mouthed, **bombastic**, and dishonest. Such nonvoters **surmise** that politicians, once elected, act in their own best interests and not in the interests of the people who put them in office. Perhaps they find examples of such behavior among elected officials, but the right to vote is one that should be exercised and appreciated regardless of personal opinion about the characters of the politicians. What nonvoters do not recognize is the plight of people who cannot vote at all. Over many **millennia** and in societies all across the globe, voting was not regarded as an **intrinsic** and inherent right of citizens—except in rare instances. First, absolute monarchs ruled and made decisions by claiming the divine right of kings they believed they alone enjoyed. Aristocrats concurred, and, like the czars, queens, kings, and emperors

everyone should vote

they served, they believed that common people were too **callow** and uneducated to govern themselves. Unless these rulers and their scions were compassionate and astute, life for their powerless subjects was a struggle. The same was true for citizens ruled by unrestrained, powerful tyrants, like Nazi Germany's Adolf Hitler and Russia's Joseph Stalin. Even in the emerging democracy in America, the country's founders vigorously debated who could and could not become enfranchised. In 1789, only white men who owned property could rightfully take part in the voting process—hardly the **epitome** of democracy, but a start.

argue

Some nonvoters **inveigh** against the Electoral College, claiming that this body of electors, not the majority of individual voters, actually chooses the President. Under the current system, voters in presidential elections vote not for a candidate but for a slate of electors who are affiliated with a certain party and who promise to cast their ballots for that party's standard-bearer. In a very closely contested election, a candidate with a slight majority of popular votes might lose the election because of the way the Electoral College has voted. This has happened more than once in the country's history.

Today, in many countries, totalitarian dictators still make all decisions for the citizenry **ex officio**, whether or not the people support those decisions. In such societies, citizens are helpless against the **stringent** laws and rigid strictures that **infringe** upon most aspects of their lives. Those residing in one-party "democracies," in which autocrats pay lip service to democratic ideals but treat opposing candidates as **interlopers**, have it no better. Nonvoters should be urgently **exhorted** to consider the alternatives to democracy before they refuse to go to the polls to cast a ballot.

Voting is a process, not a panacea. A single vote will neither herald positive change nor instantly **ameliorate** poor conditions, but voting is the best chance to achieve either outcome. In America, responsible citizens are granted the right to vote at age eighteen; and this right is a privilege and a duty that should be exercised and protected.

Left: A college student encourages people to vote.
Above: A man registers to vote in Florida.

Audio

For iWords and audio passages, go to SadlierConnect.com.

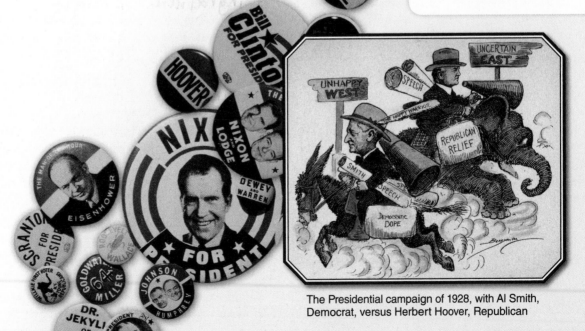

The Presidential campaign of 1928, with Al Smith, Democrat, versus Herbert Hoover, Republican

Unit 2 ■ 25

Definitions

Note the spelling, pronunciation, part(s) of speech, and definition(s) of each of the following words. Then write the appropriate form of the word in the blank space in the illustrative sentence(s) following.

1. aplomb
(ə pläm′)

(*n.*) poise, assurance, great self-confidence; perpendicularity
Considering the family's tense mood, you handled the situation with __aplomb__ .

2. bombastic
(bäm bas′ tik)

(*adj.*) pompous or overblown in language; full of high-sounding words intended to conceal a lack of ideas
He delivered a __bombastic__ speech that did not even address our problems.

3. epitome
(i pit′ ə mē)

(*n.*) a summary, condensed account; an instance that represents a larger reality
Admitting when you have been fairly defeated is the __epitome__ of sportsmanship.

4. exhort
(eg zôrt′)

(*v.*) to urge strongly, advise earnestly
With dramatic gestures, our fans vigorously __exhort__ the team to play harder.

5. ingratiate
(in grā′ shē āt)

(*v.*) to make oneself agreeable and thus gain favor or acceptance by others (sometimes used in a critical or derogatory sense)
It is not a good idea to __ingratiate__ oneself by paying cloying compliments.

6. intrinsic
(in trin′ sik)

(*adj.*) belonging to someone or something by its very nature, essential, inherent; originating in a bodily organ or part
It had been my father's favorite book when he was my age, but for me it held little __intrinsic__ interest.

7. inveigh
(in vā′)

(*v.*) to make a violent attack in words, express strong disapproval
You should not __inveigh__ against the plan with quite so much vigor until you have read it.

8. millennium
(*pl.*, **millennia**)
(mə len′ ē əm)

(*n.*) a period of one thousand years; a period of great joy
In 1999 an argument raged over whether 2000 or 2001 would mark the beginning of the new __millennium__ .

9. precipitate
(*v.*, pri sip′ ə tāt;
adj., *n.*,
pri sip′ ət ət)

(*v.*) to fall as moisture; to bring about suddenly; to hurl down from a great height; to give distinct form to; (*adj.*) characterized by excessive haste; (*n.*) moisture; the product of an action or process

Scholars often disagree over which event or events _*precipitate*_ an historic moment.

I admit that my outburst was _*precipitate*_ .

Too many eggs in this particular pudding will leave a messy _*precipitate*_ in the baking pan.

10. stringent
(strin′ jənt)

(*adj.*) strict, severe; rigorously or urgently binding or compelling; sharp or bitter to the taste

Some argue that more _*stringent*_ laws against speeding will make our streets safer.

Using Context

*For each item, determine whether the **boldface** word from pages 26–27 makes sense in the context of the sentence. Circle the item numbers next to the six sentences in which the words are used correctly.*

(1.) Stellar grades and diverse volunteer work make her the **epitome** of a desirable applicant.

2. "I wonder if our food will come in this **millennium**," I joked after waiting in line to order.

3. He reacted with such **aplomb** when he was told that he could not order his favorite dessert.

4. Change happens if you have **intrinsic** motivation, so there is no need for external forces to encourage you.

5. The enthusiasm of my friends was helpful to **inveigh** me to run for class president.

(6.) Her mind is so **stringent** that she has so far been able to master four languages.

(7.) My doctors **exhorted** me from running for a few weeks after I sprained my ankle.

(8.) It is tough to make any of my ideas heard in meetings when some of my peers are simply focused on making **bombastic** interjections just to hear themselves talk.

(9.) The union hopes that the proposed construction projects will **precipitate** a hiring frenzy.

(10.) Be wary of those who try to **ingratiate** themselves with you, as they may have an ulterior motive.

Choosing the Right Word

*Select the **boldface** word that better completes each sentence. You might refer to the passage on pages 24–25 to see how most of these words are used in context. Note that the choices might be related forms of the Unit words.*

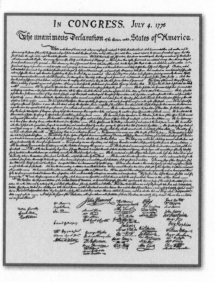

1. In stating that "All men are created equal and endowed . . . with certain inalienable rights," the Declaration of Independence proclaims the (**intrinsic, stringent**) value of every human being.

2. When the bridge suddenly collapsed in the high winds, the people on it at the time were (**inveighed, precipitated**) to their deaths in the watery abyss below.

3. We are all ready and willing to do what must be done; what we need is leadership—not (**exhortation, aplomb**)!

4. Kathy baked cookies for her book club, hoping to (**precipitate, ingratiate**) herself so that she would be nominated as president.

5. Although the music—an étude by Schumann—was not familiar to him, the pianist followed the sheet music and played the piece with great (**aplomb, epitome**).

6. His message may seem (**bombastic, intrinsic**), but there is a solid framework of practical ideas underlying the rather pompous language.

7. It is easy to (**inveigh, precipitate**) against "dirty politics," but less easy to play a positive role, however small, in the political process.

8. The song had a pleasant, (**stringent, ingratiating**) melody that gained it quick popularity and then caused it to be forgotten just as quickly.

9. This famous definition by a British general (**epitomizes, exhorts**) the nature of war: "Long periods of intense boredom punctuated by short periods of intense fear."

10. She handled a potentially embarrassing situation with cool (**millennium, aplomb**).

11. Do we need new laws to combat crime, or rather, more (**ingratiating, stringent**) enforcement of the laws we already have?

12. "I'm sure your every wish will be granted," I assured the demanding child, my tongue firmly in my cheek, "when and if the (**exhortation, millennium**) ever comes!"

Completing the Sentence

Choose the word from the word bank that best completes each of the following sentences. Write the correct word or form of the word in the space provided.

aplomb	epitome	ingratiate	inveigh	precipitate
bombastic	exhort	intrinsic	millennium	stringent

1. Addressing the school assembly for the first time was a nerve-racking experience, but I managed to deliver my speech with a reasonable amount of _____.

2. "The rash and _____ actions of that young hothead almost cost us the battle, to say nothing of the war," the general remarked sourly.

3. A combination of years of practice and _____ athletic ability has made her one of the best basketball players on the team.

4. The prophets of old fervently _____ the people to amend their lives.

5. Representing an organization of senior citizens, the rally's keynote speaker _____ vehemently against conditions that rob the elderly of their dignity and independence.

6. Though fossils show that human beings have been on earth a very, very long time, the earliest written records of their activities date back only about five _____.

7. The voters of this city are looking for practical answers to urgent questions and will not respond to that kind of _____ and pretentious claptrap.

8. How can we have any respect for people who try to _____ themselves with their superiors by flattery and favors?

9. "If you think my training rules are too _____ and confining," the coach said, "then you probably shouldn't be a candidate for the team."

10. That dancer is very talented, but isn't it going rather far to call her "the very _____ of feminine beauty and grace"?

Definitions

Note the spelling, pronunciation, part(s) of speech, and definition(s) of each of the following words. Then write the appropriate form of the word in the blank space in the illustrative sentence(s) following.

1. ameliorate
(ə mēl′ yə rāt)

(*v.*) to improve, make better, correct a flaw or shortcoming

A hot meal can _____ the discomforts of even the coldest day.

2. callow
(kal′ ō)

(*adj.*) without experience; immature, not fully developed; lacking sophistication and poise; without feathers

They entered the army as _____ recruits and left as seasoned veterans.

3. drivel
(driv′ əl)

(*n.*) saliva or mucus flowing from the mouth or nose; foolish, aimless talk or thinking; nonsense; (*v.*) to let saliva flow from the mouth; to utter nonsense or childish twaddle; to waste or fritter away foolishly

The gnawed bone was covered in _____.
We kept silent and let him _____ on.

4. ex officio
(eks ə fish′ ē ō)

(*adj., adv.*) by virtue of holding a certain office

The President is the _____ commander-in-chief of the armed forces in time of war.

5. infringe
(in frinj′)

(*v.*) to violate, trespass, go beyond recognized bounds

If you _____ on my responsibilities, will you also take the blame for any mistakes?

6. interloper
(in′ tər lōp ər)

(*n.*) one who moves in where he or she is not wanted or has no right to be, an intruder

Eager to see the band perform, the crowd resented the opening singer as an _____.

7. lassitude
(las′ ə tüd)

(*n.*) weariness of body or mind, lack of energy

On some days I am overcome by _____ at the thought of so many more years of schooling.

8. occult
(ə kəlt′)

(*adj.*) secret, hidden from view; not detectable by ordinary means; mysterious, magical, uncanny; (*v.*) to hide, cover up; eclipse; (*n.*) matters involving the supernatural

The moon was _____ by the planet.
Much of his talk about the _____ seems grounded in nothing but trick photography and folklore.

9. permeate
(pər′ mē āt)

(*v.*) to spread through, penetrate, soak through

The rain _____ all of my clothing and reduced the map in my pocket to a pulpy mass.

10. surmise
(sər mīz′)

(*v.*) to think or believe without certain supporting evidence; to conjecture or guess; (*n.*) likely idea that lacks definite proof

I cannot be sure, but I _____ that she would not accept my apology even if I made it on my knees.

The police had no proof, nothing to go on but a suspicion, a mere _____.

Using Context

*For each item, determine whether the **boldface** word from pages 30–31 makes sense in the context of the sentence. Circle the item numbers next to the six sentences in which the words are used correctly.*

1. We cannot allow feelings of hatred and intolerance to continue to **permeate** throughout our society.

2. Although I'm qualified for the job, I worry that I will get so nervous in the interview that I'll **drivel** on about irrelevant facts and look foolish.

3. The rain that began to pour on me after a terrible day only served to **ameliorate** my mood.

4. All department heads will be in a board meeting this afternoon, as they are **ex officio** members of the board.

5. If you do not **infringe** all the rules for my guest house, you will be asked to leave and find other accommodations.

6. Since she is never late to anything, I can only **surmise** that something beyond her control is holding her up right now.

7. His **callow** response to my greeting hinted that he woke up on the wrong side of the bed.

8. When some people have an extensive to-do list, they are motivated to get started right away, but others can be overcome with **lassitude** just by thinking about all the tasks in front of them.

9. After a long week, I was happy to have an **occult** evening at home by myself to relax and unwind.

10. Even though they were the ones who had invited me to lunch, they left me out of the conversation so much that I felt like an **interloper.**

Choosing the Right Word

Select the **boldface** word that better completes each sentence. You might refer to the passage on pages 24–25 to see how most of these words are used in context. Note that the choices might be related forms of the Unit words.

1. Marian Wright Edelman has never succumbed to (**drivel, lassitude**) but has instead remained a tireless advocate of children's rights since the 1960s.

2. I can usually forgive a(n) (**callow, ex officio**) display of feeble jokes and showing off—but not by someone who has passed his fortieth birthday!

3. A sour odor of decay, stale air, and generations of living (**permeated, occulted**) every corner of the old tenement.

4. I trust that we shall have the will to improve what can now be improved and the patience to bear what cannot now be (**ameliorated, surmised**).

5. I (**surmised, infringed**) that you did well on your test when you bolted through the front door as though you had just won the lottery.

6. After the unexpected defeat, the members of the team wanted to be alone and regarded anyone who entered the locker room as a(n) (**interloper, lassitude**).

7. In this situation we cannot act on the basis of what may be (**surmised, infringed**), but only in accordance with what is definitely known.

8. Because I believe in spreading governmental powers among several officials, I am opposed to having the Mayor serve as (**callow, ex officio**) head of the Board of Education.

9. The neighbor's unruly bushes and vines are beginning to (**surmise, infringe**) on our side of the property.

10. The large trees that surrounded the strange mansion (**occulted, ameliorated**) our view of the building.

11. After the speaker had droned on pointlessly for half an hour, an angry man in the front row stood up and said, "Must we continue to listen to all this childish (**lassitude, drivel**)?"

12. One way to (**permeate, ameliorate**) your fears of giving a speech is to put your audience at ease with a personal anecdote.

Completing the Sentence

Choose the word from the word bank that best completes each of the following sentences. Write the correct word or form of the word in the space provided.

ameliorate	drivel	infringe	lassitude	permeate
callow	ex officio	interloper	occult	surmise

1. The Vice President of the United States, the Secretary of State, and the Secretary of Defense are _____ members of the National Security Council.

2. He tries to give the impression of being a true man of the world, but his conduct clearly shows him to be a(n) _____ and somewhat feckless youth.

3. The people trying to "crash" our dance may think of themselves as merry pranksters, but they are really _____ who would prevent us all from having a good time.

4. We do not know what her motives were, but we may _____ that she was mainly concerned for the child's well-being.

5. Throughout the dictator's long reign, some of his most trusted advisors engaged in behind-the-scenes conspiracies and _____ schemes without his knowledge.

6. They have a great deal to say on the subject, but unfortunately most of it is meaningless _____.

7. After completing those long, grueling exams, I was overwhelmed by a(n) _____ so great that I felt I would never be able to study again.

8. I refuse to accept the idea that conditions in this slum have deteriorated so far that nothing can be done to _____ them.

9. We looked up hungrily as the delightful odor of broiled steak and fried onions _____ the room.

10. A good definition of *freedom* is: "The right to do anything you wish as long as you do not _____ on the rights of others."

Synonyms

Choose the word or form of the word from this Unit that is the same or most nearly the same in meaning as the **boldface** word or expression in the phrase. Write that word on the line. Use a dictionary if necessary.

1. to **create** a reaction _____
2. thought the idea to be **hogwash** _____
3. **encroach** on the liberties of its citizens _____
4. overwhelmed by **fatigue** _____
5. a stain that **leaked through** _____
6. hints of a **concealed** presence _____
7. a **natural** interest in the arts _____
8. to **rail** against a harmless mistake _____
9. in the next **thousand years** _____
10. a smile meant to **flatter** _____
11. **implore** drivers to follow parking rules _____
12. caught the **trespasser** sneaking in _____
13. **inferred** that the dog ate the cookies off the plate _____
14. the **model** of what not to wear _____
15. serves as the **official head** of the Senate _____

Antonyms

Choose the word or form of the word from this Unit that is most nearly opposite in meaning to the **boldface** word or expression in the phrase. Write that word on the line. Use a dictionary if necessary.

1. a **mature** young man _____
2. a **lax** requirement _____
3. **plain and simple** language _____
4. a line delivered with **self-doubt** _____
5. **exacerbate** his condition _____

Writing: Words in Action

Suppose you want to persuade the citizens in your community to vote. Write a public service announcement explaining why voting is an important act of citizenship that should be exercised. Use at least two details from the passage (pages 24–25) and three or more words from this Unit.

Vocabulary in Context

*Some of the words you have studied in this Unit appear in **boldface** type. Read the passage below, and then circle the letter of the correct answer for each word as it is used in context.*

The statistics on American political elections are sufficient to shake the **aplomb** of many observers. The cost and duration of these contests have **precipitated** much commentary recently. The 2012 presidential campaigns, for example, cost $2 billion, and an additional $5 billion was spent to pay for all elections in that year. Compare France, which caps presidential campaign costs at $30 million. From one perspective, the reasons for such monumental costs are not **occult.** The population and geographical area of the United States are **intrinsic** factors that make elections expensive. Although many critics dismiss television campaign commercials as **drivel,** the temptation for many candidates to **ingratiate** themselves with voters is often too strong to resist. The result is that tens of millions of dollars are spent to disseminate political messages on the airwaves.

The duration of campaigns is another source of concern. In France and Britain, election campaigns for president and prime minister, respectively, are restricted to several weeks. In the United States, the presidential cycle now exceeds eighteen months. In 1960, John F. Kennedy announced his candidacy just eleven months before the election. Today, however, more and more states are holding earlier primaries and caucuses to gain electoral influence. This frontloaded primary schedule compels candidates to employ earlier electioneering and fundraising strategies. Some observers credit the more protracted schedule with benefits: for example, national exposure of comparatively unknown figures (at the time) such as Jimmy Carter and Bill Clinton. But the disadvantages of a marathon campaign season are clear. Campaigning and fundraising are full-time jobs, forcing potential candidates to set aside their other commitments. For incumbents, this means subordinating the job of governing to the reelection imperative.

---

1. If your **aplomb** is shaken, you do not have
   a. confusion
   b. self-confidence
   c. embarrassment
   d. shock

2. The word **precipitate** most nearly means
   a. produce
   b. reflect
   c. revoke
   d. invite

3. If an explanation is **occult,** it is
   a. rational
   b. transparent
   c. refractory
   d. mysterious

4. **Intrinsic** factors may be described as
   a. inherent
   b. external
   c. secondary
   d. supernatural

5. **Drivel** is
   a. irresponsibility
   b. nonsense
   c. camaraderie
   d. eloquence

6. If you **ingratiate** yourself with others, you
   a. grow overly familiar
   b. boast shamelessly
   c. make yourself agreeable
   d. invite cooperation

Read the following passage, taking note of the **boldface** words and their contexts. These words are among those you will be studying in Unit 3. It may help you to complete the exercises in this Unit if you refer to the way the words are used below.

Trapped in a Cave, Foiled by a Circus

<Journal Entries>

Feb. 2, 1925

Good thing I made a reservation before leaving Chicago, because the hotel here is packed full, and a whole army of people has invaded little Cave City. As I hightailed it over to Sand Cave for an update on the news, I saw some people setting up tents, and others living out of their cars and trucks. Everyone's talking about Floyd Collins. The poor spelunker **inadvertently** became trapped in a cave, and now, after just three days, he's become the biggest sensation since the sinking of the *Titanic!* *Big event*

I interviewed a town official right away, and he told me Floyd was just a poor Kentucky farmer when he discovered Crystal Caves on his family's land eight years ago. To attract more tourists to the area, Floyd went looking for new caves, and that's when he found Sand Cave. Then his luck gave out, and here we are, waiting for Floyd to come out. *Missing*

Feb. 3, 1925

Bad news travels fast. There must be tens of thousands of ordinary folk in Cave City today, not to mention the Red Cross and the National Guard, plus hundreds of reporters like me.

lots of people
And let's not forget the stalls set up to feed and entertain all these bystanders! Everyone needs to eat, I suppose, but I suspect at least a few of these "entrepreneurs" don't just sell, but **peculate**, in taking cash from everybody.

William Burke Miller, a young Louisville newspaperman whom everyone calls "Skeets," squeezed down the narrow passageway and made contact with Floyd. Although Skeets was sent to cover the story, his being here is far from **adventitious**, since his small stature allows him access to the cave while the rest of us stand by, feeling useless. He's been bringing food down to Floyd, then interviewing him. People all around the world are now reading his dispatches.

Floyd is stuck
Feb. 4, 1925

Radio reports say that even Congress is getting updates on Floyd! Meanwhile, Skeets keeps bringing down sandwiches, water, and comfort. Floyd remains stuck, so workers are still trying to dig him out. Floyd's **sangfroid** in the midst of this circus is admirable.

Traffic jam outside of Cave City, Kentucky, 1900

Floyd Collins exploring another cave, shortly before his fatal accident in 1925

Feb. 5, 1925

Interviewed Homer Collins, Floyd's younger brother. "To what do you **ascribe** Floyd's composure in these difficult circumstances?" I asked. Homer: "Well, I reckon Floyd has always been brave in caves, even as a youngster."

he is calm

Feb. 6, 1925

There are so many journalists here, some will do anything to get a scoop. I've seen a few hard-bitten reporters, pretending to be concerned, and kowtowing to locals just to get a quotation for the evening edition; but normally, their prose is so full of **vitriol** that it would make a grown man cry. *fake*

Feb. 8, 1925

I **commiserated** with Homer, who is now **enjoined** from helping in the rescue. Others have taken control—they pushed him aside, even though Homer knows more about caving than they do—but their attempts to reach Floyd have failed miserably. The tunnel used to reach Floyd collapsed, so they'll have to dig a **circuitous** route to the trapped man.

the people failed

Feb. 10, 1925

The collapse of the shaft that had been drilled through the rock has shut Floyd off from the outside.

Floyd Collins

Feb. 11, 1925

I tried to **wheedle** an interview with Miss Jane, Floyd's stepmother. Another reporter got to her first, so I eavesdropped. I didn't catch everything she said, but let's just say she has a **tenuous** hold on reality and a **proclivity** for bending the truth. She seems a bit off in the head, so she is not exactly a reliable source. *she's gone crazy*

Feb. 12, 1925

A few of us quizzed the mayor of Cave City about **expediting** the rescue. So far, all attempts have been **nominal** and feeble. The mayor and his minions are doing their utmost to **ferment** excitement about this crisis and keep the hucksters happy. It sometimes seems as if they are more interested in bringing attention to their town than in rescuing Floyd. It's a sad state of affairs.

Feb. 14, 1925

ready to get him

The new shaft is completed, and rescuers will attempt to reach Floyd. It's been two weeks since he became trapped. Time waits for no man. We need a miracle now.

Feb. 17, 1925

Floyd is dead. I **abominate** what happened here. I witnessed a circus, not a rescue. Some of the participants in this sideshow displayed remorse, but this is a poor way to **expiate** their guilt for the role they played in this travesty. Most of the rest merely shook their heads and walked away.

A doctor listens to Floyd Collins's heartbeat through an amplifier in Sand Cave, Kentucky, 1925.

Audio

For iWords and audio passages, go to SadlierConnect.com.

[handwritten: ☆= maybe sentences]

Definitions

Note the spelling, pronunciation, part(s) of speech, and definition(s) of each of the following words. Then write the appropriate form of the word in the blank space in the illustrative sentence(s) following.

[handwritten: Quiz]
[handwritten: Matching 3 pts]
[handwritten: 5 words not hold]
[handwritten: 5 sentences 8 pts]
[handwritten: 5 parts of speech 3 pts]

[handwritten: ends in -tion = noun 9/10   -ous = adjective 9/10]

1. abominate ☆
(ə bäm' ə nāt)

(v.) to have an intense dislike or hatred for
I _abominate_ cruelty yet do not always notice when I have said something inadvertently cruel.

2. adventitious
(ad ven tish' əs)

(adj.) resulting from chance rather than from an inherent cause or character; accidental, not essential; (medicine) acquired, not congenital,
It was no _adventitious_ meeting that led to their writing songs together, for in fact they were cousins.

3. commiserate ☆
(kə miz' ə rāt)

(v.) to sympathize with, have pity or sorrow for, share a feeling of distress
The family _commiserate_ with her after the loss of her old and faithful dog.

4. enjoin ☆
(en join')

(v.) to direct or order; to prescribe a course of action in an authoritative way; to prohibit
I _enjoin_ them to stop spending so much money or to face the consequences.

5. expiate
(ek' spē āt)

(v.) to make amends, make up for; to avert
They seemed more than willing to _expiate_ their guilt by whatever means necessary.

6. inadvertent ☆
(in əd vər' tənt)

(adj.) resulting from or marked by lack of attention; unintentional, accidental
The poor fellow was stronger than he realized, and the damage he did was _inadvertent_.

7. noncommittal
(nän kə mit' əl)

(adj.) not decisive or definite; unwilling to take a clear position
We questioned her quietly, carefully, and at length, but her answers remained _noncommittal_.

8. proclivity
(prō kliv' ə tē)

(n.) a natural or habitual inclination or tendency (especially of human character or behavior)
Curious, patient, and fond of long walks outdoors, she soon displayed a _proclivity_ for nature study.

[handwritten: -ate = verb 9/10]

9. sangfroid
(sän frwä')

(*n.*) composure or coolness, especially in trying circumstances
Even when they forget their lines, experienced actors can usually perform with __Sangfroid__ .

10. tenuous
(ten' yü əs)

(*adj.*) thin, slender, not dense; lacking clarity or sharpness; of slight importance; lacking a sound basis, poorly supported
My grasp of trigonometry was __tenuous__ until I attended the remedial study sessions.

Using Context

*For each item, determine whether the **boldface** word from pages 38–39 makes sense in the context of the sentence. Circle the item numbers next to the six sentences in which the words are used correctly.*

1. She had never seen a musical before, but the **sangfroid** that showed on her face during the curtain call showed how much she enjoyed it.

2. I know your criticism of my beliefs may have been **inadvertent** as we only just met, but that should teach you to be careful about what you say around people you don't know.

3. His **tenuous** spirit shows that he works hard and never gives up on his goals.

4. When I signed up to audition for the spring musical, I found myself in the **adventitious** position of having the first slot.

5. When I lost my dog, only my friends who had ever loved an animal could truly **commiserate** with me.

6. I asked my new friend to **enjoin** our book club, but she said she wouldn't be able to fit it into her schedule.

7. My friends think that comedian is funny, but I **abominate** the offensive jokes in his routine.

8. When my two friends argue, I try to remain neutral and give **noncommittal** responses when each of them tries to get me on his side.

9. I can certainly pay to fix the window I accidentally broke, but nothing can **expiate** my guilt and sorrow.

10. Her **proclivity** for music at such a young age may predict a future career as a concert pianist.

Choosing the Right Word

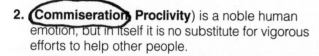

*Select the **boldface** word that better completes each sentence. You might refer to the passage on pages 36–37 to see how most of these words are used in context. Note that the choices might be related forms of the Unit words.*

1. It may be an exaggeration to say that American architect Frank Lloyd Wright (**abominated**, **enjoined**) classical European building designs, but he certainly deviated from them.

2. (**Commiseration**, **Proclivity**) is a noble human emotion, but in itself it is no substitute for vigorous efforts to help other people.

3. I learned that I would have to make a choice between my strong aversion to hard work and my equally strong (**proclivity**, **sangfroid**) for expensive living.

4. After he had seen the error of his ways, the villain attempted to (**expiate**, **enjoin**) the dark deeds of his past by acts of kindness and mercy.

5. Her investments proved to be profitable, but they were (**adventitious**, **tenuous**) rather than the result of knowledge and planning.

6. Even criminals who displayed (**sangfroid**, **proclivity**) would crack under pressure when confronted by the legendary prosecuting attorney.

7. When I spoke to Mother about going on the spring trip to Washington, her only reply was a (**adventitious**, **noncommittal**) "We'll see."

8. Peace negotiations between the two countries were already (**noncommittal**, **tenuous**) when the border dispute broke out.

9. It is only in my fantasies that I display the (**proclivity**, **noncommittal**) associated with movie heroes who are "as cool as a cucumber."

10. Experienced lawyers know that the line between literal truth and slight but significant distortion of the facts is often a(n) (**inadvertent**, **tenuous**) one.

11. They are conscientious objectors to military service because they are (**enjoined**, **abominated**) by a deep personal conviction not to take a human life.

12. An experienced politician always tries to avoid making (**adventitious**, **inadvertent**) remarks that may offend some voters.

Completing the Sentence

Choose the word from the word bank that best completes each of the following sentences. Write the correct word or form of the word in the space provided.

[redacted]

1. Who in the world can hope to match the unshakable sangfroid of the indestructible James Bond in moments of great peril?

2. If, as you say, your slamming of the door on the way out was completely inadvertent, then you should be more careful in the future.

3. Since she seems to have a strong prodivity both for science and for service to others, I think that she should plan to study medicine.

4. He claims to be a close friend of the senator, but I believe that the connection between them is extremely tenuous.

5. We must distinguish between the truly basic policies of our political party and those that are adventitious and have little connection with the essential program.

6. Declaring the boycott to be illegal, the judge enjoined the labor union from striking against the employing firm.

7. Only someone who has suffered from bursitis can fully commiserate with me when I am in the throes of an acute attack.

8. No matter what their other likes or dislikes are, most Americans thoroughly abominate slavery in all its forms.

9. She expiated the crime committed during her youth by a lifetime of service to humanity.

10. We had hoped to learn his opinion of the new energy program, but he remained completely noncommittal during the interview.

End Set A

Definitions

Note the spelling, pronunciation, part(s) of speech, and definition(s) of each of the following words. Then write the appropriate form of the word in the blank space in the illustrative sentence(s) following.

1. acculturation
(ə kəl chə rā′ shən)

(*n.*) the modification of the social patterns, traits, or structures of one group or society by contact with those of another; the resultant blend

Every immigrant group newly arrived in another country goes through a slow process of _acculturation_.

2. ascribe
(ə skrīb′)

(*v.*) to assign or refer to (as a cause or source), attribute

You may _ascribe_ these holes to gophers or elves, but I blame the dog from next door.

3. circuitous
(sər kyü′ ə təs)

(*adj.*) roundabout, not direct

I followed a _circuitous_ path through the woods, not because I feared pursuit, but because I was lost.

4. expedite
(ek′ spə dīt)

(*v.*) to make easy, cause to progress faster

The pleasant background music did not _expedite_ my work but instead distracted me.

5. ferment
(*n.*, fər′ ment; *v.*, fər ment′)

(*n.*) a state of great excitement, agitation, or turbulence; (*v.*) to be in or work into such a state; to produce alcohol by chemical action

Caught in the _ferment_ of revolution, the young men enlisted with the local militias.

If left for a time, cider will eventually _ferment_.

6. nominal
(näm′ ə nəl)

(*adj.*) existing in name only, not real; too small to be considered or taken seriously

The new health clinic for lower-income residents charges only _nomial_ fees.

7. peculate
(pek′ yü lāt)

(*v.*) to steal something that has been given into one's trust; to take improperly for one's own use

Investigators discovered that the clerk came up with a scheme to _peculate_ from the company.

8. seditious
(sə dish′ əs)

(*adj.*) resistant to lawful authority; having the purpose of overthrowing an established government

Dictators usually begin their reigns by searching out and silencing _seditious_ opinion.

9. **vitriolic**
(vi trē äl' ik)

(*adj.*) bitter, sarcastic; highly caustic or biting (like a strong acid)
Though hurt by his **vitriolic** language, I had to admit that some of his points were valid.

10. **wheedle**
(whēd' əl)

(*v.*) to use coaxing or flattery to gain some desired end
The spy used charm and flattery in order to **wheedle** the information from the diplomat.

Using Context

*For each item, determine whether the **boldface** word from pages 42–43 makes sense in the context of the sentence. Circle the item numbers next to the six sentences in which the words are used correctly.*

1. The columnist was reprimanded for acting in a **seditious** manner for merely questioning some recent decisions made by the President.

2. Before I studied abroad I was worried that there would be a long period of **acculturation**, but I felt at home almost immediately after I arrived.

3. I admire her attempt to analyze the novel in ways that had not been done before, but her logic to get there was so **circuitous** that I could not follow how she got from point *A* to point *B*.

4. We were making great time on our journey until traffic on the bridge threatened to **expedite** us.

5. I'm happy to study with you for the test if that's what you want, so there's no need for you to **wheedle** me into helping you by telling me how smart I am.

6. I know his actions hurt you, but you should not **ascribe** intent until you find out his reasons for behaving in such a way.

7. The **nominal** size of the sailboat soothed any fears I had about being out on the water, as it looked like the vessel could weather any storm.

8. The audience was in a **ferment** even before the band came out on stage, caught up in the anticipation of seeing the group perform for the first time in ten years.

9. After seeing me admire her antique locket, my grandmother showed me her entire jewelry collection and allowed me to **peculate** anything that caught my eye.

10. The **vitriolic** sound of some soothing music is all that will calm me down whenever I wake up from a nightmare.

Choosing the Right Word

*Select the **boldface** word that better completes each sentence. You might refer to the passage on pages 36–37 to see how most of these words are used in context. Note that the choices might be related forms of the Unit words.*

1. With the deadline fast approaching, the local newspaper office was in a (**sedition, ferment**) of last-minute activity and preparation.

2. This is a (**nominal, circuitous**) route, but we avoid the traffic jams on the Interstate.

3. The sordid and (**nominal, vitriolic**) language from both candidates is offensive and takes the focus away from the issues.

4. I was simply unable to follow the (**circuitous, nominal**) reasoning by which she "proved" that a straight line is not necessarily the shortest distance between two points.

5. Modern American society can justly be said to be the end point of the (**ferment, acculturation**) of diverse groups of immigrants.

6. (**Peculation, Sedition**) was a common offense among Roman provincial governors, who, when asked how they made their fortunes, often replied, "In the provinces."

7. Although the queen or king is the (**nominal, seditious**) head of state, the prime minister is the real leader of the British government.

8. Because he has been able to (**peculate, wheedle**) almost anything he wants out of his parents, he is quite unprepared now to face the harsh realities of life.

9. You are following an all too familiar pattern in (**ascribing, expediting**) your failures to everyone except yourself.

10. Although that critic is feared for (**circuitous, vitriolic**) reviews, I have learned that there is usually a sound basis for her unfavorable judgments.

11. The worst way I can think of to (**expedite, ascribe**) this program would be to set up another new Committee on New Programs.

12. Our military is prepared to deal with external aggression, but our best defense against (**sedition, peculation**) at home is the loyalty of the American people.

Completing the Sentence

Choose the word from the word bank that best completes each of the following sentences. Write the correct word or form of the word in the space provided.

acculturation	**circuitous**	**ferment**	**peculate**	**vitriolic**
ascribe	**expedite**	**nominal**	**seditious**	**wheedle**

1. Much of the money that the "robber barons" _____ from the public trust was never recovered—or even missed!

2. Some people say that they cannot understand her defeat in the election, but I _____ it to her failure to discuss the issues in simple, down-to-earth terms.

3. Certain languages such as Afrikaans are the product of _____ and were created when two societies merged.

4. We Americans do not believe that honest criticism of our public officials, no matter how severe, should be regarded as _____.

5. While he remained the _____ leader of the group, the real power passed into the hands of his wily aide.

6. You could have indicated frankly what you thought was wrong without embittering them with such _____ criticism.

7. As charming, clever, and persuasive as you may be, you will certainly not _____ me into lending you my tennis racquet.

8. Her line of questioning was so _____ that I began to suspect that she was not sure of what she was trying to prove.

9. The new computerized referral system will greatly _____ the processing of complaints by customers.

10. Wines from that part of France are produced by _____ the juice of the luscious grapes that grow on the hillsides.

Synonyms

*Choose the word or form of the word from this Unit that is the same or most nearly the same in meaning as the **boldface** word or expression in the phrase. Write that word on the line. Use a dictionary if necessary.*

1. exhibited **self-assurance** during the crisis   _____

2. an **inconsequential** ruler   _____

3. the **assimilation** of American students in Spain   _____

4. a **rancorous** tone of voice   _____

5. a **treasonable** act   _____

6. **embezzle** from the treasury   _____

7. mail that needs to be **rushed**   _____

8. **identify with** your disappointment   _____

9. was **cajoled** into agreeing   _____

10. a **fortuitous** circumstance   _____

11. to **atone** for her unkindness   _____

12. signs of rising **unrest**   _____

13. an **unplanned** meeting   _____

14. **credit** his failures to bad luck   _____

15. **vacillating** in her answer   _____

Antonyms

*Choose the word or form of the word from this Unit that is most nearly opposite in meaning to the **boldface** word or expression in the phrase. Write that word on the line. Use a dictionary if necessary.*

1. **solid** evidence against the defendant   _____

2. took a **straight** route   _____

3. the **inability** to complain   _____

4. **permit** you to move forward with the plan   _____

5. **love** political speeches   _____

Writing: Words in Action

Write a brief essay in which you compare risk-takers to those who act recklessly. Support your ideas with specific examples from your observations, studies, and the reading (refer to pages 36–37). Write at least three paragraphs, and use three or more words from this Unit.

Vocabulary in Context

*Some of the words you have studied in this Unit appear in **boldface** type. Read the passage below, and then circle the letter of the correct answer for each word as it is used in context.*

Art has always been a way to converse without words—for example, graffiti art can be seen as a **seditious** form of communication against established rules. Art fulfills an innate need to produce and express, and recently, researchers have discovered evidence that this need goes all the way back to ancient Indonesian cave paintings. On Sulawesi, an island in Indonesia, Maxime Aubert, an Australian geochemist and archaeologist, **enjoined** a group of Australian and Indonesian researchers to date a cave painting of a babirusa, a "pig-deer" that was commonly seen throughout the Indonesian valleys. Aubert led his team with **sangfroid**, even as he used a new technique called uranium-thorium dating that measured how uranium decayed as it turned to thorium. This process enabled the scientists to **ascribe** an approximate age to the cave painting's calcium carbonate top layer. The babirusa that Aubert's team found was 35,400 years old—the oldest known example of figurative art anywhere in the world.

Aubert's research shattered previous conceptions about the origins of art. Prior to Aubert's expedition, the oldest known art was thought to be in the Chauvet Cave in France. There are interesting similarities between Sulawesian and European figurative art, possibly due to **acculturation** before these groups separated onto different continents. While some scientists still believe that cave art originated in Africa, other scientists are **noncommittal** about where art began. Even though the origin point is still under debate, it is clear that early cave art paved the way for future forms of visual expression.

---

1. The word **seditious** most nearly means
   a. fearful of taking risks
   b. hesitant to take action
   c. resistant to lawful authority
   d. compliant with guidelines

2. When you **enjoin** a group of people, you
   a. exploit them
   b. direct them
   c. appeal to them
   d. collaborate with them

3. A person behaving with **sangfroid** is
   a. tentative
   b. silent
   c. vulnerable
   d. composed

4. To **ascribe** an attribute is to
   a. assign it
   b. fabricate it
   c. disguise it
   d. own it

5. **Acculturation** occurs when one group's social patterns are
   a. unchanged
   b. eliminated
   c. modified
   d. opposed

6. Someone who is **noncommittal** is
   a. lacking in motivation
   b. unwilling to pledge
   c. firm in resolve and beliefs
   d. hasty in forming an opinion

Vocabulary for Comprehension
Part 1

*Read this passage, which contains words in **boldface** that appear in Units 1–3. Then choose the best answer to each question based on what is stated or implied in the passage. You may refer to the passage as often as necessary.*

Questions 1–10 are based on the following passage.

Obstacles, discrimination, and rejection have always been pitfalls on the immigrant road to a new life in a new world, and these were among the central themes of

(5) the early twentieth-century writer Sui Sin Far. Born Edith Maud Eaton in England in 1865, she had a British father and a Chinese mother.

The Eaton family did not live a life of

(10) **decadence**, yet their fortunes were precarious. Edith's father, Edward, a struggling landscape painter, found it difficult to provide for his family of fourteen, and decided to emigrate to the New

(15) World—first to Hudson, New York, and then to Montreal, Canada, settling down there when Edith was about eight years old. While still teenagers, Edith and her sister Winifred showed a **proclivity** for

(20) literature and wrote for their local newspaper. In her early twenties, Edith left Montreal for the West Coast of the United States, living in Los Angeles, San Francisco, and Seattle. It was in this

(25) period that she espoused the cause of the Chinese in America, determined to **ameliorate** the climate of discrimination.

Chinese immigrants began arriving in significant numbers in the 1850s, largely

(30) settling in western cities like San Francisco. Overwhelmingly male, they first worked on the railroads or in mining; later, they worked in agriculture, light manufacturing, restaurants and laundries. Almost from the

(35) first, they were the target of **vitriolic** attacks from such groups as the Workingmen's Party, who **inveighed** against their supposed servitude and questioned their

loyalty. Such **stringent** criticism was almost

(40) surely motivated by economic resentment. The Chinese, it was said, undercut salaries by working for starvation wages. This **lurid** vendetta reached a climax in 1882 when Congress passed the Chinese Exclusion

(45) Act, the first federal legislation in American history to target an ethnic group. Chinese immigration was halted for ten years, and all Chinese were branded as "aliens ineligible for citizenship." Later renewals

(50) and extensions of the act effectively suspended Chinese immigration until 1943.

Edith Maud Eaton mounted a lonely but eloquent counteroffensive. She first asserted her Chinese identity by adopting

(55) the pseudonym Sui Sin Far, meaning "narcissus" flower. In stories and articles that were widely published, she wrote of the social toll exacted by racial insensitivity. In her ironically titled story "In the Land of

(60) the Free," she presented a sympathetic portrait of a Chinese mother, hoping to counter negative stereotypes. Eaton dramatized the plight of Eurasians like herself. Perhaps the climax of Eaton's

(65) achievement on this subject was the publication in 1912 of a novel titled *Mrs. Spring Fragrance*, which consisted of linked short stories.

Eaton's pioneering aspiration was to

(70) serve as a bridge between East and West. She died in 1914. Although it would be years before **acculturation** of the Chinese in the United States reached stable levels, Eaton may be credited as the first author

(75) to have realistically portrayed the dilemmas and conflicts of this immigrant group and to have encouraged **approbation** rather than stigma.

1. The primary purpose of the passage is to
  A) give a history of Chinese immigration to the United States.
  B) explain why Edith Maud Eaton chose a Chinese pseudonym for her writing.
  C) offer a brief overview of Edith Maud Eaton's writing and its social context.
  D) describe the conflicts that resulted in passage of the Chinese Exclusion Act.

2. In the first paragraph, the author suggests that immigrant life is often
  A) arduous.
  B) expensive.
  C) melancholy.
  D) unpredictable.

3. Based on the first two paragraphs, it can reasonably be inferred that Edith's determination to focus on the plight of Chinese immigrants in America was at least partially due to
  A) her family's financial troubles.
  B) her experience writing for the local newspaper.
  C) her desire to become a famous writer.
  D) her own ethnic heritage and her family's experience as immigrants.

4. As it is used in line 19, "proclivity" most nearly means
  A) penchant.
  B) antipathy.
  C) curiosity.
  D) antagonism.

5. The third paragraph (lines 28–51) of the passage serves to
  A) explain the reasons for Chinese immigration to America in the 1850s.
  B) sketch briefly the early history of Chinese immigration and describe the hostility it provoked.
  C) analyze the economic claims made against Chinese immigrants.
  D) refute popular stereotypes about Chinese immigrants in the West.

6. As it is used in line 35, "vitriolic" most nearly means
  A) exaggerated.
  B) sentimental.
  C) self-serving.
  D) caustic.

7. In the third paragraph (lines 28–51), the author asserts that one reason for hostility toward the Chinese in the late 1800s was almost certainly
  A) political.
  B) racial.
  C) philosophical.
  D) economic.

8. Which choice provides the best evidence for the answer to the previous question?
  A) Lines 31–34 ("Overwhelmingly . . . laundries")
  B) Lines 34–39 ("Almost. . . loyalty")
  C) Lines 39–40 ("Such . . . resentment")
  D) Lines 42–46 ("This lurid . . . group")

9. The author most likely refers to Eaton's story "In the Land of the Free" as "ironically titled" (line 59) in order to suggest that
  A) China was ruled by a totalitarian government at the time.
  B) the Chinese mother in the story was a recent immigrant.
  C) negative stereotypes clashed with America's self-image as the home of freedom.
  D) the "Star-Spangled Banner" had not yet been adopted as the national anthem.

10. As it is used in line 78, "approbation" most nearly means
  A) conviction.
  B) sanction.
  C) censure.
  D) vindication.

Vocabulary for Comprehension
Part 2

*Read this passage, which contains words in **boldface** that appear in Units 1–3. Then choose the best answer to each question based on what is stated or implied in the passage. You may refer to the passage as often as necessary.*

Questions 1–10 are based on the following passage.

When President Theodore Roosevelt appropriated a phrase from John Bunyan's famous religious allegory *Pilgrim's Progress* (1678) to describe
(5) some American journalism of the early 1900s, citizens of the time wondered whether Roosevelt's use of the term "muckraking" was complimentary or scornful. Today, muckraking has assumed
(10) generally positive connotations. Following the era of "yellow journalism" in the 1890s, when sensationalized headlines were used to increase newspaper circulation, the muckrakers drew attention to injustice,
(15) corruption, the abuse of **prerogative,** and health hazards that shook the public conscience. Not only was muckraking eminently profitable for publishers; the **ferment** it incited also often led to lasting
(20) reforms in American public policy.

Consider Upton Sinclair, often featured as the **epitome** of muckrakers for his pioneering novel *The Jungle* (1906). This work, which focused on the exploitation
(25) of immigrant workers in the Chicago stockyards, as well as on the appallingly unsanitary conditions there, elicited widespread indignation. Within a year, to **assuage** the public outcry, Congress
(30) passed the Pure Food and Drug Act and the Meat Inspection Act. Perhaps to tone down his **bombastic** approach, Sinclair said, "I aimed at the public's heart and by accident I hit it in the stomach." During his
(35) career, Sinclair continued to **expostulate** against economic and social injustice.

Upton Sinclair's work should be viewed in comparison with one of his most significant precursors, Ida M. Tarbell. Like
(40) Sinclair, Tarbell was a college graduate, a relatively rare achievement for a woman of her time. The daughter of a small oil company executive in Pennsylvania, she traveled to Paris to enroll in the Sorbonne
(45) and support herself through freelance journalism. Her magazine work attracted the attention of Samuel Sidney McClure, who hired her as an editor for his newly founded magazine in 1894. With
(50) admirable **aplomb,** she doubled the circulation of *McClure's Magazine* with her biographical series on Abraham Lincoln and Napoleon.

But Tarbell was not destined to linger
(55) in the archives of historical biography. Possibly motivated to **intercede** in a personal cause—her father had been driven out of business by the monopolistic practices of John D. Rockefeller—she
(60) embarked in 1902 on a multipart project entitled *The History of the Standard Oil Company*. Part chronicle and part exposé, this remarkable profile of America's most colossal firm of the era was a sensation.
(65) It was good reading but more than that: like Sinclair, Tarbell aroused public indignation, to the extent that in 1911 the Supreme Court ruled Standard Oil was in violation of antitrust legislation, a ruling
(70) that compelled the company to break up. With remarkable **sangfroid,** Tarbell had gone up against America's most formidable tycoon of industry, and she had won. Her victory can be ascribed
(75) not to sensationalism, but to a meticulous, hard-boiled but even-handed dedication to detail, and to an egalitarian sense of fairness. She was prepared to admit that John D. Rockefeller was a brilliant

(80) business executive and that capitalism was the best possible system for the American economy. Only about Standard Oil she wrote, "They had never played fair, and that ruined
(85) their greatness for me."

1. The primary purpose of the passage is to present
   A) a position and specific examples that defend it.
   B) biographical sketches that illustrate a type of journalism.
   C) contributing causes that explain a puzzling effect.
   D) a problem and several potential solutions.

2. In the first paragraph, the author suggests that the muckrakers had some elements in common with
   A) the agenda of the Progressive movement in politics.
   B) the platform of Theodore Roosevelt's opponents.
   C) the tactics and tone of yellow journalism.
   D) the strategies of news organizations.

3. As it is used in line 19, "ferment" most nearly means
   A) excitement.
   B) disobedience.
   C) tranquility.
   D) respite.

4. It can reasonably be inferred from the second paragraph that Upton Sinclair's novel *The Jungle* dealt with abuses in which of the following industries?
   A) Pharmaceutical
   B) Logging
   C) Meatpacking
   D) Railroad

5. Which choice provides the best evidence for the answer to the previous question?
   A) Lines 23–28 ("This work . . . indignation")
   B) Lines 28–31 ("Within. . . Act")
   C) Lines 31–34 ("Perhaps. . . stomach'")
   D) Lines 34–36 ("During . . . injustice")

6. As it is used in line 29, "assuage" most nearly means
   A) exacerbate.
   B) analyze.
   C) calm.
   D) register.

7. The author asserts all of the following about Ida Tarbell EXCEPT
   A) like Upton Sinclair, she was a college graduate.
   B) as a young writer, she was offered a job at *McClure's Magazine*.
   C) she authored a biographical series on Abraham Lincoln.
   D) she was personally acquainted with John D. Rockefeller.

8. Which of the following does the author point out as a similarity between Upton Sinclair and Ida Tarbell?
   A) The published work of both writers resulted in important reforms.
   B) Both writers were publicly recognized only long after their death.
   C) Both Sinclair and Tarbell were notable for their caustic writing style.
   D) Neither writer enjoyed any influence with President Theodore Roosevelt.

9. As it is used in line 71, "sangfroid" most nearly means
   A) poise.
   B) enthusiasm.
   C) patience.
   D) gratitude.

10. The author most likely includes the quotation from Tarbell in lines 83–85 to
   A) illustrate a biased perspective.
   B) emphasize Tarbell's commitment to fairness.
   C) refute a common preconception about muckraking.
   D) demonstrate Tarbell's commitment to accurate research.

Synonyms

*From the word bank below, choose the word that has the same or nearly the same meaning as the **boldface** word in each sentence and write it on the line. You will not use all of the words.*

acculturation	circuitous	expedite	precipitate
ascribe	commiserate	expostulate	seditious
bombastic	drivel	occult	unctuous
callow	epitome	permeate	vitriolic

1. We did not expect the valedictorian, who was normally shy and kept to himself, to give such a **pretentious** speech at graduation. _____

2. I hoped that my helping her would **facilitate** the process, but it took her so long to explain everything that I felt like more of a hindrance. _____

3. His comments about the article were certainly accurate, but I don't think such an **acerbic** tone was warranted. _____

4. After being up all night, I am so exhausted that everything coming out of my mouth sounds like **nonsense**. _____

5. As someone who has had to transfer to a new school, I can **empathize** with anyone who struggles with being the new kid. _____

6. You could have just asked me directly for help rather than using **indirect** language and giving me hints. _____

7. My colleague was trying to impress our new boss by doing her favors, but she just came across as a **fawning** flatterer. _____

8. My sister and I **argue** with our parents about moving to a new house, but they still refuse to hear to our reasoning. _____

9. The rescue dog's **adaptation** to us was a slow process, but after a few weeks he began to feel more comfortable. _____

10. Just when I think the day can't get any worse, I see ink from the pens in my pocket **soak through** the fabric of my shirt. _____

11. Reviewers say that the movie about the tragic love story will **provoke** feelings of grief in even the most stoic of viewers. _____

12. The replacement ran onto the field to take over after the starting quarterback was injured, hoping he would not seem like an **inexperienced** athlete. _____

Two-Word Completions

Select the pair of words that best completes the meaning of each of the following sentences.

1. Though my teaching job entails numerous responsibilities, it also brings with it certain _____, one of which is the right to use school equipment, services, and facilities during the _____ between semesters or the summer break.
   a. simulations . . . millennia
   b. ameliorations . . . proclivities
   c. prerogatives . . . hiatus
   d. surmises . . . innuendoes

2. Though the Prime Minister actually directs the British government, the reigning monarch is the _____ head of state and, by virtue of that position, also the _____ leader of the Anglican Church.
   a. adventitious . . . noncommittal
   b. nominal . . . ex officio
   c. tenuous . . . inadvertent
   d. intrinsic . . . occult

3. Some senators favored the new budget proposal and in the warmest terms _____ their colleagues to pass the measure. Others disliked the idea and just as vehemently _____ against its adoption.
   a. assuaged . . . interceded
   b. wheedled . . . enjoined
   c. elicited . . . infringed
   d. exhorted . . . inveighed

4. "The general's death-defying feats of gallantry in the recent war certainly deserve our _____," the article declared. "But, by the same token, his wanton acts of cruelty _____ our severest censure."
   a. aplomb . . . expiate
   b. sangfroid . . . elicit
   c. umbrage . . . enjoin
   d. approbation . . . merit

5. While the Roman people remained vigorous and aggressive, their empire flourished. Once they began to sink into a sort of physical and spiritual _____, however, the empire became feeble and _____.
   a. lassitude . . . decadent
   b. aplomb . . . jaded
   c. ferment . . . adventitious
   d. umbrage . . . petulant

6. As a result of the recent actions of several _____, who have since been indicted, the bank has instituted a new set of _____ guidelines regarding the transfer of funds.
   a. coalitions . . . lurid
   b. interlopers . . . hackneyed
   c. provincials . . . ingratiating
   d. peculators . . . stringent

7. "A(n) _____ government will prove workable only as long as its members are able to _____ party differences," the professor remarked. "As soon as they become entangled in factional disputes, the partnership will begin to collapse."
   a. seditious . . . ameliorate
   b. coalition . . . transcend
   c. provincial . . . surmise
   d. ex officio . . . abominate

Idioms

In the essay "Why Vote?" (see pages 24–25), the author talks about autocrats who "pay lip service to" democratic ideals. What the writer means is that the autocrats talk about the importance of democratic ideals, but they do not put these ideals into practice.

The phrase "pay lip service to" is an **idiom**—an expression that is not meant to be taken literally. Like other types of figurative language, idioms ask the reader or listener to associate two unlike things and create a mental image. Even if you have never heard a particular idiom before, you may be able to determine its meaning from its imagery or from the surrounding context. Some idioms, however, defy easy interpretation and must simply be memorized.

Choosing the Right Idiom

Read each sentence. Use context clues to figure out the meaning of each idiom in **boldface**. *Then write the letter of the definition for the idiom in the sentence.*

1. Renee has been **pounding the pavement** every day, but she still cannot find a job. _____

2. It is so typical of Mandy to **pass the buck** and assign her work to other members in the group. _____

3. Though many politicians enjoy **sitting on the fence**, this election will require candidates to be more committed. _____

4. Quit **dragging your feet** and decide which college you want to attend. _____

5. Anna has **burned so many bridges**, I'm surprised anyone in this town wants to hire her. _____

6. My trainer has a **bee in her bonnet** about sugar, and she advises against drinking soda or eating foods that are sweetened. _____

7. You can tell by the intricate details in the carving that Marco put a lot of **blood**, **sweat**, **and tears** into building his boat. _____

8. Of course I will not tell a soul how much you spent on those jeans. **My lips are sealed**! _____

9. You can count on Jonas to **go the extra mile** and produce a spectacular play. _____

10. Chad got a job at the bank during a hiring freeze because his father, a high-level manager, **pulled strings**. _____

a. refusing to take sides on an issue

b. alienated or destroyed prior relationships

c. diligently seeking something, such as a job

d. an idea that occupies one's thoughts; an obsession

e. do more than is expected

f. used political or personal influence to obtain something

g. avoid responsibility by giving it to others

h. tremendous hard work and effort

i. postponing or delaying a decision or action

j. a promise to maintain a secret

Classical Roots

cede, cess, ceas—to happen, yield, go

The root *cede* appears in **intercede** (page 14). The literal meaning is "to go between," but the word now means "to ask a favor from one person for another." Some other words based on the same root are listed below.

accede	cessation	decease	predecessor
accessory	concession	precedence	recession

From the list of words above, choose the one that corresponds to each of the brief definitions below. Write the word in the blank space in the illustrative sentence below the definition. Use an online or print dictionary if necessary.

1. an admission, anything yielded, a compromise; a franchise
There is always a line at the food _____.

2. a withdrawal, departure; a period of economic slump
Millions of workers were unemployed during the _____.

3. something added, a finishing touch; a helper in a crime
Her sister was held by the police as a(n) _____.

4. a stopping, ceasing
The ambassador called for a(n) _____ of hostilities.

5. death ("*going away*")
Marcia will inherit the estate after her aunt's _____.

6. someone or something that comes before another in time, especially in an office or position ("*one who leaves before*")
Starting today, I will take over from my _____.

7. to give in, agree; to attain ("*to yield to*")
The king's subjects are expected to _____ to all his requests.

8. priority in order, rank, or importance
Studying for finals must take _____ over everything else.

*Read the following passage, taking note of the **boldface** words and their contexts. These words are among those you will be studying in Unit 4. It may help you to complete the exercises in this Unit if you refer to the way the words are used below*

Ada Byron: Visionary Mathematician

<Biographical Sketch>

Ada Byron was born in London, England, in 1815, the daughter of the famed poet Lord Byron and his wife, Anna Milbanke. Ada's parents separated months after she was born. She never knew her father, who left England in 1816 and died when Ada was only nine years old. By the time they separated, Anna Milbanke had a thoroughly negative view of Lord Byron, believing him to be an unfaithful and **scurrilous** man. She feared that Ada might inherit the wild poetic **propensities** of her father, and she hoped that rigorous training in mathematics would discourage the development of unruly tendencies in her daughter. Thus, Ada spent much of her early life in the intelligent **aura** of **erudite** tutors, including some of the most brilliant mathematical minds of her day.

Ada was a **sedulous** student who excelled in mathematics, and she grew to become a talented and insightful mathematician. But the apple doesn't fall far from the tree. Ada's fretful mother was **querulous** about her daughter's poetic tendencies and **remonstrated** with her about their dangers, but Ada refused to **repudiate** her poetic qualities. And so Ada Byron became a gifted mathematician with a vivid imagination and a flair for language. She proved especially skillful at expressing mathematical concepts in writing. Though she suffered from illnesses throughout her life, she had a **resilient** spirit and remained focused on her studies and her rich social life.

When Ada was only seventeen years old, she met Charles Babbage. Babbage was a professor of mathematics who was designing an "analytical engine," a mechanical computing machine that was an **archetype** of the modern computer. Ada was fascinated by Babbage's description of the machine. She corresponded with him for the rest of her life, discussing mathematics, logic, and the operation of the analytical engine. In 1842, when an article about Babbage's machine was published in French,

Ada Byron

he asked Ada to translate it into English and to add her own explanatory notes to the English translation.

Babbage was not an **affable** man. He often **aggrandized** his own accomplishments and neglected to give credit to others. But he was so impressed with Ada's work that he conceded she might have understood his machine even better than he did, and that she was "far, far better at explaining it." Many mathematicians of the day had only an imperfect understanding of Babbage's machine, considering it an **inscrutable** and impractical device. Ada's notes provided a clear explanation for her contemporaries and included descriptions of procedures that are today considered to be

the first computer programs. In addition, Ada imagined applications of the machine that went beyond the **insular** field of mathematics. She foresaw that it could be used to compose music and could be put to a wide range of other symbolic uses.

Charles Babbage may have been the first person to design a computer, but Ada Byron was the first person to recognize the full potential of his machine. Especially remarkable in an age in which women were discouraged from participating in mathematics and the sciences, Ada's profound mathematical understanding, her eloquence in explaining the operation of Babbage's analytical engine, and her visionary insight into its many uses are accomplishments that continue to **reverberate** throughout history.

Charles Babbage

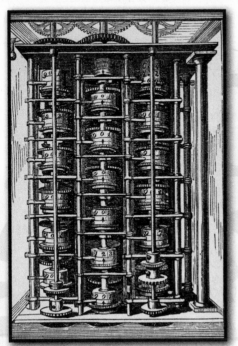

Charles Babbage designed a calculating machine called the Difference Engine before designing the analytical engine.

Audio

For iWords and audio passages, go to **SadlierConnect.com**.

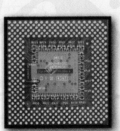

Procedures like those described by Ada Byron are performed by computer processors today.

Definitions

Note the spelling, pronunciation, part(s) of speech, and definition(s) of each of the following words. Then write the appropriate form of the word in the blank space in the illustrative sentence(s) following.

1. **aggrandize**
   (ə gran′ dīz)

   (*v.*) to increase in greatness, power, or wealth; to build up or intensify; to make appear greater

   John D. Rockefeller worked to _aggrandize_ his empire by purchasing oil wells, refineries, and pipelines.

2. **amorphous**
   (ə môr′ fəs)

   (*adj.*) shapeless, without definite form; of no particular type or character; without organization, unity, or cohesion

   The _amorphous_ body of the amoeba was fascinating to watch under the microscope.

3. **aura**
   (ôr′ ə)

   (*n.*) that which surrounds (as an atmosphere); a distinctive air or personal quality

   What people thought was her _aura_ of mystery was actually a mask for her shyness.

4. **erudite**
   (er′ yü dīt)

   (*adj.*) scholarly, learned, bookish, pedantic

   For my paper, I would like to find an _erudite_ history of the subject written in a clear and unbiased manner.

5. **inscrutable**
   (in skrü′ tə bəl)

   (*adj.*) incapable of being understood; impossible to see through physically

   I could not tell by her _inscrutable_ smile whether she was pleased or only amused with me.

6. **propensity**
   (prə pen′ sə tē)

   (*n.*) a natural inclination or predilection toward _preference_

   Queen Elizabeth I showed a strong _propensity_ for putting off decisions in the hopes that they would resolve themselves.

7. **querulous**
   (kwer′ ə ləs)

   (*adj.*) peevish, complaining, fretful _annoying_

   Some flight attendants dread a _querulous_ airline passenger more than they do rough weather.

8. **remonstrate**
   (ri män′ strāt)

   (*v.*) to argue with someone against something, protest against

   Slowly, carefully, keeping his voice down, he argued with the caller as one might _remonstrate_ with a child.

9. **resilient**
(ri zil′ yənt)

(*adj.*) able to return to an original shape or form; <u>able to</u> <u>recover quickly</u>
The development of lightweight, *resilient* _____ plastics revolutionized the design of many durable goods.

10. **sedulous**
(sej′ ə ləs)

(*adj.*) <u>persistent, showing industry and determination</u>
No one could say that he was lazy, for he was a careful, *sedulous* _____ copier of other people's work.

Using Context

*For each item, determine whether the **boldface** word from pages 58–59 makes sense in the context of the sentence. Circle the item numbers next to the six sentences in which the words are used correctly.*

(1.) I have found that people who are **erudite** are not necessarily good teachers, as they may find it difficult to break down a topic into simple terms.

(2.) Even studying with the most **sedulous** concentration will not help you if you only start preparing for an exam the night before.

3. The curtains were so **amorphous** that they were surely there for decoration rather than to keep out any light.

4. Her face is always fixed in a **querulous** expression, and when anyone addresses her she looks as if she were just startled out of a dream.

(5.) The greatest trailblazers throughout history often faced rejection, but they were **resilient** enough to keep trying.

(6.) The instructions for putting the desk together made so little sense that I deemed them **inscrutable**.

7. His **propensity** for air travel is so strong that he would prefer to go to Europe by boat than to board a plane.

(8.) Of course everyone looks to emphasize his or her strengths in a job interview, but be sure not to **aggrandize** yourself to the point of sounding arrogant.

9. The teacher will **remonstrate** with the students who answered the last question incorrectly so that they will not make the same mistake again.

(10.) The library is where I go to calm down, because as soon as I enter the building, I can sense an **aura** of peace and quiet.

Choosing the Right Word

*Select the **boldface** word that better completes each sentence. You might refer to the passage on pages 56–57 to see how most of these words are used in context. Note that the choices might be related forms of the Unit words.*

1. On its centennial, the entire country was immersed in a(n) (**propensity, aura**) of patriotism that was difficult to convey to outsiders.

2. Since he seems to have no moral standards whatsoever, it would probably be futile to (**aggrandize, remonstrate**) with him about his outrageous behavior.

3. Carefully avoiding any attempt at originality, she has fashioned her style on (**sedulous, resilient**) mimicry of other, more talented writers.

4. I tried to make some sense out of the strange orders he had given us, but his plan and purpose remained utterly (**erudite, inscrutable**).

5. When we arrived home, we were tired and depressed, but the (**querulous, resilient**) spirit of youth made things look brighter the next morning.

6. The musical composition, with no melodic pattern and no well-defined structure of development, seemed (**amorphous, querulous**) to my ear.

7. What we really resent is not sensible criticism but nagging that is petty, capricious, and (**querulous, sedulous**).

8. Throughout his career, the man has emphasized the (**aggrandizement, inscrutability**) of wealth and power at the expense of other values.

9. Lucy finally completed her (**querulous, erudite**) term paper, in which she quoted from more than a hundred sources.

10. Your (**propensity, aura**) for spending more than you can afford will lead to only one result—bankruptcy!

11. The puppy ignored the repeated (**remonstrative, erudite**) calls of its owners and ran right into the busy street, barely dodging the traffic.

12. No one could deny the (**aura, resilience**) of the small town, which once again swiftly rebuilt its downtown district after the destruction of another tornado.

Completing the Sentence

Choose the word from the word bank that best completes each of the following sentences. Write the correct word or form of the word in the space provided.

~~aggrandize~~	~~aura~~	~~inscrutable~~	~~querulous~~	~~resilient~~
~~amorphous~~	~~erudite~~	~~propensity~~	remonstrate	~~sedulous~~

1. Because of his __propensity__ for gossiping, we tried not to let him learn anything about our personal affairs.

2. As my opponent cited facts and figures without once referring to notes, I became aware of how __erudite__ she was.

3. She tried in vain to guess what surprise she might expect next from that __inscrutable__ power, Lady Luck.

4. He is really insufferable when he gets into one of those __querulous__ moods in which nothing in the world pleases him.

5. Perhaps she had less native ability than some of her classmates, but her powers of concentration and __sedulous__ study program enabled her to finish first in the class.

6. You used your admittedly remarkable talents only to __aggrandize__ yourself, not to benefit the society that was so kind to you.

7. The program he suggested was so barren of guiding ideas and specific proposals that I felt justified in referring to it as __amorphous__.

8. Since our efforts to __remonstrate__ with the factory managers about pollution of the lake have been ineffective, we are now considering legal action.

9. This jacket is made of a material so __resilient__ that it sheds wrinkles and keeps its shape even when one has worn it for days.

10. On his combat uniform, he wore absolutely no insignia of rank, but he was surrounded with an unmistakable __aura__ of authority.

Definitions

Note the spelling, pronunciation, part(s) of speech, and definition(s) of each of the following words. Then write the appropriate form of the word in the blank space in the illustrative sentence(s) following.

1. **affable**
   (af′ ə bəl)

   (*adj.*) courteous and pleasant, sociable, easy to speak to
   We spent a pleasant afternoon with our
   affable neighbors.

2. **archetype**
   (är′ kə tīp)

   (*n.*) an original model on which something was patterned or replicated; the ideal example of a particular type of person or thing *as it is*
   Sherlock Holmes was an _archetype_ of a clever detective who always solves the case.

3. **contraband**
   (kän′ trə band)

   (*n.*) illegal traffic, smuggled goods; (*adj.*) illegal, prohibited
   Three jeweled combs from the seventeenth century were among the _contraband_ seized by the police.

4. **gossamer**
   (gäs′ ə mər)

   (*adj.*) thin, light, delicate, insubstantial; (*n.*) a very thin, light cloth
   Ghosts are often depicted in literature as wearing _gossamer_ clothing that makes them seem all the more ethereal.
   The book was so old that each finely printed page seemed only the weight of _gossamer_.

5. **insular**
   (in′ syə lər)

   (*adj.*) relating to, characteristic of, or situated on an island; narrow or isolated in outlook or experience
   You seem too sophisticated to hold such _insular_ opinions.

6. **irrevocable**
   (i rev′ ə kə bəl)

   (*adj.*) incapable of being changed or called back *permanite*
   We tend to think of court verdicts as _irrevocable_, but they are often overturned by higher courts.

7. **repudiate**
   (ri pyü′ dē āt)

   (*v.*) to disown, reject, or deny the validity of
   He was forced to _repudiate_ a statement he had made before he'd had all the information.

8. **reverberate**
   (ri vər′ bə rāt)

   (*v.*) to re-echo, resound; to reflect or be reflected repeatedly
   From the construction site, the noise of bulldozers and dump trucks _reverberate_ across the valley.

9. scurrilous
(skər′ ə ləs)

(*adj.*) coarsely abusive, vulgar or low (especially in language), foul-mouthed

Days passed and unrest grew, and soon the rebels began a _scurrilous_ attack on their absent leader.

10. sleazy
(slē′ zē)

(*adj.*) thin or flimsy in texture; cheap; shoddy or inferior in quality or character; ethically low, mean, or disreputable

My grandmother made her clothes at home in order to avoid the _sleazy_ goods sold in the general store.

Using Context

*For each item, determine whether the **boldface** word from pages 62–63 makes sense in the context of the sentence. Circle the item numbers next to the six sentences in which the words are used correctly.*

1. Dropping the large pile of books was embarrassing enough, but when the crashing sound began to **reverberate** throughout the room and everyone looked over at me, my face turned beet red.

2. The size of the project was of **contraband** proportions, so I sighed with relief when I learned we would be working on it in groups.

3. The restaurant looks particularly **sleazy** from the outside, but what they lack in décor they make up in the best food you'll ever have.

4. Although it was written centuries ago, the story of Romeo and Juliet is the **archetype** of a tale about star-crossed lovers, on which many books and movies made today are based on.

5. His **insular** views on the world reflect how much he has traveled as well as how many people from different backgrounds he has gotten to know.

6. I was grateful that my roommate at summer camp was an **affable** young woman, and not the surly types whom I had passed on my way in.

7. None of us were expecting that what was predicted to be a quick storm would turn into a hurricane that unleashed **irrevocable** damage on our community.

8. I can **repudiate** your claim that you were studying at the library all morning, as I was there with you.

9. We tried every trick in the book to catch the mouse that had made its home in our basement, but the **scurrilous** creature was able to escape us every time.

10. The **gossamer** curtains were lovely as they blew in the breeze in the afternoon, but not as welcome the next morning when the rays of sun streamed right through them and onto my face.

Choosing the Right Word

Select the **boldface** word that better completes each sentence. You might refer to the passage on pages 56–57 to see how most of these words are used in context. Note that the choices might be related forms of the Unit words.

1. I think that nothing in Shakespeare is lighter or more delightful than the (**gossamer, sleazy**) wit and fancy of *A Midsummer Night's Dream*.

2. The four-year-old twins, Martin and Harrison, are such (**affable, irrevocable**) children that babysitting for them is a pleasure.

3. The philosopher said that the ancient question "Am I my brother's keeper?" has continued to (**reverberate, repudiate**) through the ages.

4. We cannot bar foreign influences from our shores, and we cannot treat unfamiliar ideas as (**gossamer, contraband**)!

5. The language he used in his bitter attack on us was so (**affable, scurrilous**) that I hesitate even to repeat it.

6. To keep the mosquitoes from biting us while we slept, we hung lightweight, (**scurrilous, gossamer**) mosquito netting around our cots.

7. While searching the ship's cargo, inspectors discovered a secret compartment containing (**gossamer, contraband**) animals, including several endangered species.

8. Our determination never to yield to force or the threat of force is firm and (**affable, irrevocable**)!

9. To limit the free expression of unpopular ideas is to (**repudiate, reverberate**) the basic spirit of the Bill of Rights.

10. Surrounded by people who voiced dismal ideas about the economy, Heather found their (**irrevocable, insular**) views disquieting.

11. After compiling feedback on the aircraft's design, the engineering group gathered to make improvements to the (**contraband, archetype**).

12. The pitiful derelict's only protection against the elements was a cheap overcoat made out of some kind of (**affable, sleazy**) material that wouldn't keep the cold out in a heat wave.

Completing the Sentence

Choose the word from the word bank that best completes each of the following sentences. Write the correct word or form of the word in the space provided.

affable	contraband	insular	repudiate	scurrilous
archetype	gossamer	irrevocable	reverberate	sleazy

1. I am not going to _____ the ideas and standards by which I have guided my life just because they have become unpopular.

2. _____ dives full of disreputable and dangerous-looking characters have given the waterfront areas of many cities a bad reputation.

3. When asked to create a science fiction villain for a story, many writers refer to Frankenstein, the _____ of a mad doctor.

4. The drops of dew sparkled like diamonds on the _____ threads of the spider web.

5. Under the latest regulations, any shipment of arms to those countries is illegal and may be seized as _____.

6. While tsarist Russia's vast territories were almost purely continental, the British Empire included numerous _____ possessions.

7. The sharp crack of the rifle shot _____ through the hills.

8. The commitment you have made is _____ without the consent of the other party to the agreement.

9. If you happen to have a(n) _____ seatmate on a long airplane flight, you may find yourself talking more freely about personal matters than you would under other circumstances.

10. His attempts to discredit her by belittling her ability and character were nothing more than _____ abuse.

Synonyms

*Choose the word or form of the word from this Unit that is the same or most nearly the same in meaning as the **boldface** word or expression in the phrase. Write that word on the line. Use a dictionary if necessary.*

1. **expostulate** with the cashier about the charges _____

2. **academic** study of the topic _____

3. answer with an **unreadable** smile _____

4. the **prototype** of all future films _____

5. a **tawdry** appearance _____

6. tried to calm the **petulant** customer _____

7. had a festive **feeling** _____

8. sounds that **echoed** in the Grand Canyon _____

9. only a **nebulous** idea of his future _____

10. **disclaim** an earlier promise _____

11. a relaxed, **agreeable** companion _____

12. thieves smuggling **illicit** materials _____

13. solved the case by being **diligent** _____

14. said her decision was **irreversible** _____

15. **ethereal** wings of a dragonfly _____

Antonyms

*Choose the word or form of the word from this Unit that is most nearly opposite in meaning to the **boldface** word or expression in the phrase. Write that word on the line. Use a dictionary if necessary.*

1. only supports causes that **diminish** their power _____

2. used **tasteful** language _____

3. the **disinclination** to take risks _____

4. has a **cosmopolitan** existence _____

5. remained **weak** after the crisis _____

Writing: Words in Action

Suppose you had the opportunity to write to Charles Babbage about computers in the twenty-first century. Follow in Ada Byron's footsteps and compose a short letter to Babbage, explaining how computers are used today. Use at least two details from the passage (pages 56–57) and three or more words from this Unit.

Vocabulary in Context

*Some of the words you have studied in this Unit appear in **boldface** type. Read the passage below, and then circle the letter of the correct answer for each word as it is used in context.*

Although fashion design and mathematics may seem antithetical to one another, these two disciplines are more interrelated than they initially seem. After a fashion designer has the initial inspiration for a garment, the journey from concept to finished creation varies widely: some designers have the **propensity** to sketch the idea first, while others begin by draping an **amorphous** piece of fabric over a dress form or a live model. At a later stage, designers choose the best fabric to fit their vision; for some garments, a luxurious fabric like velvet suits the vision, while more ethereal designs necessitate a transparent, yet not **sleazy** material.

Nothing is **contraband** when it comes to creating the straight lines found on collars, seams, and A-line dresses; designers make use of mathematical tools like T-squares and rulers to ensure that their final garments have the optimal fit. When fitting garments to the human frame, awareness of symmetry guarantees that clothes are balanced on the body. In addition, knowledge of angles, lines, and focal points enables fashion designers to highlight some parts of the body while minimizing others. When a design—with its angles, seams, and symmetry—is near completion, it can still be altered. Thus, nothing about fashion design is **irrevocable** until the designer decides that the process is complete.

Low-dimensional topology, the mathematics of two-, three-, and four-dimensional objects in nature, is another mathematical area that is being integrated into fashion design. Some innovative low-dimensional topologic designers have incorporated linked loops of gauzy, **gossamer** material into garments, while others have used knots and braids. The intersection of mathematics and fashion has produced many breathtaking fashion trends, and continued interdisciplinary collaboration will inspire designers to create more cutting-edge fashion.

1. The word **propensity** most nearly means
   a. an aversion to
   b. a natural inclination to
   c. a passive resistance to
   d. a positive reaction to

2. An **amorphous** piece of fabric is
   a. shapeless
   b. smooth
   c. opaque
   d. heavy

3. The word **sleazy** most nearly means
   a. luxurious and expensive
   b. richly textured and ornate
   c. thin or flimsy in texture
   d. heavily patterned and decorated

4. An object that is **contraband** is
   a. useful
   b. disposable
   c. complicated
   d. prohibited

5. Something that is **irrevocable** is
   a. incapable of being changed
   b. difficult to articulate
   c. unable to express in writing
   d. impossible to break

6. A dress of **gossamer** is
   a. miniature
   b. rough
   c. delicate
   d. sturdy

*Read the following passage, taking note of the **boldface** words and their contexts. These words are among those you will be studying in Unit 5. It may help you to complete the exercises in this Unit if you refer to the way the words are used below.*

Lending a Hand to End Poverty

<Newspaper Article>

By WALTER Q. VOGEL
November 12

Washington, D.C.—A local charity that studies antipoverty programs has declared one particular activist's model a notable success. In its annual report, "Fighting Poverty Today," Global Poverty Watchers United (GPWU) hailed the work of Muhammad Yunus, whose pioneering microloan program has helped thousands of Bangladeshis rise out of poverty. The charity suggests that the concept of microcredit—lending people very small sums of money—be tried by governments around the world. "Poverty is a **scourge** that knows no borders," says the report's author, Anja Aziz-Ooka. "In every country in the world, we find people living a hardscrabble existence. For some of them, thanks to microloans, escaping poverty can be more than just a dream."

Yunus's work to alleviate poverty began in 1974 during a visit to his native Bangladesh. The American-educated economist was shocked by the widespread famine he witnessed in his home country. Yunus figured that if destitute people were able to obtain small loans, they might be able to **extricate** themselves from the clutches of poverty. His first set of loans, from his own pocket, went to 42 borrowers and amounted to just $27. Yunus trusted that the majority of recipients were honest and would not **filch** these very small sums but would instead repay the money once they got on their feet.

From tiny acorns mighty oaks grow. In 1983, Yunus founded the Grameen Bank to apply the principles of microcredit throughout Bangladesh. To date, Grameen Bank has given loans to more than eight million poor people in Bangladesh, 97 percent of whom are women. The bank has found that women are more likely than men to use the loans to create a more **equitable** society and

Muhammad Yunus at a speech in Germany

better living conditions for their families. Borrowers use the loans to establish entrepreneurial ventures, such as a yogurt factory or village telephone service. The **salutary** effects of Grameen's microloans are undeniable: 58 percent of the bank's borrowers have now crossed over the poverty line and live better lives. The bank's loan repayment rate is a remarkable 97 percent.

In recognition of his efforts, Yunus was awarded the Nobel Peace Prize in 2006. As he accepted the Nobel Prize, Yunus made **scathing** comments about the living conditions that the poor must endure, and about the inequitable distribution of income worldwide. He pointed out that 60 percent of the global population lives on only 6 percent of the world's income. More than one billion people live on less than a dollar a day. His fame as a Nobel laureate and the success of the Grameen Bank have helped **blazon** the microfinance concept across the developing world. Yunus has issued a strong **caveat** to world leaders: Poverty, he believes, is a threat to peace.

This view is shared by scholars. "When human beings are trapped in a web of malnutrition, disease, and hopelessness, they lead a **sepulchral** existence," says Kevyn di Napoli, a researcher with the city Department of Social Assistance. "Poverty robs its victims of their **autonomy**, making them vulnerable to ruthless landlords and moneylenders and even the

This woman started a dressmaking shop with her loan.

This woman started a poultry farm with her Grameen loan.

bullies of organized crime." As a result, he notes, the desperately poor may become hostile and angry. "Inevitably, simply to survive, some will **flout** the law and social convention alike by turning to a life of crime."

One of Yunus's basic **precepts** is that poverty is the creation of poorly designed social and economic systems. Before the rise of microloan programs, it was **axiomatic** in banking circles that prospective borrowers had to have a job and collateral. Change in traditional banking practices has come at a **soporific** pace, says GPWU's Aziz-Ooka. "Too many bankers have been unimaginative, **straitlaced**, and unwilling to experiment with bold, new ideas." Clearly, microfinance is no **transient** phenomenon, as Yunus's forty years of success shows (he retired in 2011). Similar programs are being created across the developing world, from Malawi in Africa to Bolivia in South America. As Yunus asserted in his Nobel Prize acceptance speech, "We can create a poverty-free world if we collectively believe in it."

Audio

For iWords and audio passages, go to SadlierConnect.com.

Definitions

Note the spelling, pronunciation, part(s) of speech, and definition(s) of each of the following words. Then write the appropriate form of the word in the blank space in the illustrative sentence(s) following.

1. amnesty (am′ nə stē)	(*n.*) a general pardon for an offense against a government; in general, any act of forgiveness or absolution Many political prisoners were freed under the _____ granted by the new regime.
2. blazon (blāz′ ən)	(*v.*) to adorn or embellish; to display conspicuously; to publish or proclaim widely They will _____ the results of the election across the Internet and every television set in the land.
3. equitable (ek′ wə tə bəl)	(*adj.*) fair, just, embodying principles of justice He did more work, so a sixty-forty split of the profits seemed an _____ arrangement.
4. filch (filch)	(*v.*) to steal, especially in a sneaky way and in petty amounts If you _____ pennies from the cash drawer, you will be tempted to steal larger amounts one day.
5. fractious (frak′ shəs)	(*adj.*) tending to be troublesome; unruly, quarrelsome, contrary; unpredictable It seems as if even the smoothest-running organizations contain one or two _____ elements.
6. precept (prē′ sept)	(*n.*) a rule of conduct or action Many philosophies follow the _____ that it is important to treat others as you would like to be treated.
7. scathing (skā′ thiŋ)	(*adj.*) bitterly severe, withering; causing great harm Sometimes a reasoned discussion does more to change people's minds than a _____ attack.
8. soporific (säp ə rif′ ik)	(*adj.*) tending to cause sleep, relating to sleepiness or lethargy; (*n.*) something that induces sleep He claimed that the musical was _____ and that he had slept through the entire second act. Shakespeare's Juliet drinks a _____ so as to appear to be dead—a trick she is soon to regret.

9. straitlaced
(strāt′ lāst)

(*adj.*) extremely strict in regard to moral standards and conduct; prudish, puritanical

Travelers may find people overseas _____ in some ways but surprisingly free in others.

10. vapid
(vap′ id)

(*adj.*) dull, uninteresting, tiresome; lacking in sharpness, flavor, liveliness, or force

While critics called the movie _____, I thought the performers were very compelling.

Using Context

*For each item, determine whether the **boldface** word from pages 70–71 makes sense in the context of the sentence. Circle the item numbers next to the six sentences in which the words are used correctly.*

1. I enjoy watching costume dramas and seeing the **straitlaced** behaviors and customs, but I could never live like that.

2. I often look for a moment of **amnesty** by eating lunch in the empty cubicle.

3. Although I do not think the book lives up to the author's previous works, it did not deserve such **scathing** reviews.

4. The actress's manager tried to contain the story about her private life, but still the gossip columnist was able to **blazon** it across social media for everyone to read.

5. When the petty thieves tried to **filch** a few dollars from the donation can, they accidentally knocked it over, calling attention to their intended misdeed.

6. Although the movie was filled with exciting graphics and an interesting score, the plot itself was decidedly **vapid**.

7. The jury's **equitable** decision to convict the suspect, despite his alibi, will be protested by local advocates for justice.

8. As a new rider, the trainer gave me the most **fractious** horse so that I would feel at ease.

9. I can certainly appreciate most classical music, but sometimes the melodies are so **soporific** that I begin to drift off.

10. I have found that when I go into a situation with a negative **precept** of what will happen, I usually end up having a bad time.

Choosing the Right Word

*Select the **boldface** word that better completes each sentence. You might refer to the passage on pages 68–69 to see how most of these words are used in context. Note that the choices might be related forms of the Unit words.*

1. I now know that Jonathan Swift's *Gulliver's Travels*, far from being a "children's book," is a work of mature and (**scathing, vapid**) satire.

2. Today our intricate network of mass communications can (**blazon, filch**) news of national importance across the country in a matter of minutes.

3. We had many talented players, but the (**fractious, scathing**) behavior of a few individuals impaired our team spirit and led to a losing season.

4. Instead of brooding about past wrongs, I suggest that you declare a personal (**amnesty, precept**) and start thinking about the future.

5. In spite of the tremendous sales of that novel, I found it to be mediocre and (**fractious, vapid**) in every respect.

6. The verbal sparring that took place between the two head coaches was (**blazoned, filched**) across headlines nationwide.

7. Arriving at (**fractious, equitable**) arrangements in human affairs often requires sound judgment, as well as good intentions.

8. Officials who took bribes were indicted with no hope of a(n) (**amnesty, precept**).

9. Some sadly misguided individuals seem to go through life trying to (**filch, blazon**) petty advantages from everyone they encounter.

10. You may regard her ideas as (**equitable, straitlaced**), but I think that they reflect good thinking and sound values.

11. I intend to be guided by the simple (**amnesties, precepts**) that have proven their value over long periods of human experience.

12. I didn't expect the play to be particularly stimulating, but I certainly never anticipated its overwhelmingly (**equitable, soporific**) power.

Completing the Sentence

Choose the word from the word bank that best completes each of the following sentences. Write the correct word or form of the word in the space provided.

amnesty	equitable	fractious	scathing	straitlaced
blazon	filch	precept	soporific	vapid

1. Who would have thought that the new treasurer could sink so low as to _____ money from the club's petty cash fund?

2. Her approach to the problem seems to have been guided by the time-honored _____ that "force is the remedy for nothing."

3. The fighter planes of World War II sometimes had the pictures of famous movie stars, like Betty Grable, _____ on the fuselage.

4. The _____ effect of his droning lectures surpasses that of any sleeping pill now in use.

5. Even the most talented actors could not breathe life and credibility into the _____ lines of that silly play.

6. The standards of behavior generally accepted in Victorian times would probably be rejected today as excessively _____.

7. The new government, seeking to restore normal conditions, declared a(n) _____ for all political prisoners.

8. The decision was a disappointment to me, but after thinking it over, I had to agree that it was _____.

9. My teacher's criticism of my term paper was so _____ that after reading it, I felt thoroughly crushed.

10. It became clear that the squad of police would be unable to control the small but _____ crowd of angry protesters.

Definitions

Note the spelling, pronunciation, part(s) of speech, and definition(s) of each of the following words. Then write the appropriate form of the word in the blank space in the illustrative sentence(s) following.

1. autonomy
(ô tän′ ə mē)

(*n.*) self-government, political control

After the colonies gained _____ from England, many Americans still clung to English traditions.

2. axiomatic
(ak sē ə mat′ ik)

(*adj.*) self-evident, expressing a universally accepted principle

One should not accept the idea that the camera never lies as an _____ truth.

3. caveat
(kav′ ē at)

(*n.*) a warning or caution to prevent misunderstanding or discourage behavior

The well-known Latin phrase " _____ emptor" means, "Let the buyer beware."

4. extricate
(ek′ strə kāt)

(*v.*) to free from entanglements or difficulties; to remove with effort

The ring must have slid off my finger as I was trying to _____ the fish from the net.

5. flout
(flaůt)

(*v.*) to mock, treat with contempt

She chose to ignore my advice, not because she wanted to _____ my beliefs, but because she had strong opinions of her own.

6. salutary
(sal′ yə ter ē)

(*adj.*) beneficial, helpful; healthful, wholesome

The cute new puppy had a _____ effect on her health.

7. scourge
(skərj)

(*v.*) to whip, punish severely; (*n.*) a cause of affliction or suffering; a source of severe punishment or criticism

Jonathan Swift used wit to _____ the British government for its cruel treatment of Ireland.
Competing teams consider my daughter the _____ of the soccer field.

8. sepulchral
(sə pəl′ krəl)

(*adj.*) funereal, typical of the tomb; extremely gloomy or dismal

In a severe and _____ tone of voice, my sister announced that we were out of cookies.

9. transient (tran' shənt)	(*adj.*) lasting only a short time, fleeting; (*n.*) one who stays only a short time His bad mood was _____, and by the time he'd finished his breakfast, he was smiling. Many farm hands lived the lives of _____ during the Great Depression.
10. unwieldy (ən wēl' dē)	(*adj.*) not easily carried, handled, or managed because of size or complexity We loaded the truck with the chairs and the coffee table, but the grand piano was too _____.

Using Context

*For each item, determine whether the **boldface** word from pages 74–75 makes sense in the context of the sentence. Circle the item numbers next to the six sentences in which the words are used correctly.*

1. Although exercise is the last thing I feel like doing when I'm tired, it always has a **salutary** effect on my mood.

2. He resolved to never drive a minivan again, as the one time he tried it proved too **unwieldy** for him to handle.

3. I plan to **flout** any questions about what I will do if I do not get into the only college I applied to by ignoring them.

4. Whenever I am in a tough situation, I just remind myself that everything is **transient** and that one day I'll barely remember the issues that once felt like crises.

5. The **axiomatic** way in which she answered my questions hinted that she knew more than she was letting on.

6. I wrote a letter to **scourge** our local politicians for their public support of the music program.

7. While it may be tempting to sign an extensive contract without reading the fine print, you must check for any **caveat** that may make you change your mind.

8. I felt as if I were being held in **autonomy** after listening to the lecture for four hours.

9. I thought something was wrong when I heard the **sepulchral** tone of her voice, but she merely informed me that she had a cold and would have to cancel our dinner plans.

10. I was grateful when my friend called me over to **extricate** me from a deadly conversation.

Choosing the Right Word

*Select the **boldface** word that better completes each sentence. You might refer to the passage on pages 68–69 to see how most of these words are used in context. Note that the choices might be related forms of the Unit words.*

1. The ghost of Hamlet's father whispered in (**sepulchral, salutary**) tones the story of his tragic death.

2. Unabridged dictionaries often alert the reader to common mistakes in the use of a word by including brief (**caveats, scourges**).

3. How easy it is for a nation to become trapped in an inflationary price rise; how difficult to (**flout, extricate**) itself from the upward spiral!

4. Few things are more (**salutary, unwieldy**) for a young person than an occasional painful reminder that life is not a bowl of cherries.

5. Young people, tired of being controlled by parents, teachers, and others, often have a strong impulse to gain (**caveat, autonomy**).

6. Those who consider themselves nonconformists often go to extremes in their determination to (**extricate, flout**) the conventions.

7. Appointed by the governor to be commissioner of investigations, she soon became the (**scourge, autonomy**) of dishonest and incompetent officials.

8. The rules of the club proved so (**unwieldy, salutary**) that it was all but impossible to carry on business.

9. The (**caveat, scourge**) of plagiarism is on the rise in many schools as students cut and paste from essays they download from the Internet.

10. The newly elected judge ruled his courtroom with a king's (**scourge, autonomy**), and no one dared to act in an unruly fashion.

11. The popular self-help book teaches that material things are (**transient, axiomatic**), while moral values are eternal.

12. Isn't it strange that the basic ideas that some economists regard as (**sepulchral, axiomatic**) are rejected by others as absolutely false!

Completing the Sentence

Choose the word from the word bank that best completes each of the following sentences. Write the correct word or form of the word in the space provided.

autonomy	**caveat**	**flout**	**scourge**	**transient**
axiomatic	**extricate**	**salutary**	**sepulchral**	**unwieldy**

1. Shivers went up and down our spines as, in a(n) _____ voice, the teacher spoke to us of ghosts, vampires, and the "living dead."

2. It is _____ that democracy, more than any other form of government, calls for the active participation of all the people in public affairs.

3. It was Lincoln who said, "Fondly do we hope, fervently do we pray, that this mighty _____ of war may speedily pass away."

4. Any unit of government—national or local—that _____ sound economic principles is headed for disaster.

5. I tried to warn them of the dangers involved in such an undertaking, but all my _____ and admonitions fell on deaf ears.

6. Since the close of World War II, almost one hundred former colonies have gained full _____ and joined the family of nations.

7. Failures are always unpleasant, but if you learn from them, they may have a(n) _____ effect on your future career.

8. His fame as a football star proved to be _____, and he found himself just another young man looking for a job.

9. She has made so many contradictory promises to so many people that I don't see how she can _____ herself from the situation.

10. The carton was not heavy, but it was so _____ that it took four of us to carry it to the shed.

Synonyms

*Choose the word or form of the word from this Unit that is the same or most nearly the same in meaning as the **boldface** word or expression in the phrase. Write that word on the line. Use a dictionary if necessary.*

1. an **indubitable** idea _____
2. the critic's **savage** review _____
3. an **insipid** little five-note tune _____
4. my **overly strict** grandparents _____
5. a **doleful** atmosphere during the service _____
6. eager to **scoff at** the unknown _____
7. **broadcast** across the sky _____
8. to **pocket** some coins from petty cash _____
9. a **valuable** lesson in fire safety _____
10. guided by stern **rules** _____
11. **disengage** the cat from the tree _____
12. an **acquittal** for the former rebels _____
13. an argumentative, **obstinate** congress _____
14. too **cumbersome** to carry home _____
15. a **forewarning** regarding possible difficulties _____

Antonyms

*Choose the word or form of the word from this Unit that is most nearly opposite in meaning to the **boldface** word or expression in the phrase. Write that word on the line. Use a dictionary if necessary.*

1. had an **invigorating** effect _____
2. considered a **boon** to the competitors _____
3. hired **permanent** workers _____
4. an example of municipal **dependence** _____
5. a(n) **disproportionate** settlement _____

Writing: Words in Action

Do you agree that small loans can encourage people to become more self-sufficient, or do you think such loans can make people more dependent? In a brief essay, support your opinion using examples, observations, and the reading (refer to pages 68–69). Use at least two details and three or more words from this Unit.

Vocabulary in Context

*Some of the words you have studied in this Unit appear in **boldface** type. Read the passage below, and then circle the letter of the correct answer for each word as it is used in context.*

In South Africa, the gap between the wealthy and the impoverished is the largest in the world. Two factors that contribute to this **fractious** discrepancy are race and gender. Though women comprise 52 percent of South Africa's population, white men earn 53 percent more than white women and 116 percent more than black women. This situation seems **unwieldy** at first glance, but the state of conditions has improved. Microlending programs have targeted black women in rural areas to make access to wealth more **equitable**.

New entrepreneurship organizations have partnered with companies and individuals to provide microloans to South African women in poorer, rural areas who would not normally qualify for a loan. Some recipients of microloans have invested the money in their own businesses, thus gaining financial control. Since women worldwide invest 90 percent of their income in their families, this money has precipitated a domino effect. South African recipients of microloans spend money in their households, and that action ultimately stimulates their communities. This money also helps alleviate the **scourge** of poverty in that region of the country.

Some critics consider microlending just another **vapid** form of charity, but experts would contend that microlending is a pioneering type of humanitarian aid, similar to providing **amnesty** to those who have received unfair prison sentences. By helping one person at a time, microlending is impacting individuals, families, and communities around the world. Perhaps one day there will be no need for microlending. Until that day, microlending helps address the chasm between wealth and poverty around the globe.

---

1. The word **fractious** most nearly means
   a. likely to be broken
   b. able to be overturned
   c. prone to failure
   d. tending to be troublesome

2. Something that is **unwieldy** is
   a. not easily managed
   b. easy to comprehend
   c. difficult to process
   d. easy to conceptualize

3. A situation is **equitable** if it is
   a. appropriate
   b. fair
   c. accessible
   d. knowledgeable

4. Poverty is a **scourge** because it is
   a. an investment of time
   b. a cause of suffering
   c. an effect of homelessness
   d. a denial of responsibility

5. A **vapid** idea is
   a. uninteresting
   b. unintelligible
   c. unflattering
   d. untimely

6. The word **amnesty** most nearly means
   a. an agreement between groups
   b. an act of absolution
   c. a contract for consideration
   d. a deed requiring payment

Read the following passage, taking note of the **boldface** words and their contexts. These words are among those you will be studying in Unit 6. It may help you to complete the exercises in this Unit if you refer to the way the words are used below.

Pre-Columbian America
<Blog Entry>

A teacher visiting pre-Columbian (before the time of Christopher Columbus) sites in Mexico during her summer break blogged about her experience for her students.

Near Mexico City, July 2011

Hello from Mexico! My hope is that everyone reading this blog lives my experiences **vicariously**. I'm sitting in a creaky, threadbare seat on a broiling, crowded bus. Far from feeling **ennui**, I am enjoying every minute of this sweaty bus ride because we are nearing the first great American city. Teotihuacán had 200,000 inhabitants a millennium before Columbus set foot in the Americas. It boasted broad avenues and stately pyramids as massive as the largest in Egypt. And to think that the first European arrivals cast **aspersions** on the native population groups they encountered, believing that they had landed on a continent peopled only by struggling farmers and hunter-gatherers.

Perhaps you recall learning in world history class that the European settlers, unaware of the widespread existence of formidable civilizations like this one, scorned the natives they met. These settlers directly or **surreptitiously** usurped lands that the local inhabitants had occupied for centuries, either **cajoling** them

with trinkets, or else **contriving** other ways to cheat them. Had the Europeans only seen the fine pottery, masks, advanced calendars, glorious palaces and temples! But when the Europeans arrived in North America, they saw populations already decimated by diseases brought by earlier European fishermen and explorers. Pushing the weakened natives out was a **sinecure**.

Terracotta figure of Tlaloc, god of rain and water, from Teotihuacán

Pyramid of the Sun,
Teotihuacán, Mexico

At Teotihuacán

It is not true that dead men tell no tales, because the long-gone population of Teotihuacán has left behind plenty that tells us of its great society. In front of me now is the spectacular Pyramid of the Sun. There is nothing **anomalous** about the engineering marvels at Teotihuacán. Great civilizations throughout the so-called new world lived in cities larger than those in Europe at the same time. **Fettered** by ignorance and ethnocentrism, people in Europe's capital cities would have found the idea of sophisticated cultures across the Atlantic completely **bizarre**; but had they seen the impressive Toltec, Mayan, Aztec, or Incan civilizations in their prime, they would have been **disabused** of the notion that the lands Columbus "discovered" always had been thinly populated and lightly tread upon.

I overheard a tour guide telling visitors that by the time the Europeans arrived, all the great civilizations that had built such astounding structures were crumbling or lost forever. Gone were the vast trading networks, the advanced metallurgy techniques, and the agricultural methods that **transmuted** barren land and steep hillsides into fertile growing land. Gone, too, were the all-powerful rulers who reigned as ruthlessly as did the most **heinous** kings in Europe, and who freely **castigated** their subjects for **transgressing** even the pettiest of laws. What remained were tools, pottery shards, and remnants of fine roads and great temples.

End of a Great Day

After spending the day traveling back in time, I am now on the bus back to the modern world. I saw **immutable** proof that a great city in an advanced civilization once existed here, and I wonder how many of you know of Teotihuacán or have even heard of the huge but long-gone urban centers of Chaco and Cahokia in the United States. The true history of the Americas was misunderstood not only by the first European visitors, but by people in our own time. Thankfully, this is changing as new scholarship is transforming long-held beliefs about the nature of life in the Americas before Columbus. A "lightly tread-upon" continent? No way!

Audio

For iWords)) and audio passages, go to SadlierConnect.com.

Definitions

Note the spelling, pronunciation, part(s) of speech, and definition(s) of each of the following words. Then write the appropriate form of the word in the blank space in the illustrative sentence(s) following.

1. anomalous
(ə näm' ə ləs)

(*adj.*) abnormal, irregular, departing from the usual
Feeling protective of my friend but knowing of his difficulties placed me in an _____ position.

2. bizarre
(bi zär')

(*adj.*) extremely strange, unusual, atypical
Years from now I will look at this picture and wonder what sort of _____ costume I was wearing.

3. cajole
(kə jōl')

(*v.*) to coax, persuade through flattery or artifice; to deceive with soothing thoughts or false promises
With a smile, a joke, and a second helping of pie, she would _____ him into doing what she wanted.

4. demagogue
(dem' ə gäg)

(*n.*) a leader who exploits popular prejudices and false claims and promises in order to gain power
Often a show of angry concern conceals the self-serving tactics of a _____.

5. disabuse
(dis ə byüz')

(*v.*) to free from deception or error, set right in ideas or thinking
He thinks that all women adore him, but my sister will probably _____ him of that idea.

6. fetter
(fet' ər)

(*n.*) a chain or shackle placed on the feet (often used in plural); anything that confines or restrains; (*v.*) to chain or shackle; to render helpless or impotent
_____ on the prisoners deterred escape.
It is said that good inventors do not _____ themselves with conventional thinking.

7. heinous
(hā' nəs)

(*adj.*) very wicked, offensive, hateful
A town so peaceful, quiet, and law-abiding was bound to be horrified by so _____ a crime.

8. megalomania
(meg ə lō mā' nē ə)

(*n.*) a delusion marked by a feeling of power, wealth, talent, etc., far in excess of reality
Sudden fame and admiration can make people feel unworthy—or it can bring on feelings of _____.

9. surreptitious
(sər əp tish′ əs)

(*adj.*) stealthy, secret, intended to escape observation;
made or accomplished by fraud
The movie heroine blushed when she noticed the
_____ glances of her admirer.

10. transmute
(tranz myüt′)

(*v.*) to change from one nature, substance, or form to another
To _____ distrust into cooperation along
that war-torn border will take more than talk and treaties.

Using Context

*For each item, determine whether the **boldface** word from pages 82–83
makes sense in the context of the sentence. Circle the item numbers
next to the six sentences in which the words are used correctly.*

1. His story to explain why he was late is so **bizarre** that I believe him, if only because
it is truly stranger than anything he could make up.

2. As someone who loves to clean and organize, I always **fetter** my room with junk.

3. Although I can only donate an **anomalous** amount of money to charities each year,
I know that every little bit will help.

4. The con artist pulls off his schemes by thinking of ways to **disabuse** people into trusting
him with their personal information.

5. When my little sister suddenly starts being sweet to me, I immediately assume she
is trying to **cajole** me into doing her a favor.

6. I was suspicious of why they were sneaking around in such a **surreptitious** manner,
until I learned they were planning a surprise party for me!

7. I know it was thoughtless of me to forget your birthday, but I would hardly describe it
as a **heinous** act.

8. The famous scientist displayed such **megalomania** that she could not hear a compliment
without giving credit to one of her colleagues.

9. After declaring that I would not live anywhere but the city, who would believe that my
tolerance for rural living would **transmute** into love for the great outdoors?

10. When tensions are running high, we must not let a **demagogue** seize power by
taking advantage of our fears.

Choosing the Right Word

*Select the **boldface** word that better completes each sentence. You might refer to the passage on pages 80–81 to see how most of these words are used in context. Note that the choices might be related forms of the Unit words.*

1. Have you ever heard of anything as (**bizarre, anomalous**) as an experimental technique to test the intelligence of cows?

2. If, as they now claim, they were not aware of the illegal character of their undertaking, why did they plan it so (**cajolingly, surreptitiously**)?

3. The task of education, said the speaker, is to (**cajole, transmute**) the primitive selfishness of the child into socially useful modes of behavior.

4. Her conduct after her mother's death was so (**anomalous, surreptitious**) that I must conclude she was not in full possession of her faculties.

5. A favorite ploy of the (**anomalous, demagogue**) is to appoint a convenient scapegoat upon whom a misguided populace can vent its anger.

6. For ancient Romans, fleeing from the battlefield was the most (**heinous, bizarre**) act of cowardice a soldier could commit.

7. He's so tight with his money that it's just about impossible to (**cajole, transmute**) a nickel out of him, no matter how worthy the cause.

8. Government bureaucracy was hobbling many programs with (**fetters, demagogues**) of red tape.

9. While I was sleeping soundly in my tent, oblivious to nocturnal creatures, a snake made its (**bizarre, surreptitious**) way across the campsite.

10. I spent all morning trying to (**cajole, fetter**) our frightened cat out from under the house.

11. Her opinion of her own importance is so grotesquely exaggerated that we have come to regard her as a (**megalomaniac, demagogue**).

12. My uncle Rick seems unable to (**cajole, disabuse**) himself of the idea that he is still capable of the feats he performed in his youth.

Completing the Sentence

Choose the word from the word bank that best completes each of the following sentences. Write the correct word or form of the word in the space provided.

anomalous	cajole	disabuse	heinous	surreptitious
bizarre	demagogue	fetter	megalomania	transmute

1. The speaker's blatant appeal to the emotions of the crowd smacked more of the _____ than of a true leader of the people.

2. Resorting to rather farfetched promises, I finally _____ Tina into going to the prom with me.

3. The _____ way in which they planned the undertaking shows that they were aware of its illegal character.

4. Is there any other crime in history as _____ as the attempt of the Nazis to annihilate so-called inferior racial groups?

5. Can you imagine anything as _____ as a successful drama coach who has never acted on the stage?

6. His conceit is so great and so immune to the lessons of experience that this must be considered a kind of _____.

7. At the very outset of the term, I urged you to _____ yourself of the idea that you can pass this course without hard, regular work.

8. The alchemists of the Middle Ages, who were both mystics and primitive chemists, hoped to _____ base metals into gold.

9. The Emancipation Proclamation issued by Abraham Lincoln once and for all broke the _____ that bound African Americans to a life of servitude.

10. Wearing _____ masks at Halloween is a tradition that goes back many centuries.

Definitions

Note the spelling, pronunciation, part(s) of speech, and definition(s) of each of the following words. Then write the appropriate form of the word in the blank space in the illustrative sentence(s) following.

1. aspersion
(ə spər' zhən)

(*n.*) a damaging or derogatory statement; the act of slandering or defaming

Think twice before casting _____ on his honesty, for he might be telling the truth.

2. brusque
(brəsk)

(*adj.*) abrupt, blunt, with no formalities

His request for a large loan for an indefinite length of time was met with a _____ refusal.

3. castigate
(kas' tə gāt)

(*v.*) to punish severely; to criticize severely

After he _____ the unruly children, they settled down to study quietly.

4. contrive
(kən trīv')

(*v.*) to plan with ingenuity; to bring about through a plan

She can _____ wonderful excuses; but when she tries to offer them, her uneasiness gives her away.

5. ennui
(än wē')

(*n.*) weariness and dissatisfaction from lack of occupation or interest, boredom

Some people seem to confuse sophistication with

_____.

6. immutable
(i myü' tə bəl)

(*adj.*) not subject to change, constant

Scientists labored to discover a set of

_____ laws of the universe.

7. insurgent
(in sər' jənt)

(*n.*) one who rebels or rises against authority; (*adj.*) rising in revolt, refusing to accept authority; surging or rushing in or on

George Washington and his contemporaries were

_____ against Britain.

The army was confident that they could crush the

_____ forces.

8. sinecure
(si' nə kyür)

(*n.*) a position requiring little or no work; an easy job

The office of Vice President of the United States was once considered little more than a _____.

9. transgress
(tranz gres')

(*v.*) to go beyond a limit or boundary; to sin, violate a law
The penitent citizens promised never again to
_____ the laws of the land.

10. vicarious
(vī kâr' ē əs)

(*adj.*) performed, suffered, or otherwise experienced by
one person in place of another
In search of _____ excitement, we
watched movies of action and adventure.

Using Context

For each item, determine whether the **boldface** *word from pages 86–87 makes sense in the context of the sentence. Circle the item numbers next to the six sentences in which the words are used correctly.*

1. Her knowledge on the subject, combined with her exceptional rhetorical skills, make her an **immutable** opponent in a debate.

2. Our professor seems to suffer from such **ennui** after so many years of teaching that even on the first day of class he seemed to be half asleep.

3. Her emails are always filled with exclamation points and friendly greetings, so I was surprised by her **brusque** behavior when we finally met in person.

4. After the poor service he received at the new restaurant, the diner spoke with the manager to make an **aspersion** against the staff, hoping that he would not have to pay for his meal.

5. During the graduation ceremony, we will **castigate** any faculty members who are retiring by having some of their students say a few words about their legacy.

6. Your ability to **contrive** stories about other people actually makes you a liar and not, as you argue, a "superb storyteller."

7. "Being an assistant may seem like a **sinecure**, but I always do as much work as I can in a day," she said as she flipped through a magazine at her desk.

8. The teacher pointed out general areas we should focus on when studying for the exam so that we do not waste time reviewing **vicarious** information.

9. Many young children will try to **transgress** the boundaries set by their parents, but that is just their way of testing the limits and not an indication that they will be rebellious adolescents.

10. The mayor planned to have double the police protection during his speech, as he knew that **insurgent** groups would attend in order to protest his announcement.

Choosing the Right Word

*Select the **boldface** word that better completes each sentence. You might refer to the passage on pages 80–81 to see how most of these words are used in context. Note that the choices might be related forms of the Unit words.*

1. Laura Ingalls Wilder's *Little House on the Prairie* books were so vivid that, as a child, I felt I was (**vicariously, immutably**) experiencing the realities of pioneer life.

2. In *Gulliver's Travels* and other writings, Jonathan Swift (**transgressed, castigated**) the human race for its follies and wickedness.

3. With the innumerable activities open to a young person like you, I can't understand why you should suffer from (**ennui, aspersion**).

4. By casting (**sinecures, aspersions**) on the ability and character of others, you reveal the misgivings you have about yourself.

5. A(n) (**insurgent, vicarious**) group at the convention refused to accept the choices of the regular party leaders.

6. She may have kept within the letter of the law, but there is no doubt that she has (**contrived, transgressed**) the accepted moral code.

7. Many of Mark Twain's contemporaries found his essays amusing, but others cringed at his (**immutable, brusque**) commentary.

8. I cannot understand how she was able to (**castigate, contrive**) a meeting between two people who had refused to have anything to do with each other.

9. What hurt my feelings was not so much his refusal to give me a job as the (**brusque, vicarious**) way in which he told me that he had nothing for me.

10. Although her new position bore a high-sounding title, it was really little more than a(n) (**insurgent, sinecure**).

11. The institutions of our society, far from being (**immutable, insurgent**), are in the process of change at this very moment.

12. The coach put his faith in his team, hoping they would not (**contrive, transgress**) the bounds of their training and violate protocol.

Completing the Sentence

Choose the word from the word bank that best completes each of the following sentences. Write the correct word or form of the word in the space provided.

aspersion	castigate	ennui	insurgent	transgress
brusque	contrive	immutable	sinecure	vicarious

1. The one fact about nature that seems completely _____ is that everything is subject to change.

2. Rude questions call for _____ answers, and mine is "No!"

3. Anyone who refers to my job as a(n) _____ should spend just one day in my place!

4. I find it hard to understand how they were able to _____ such an elaborately underhanded scheme in so short a time.

5. In her determination to be blunt and honest, she has _____ the limits of good taste.

6. Although most of us lead a quiet, humdrum sort of life, we can all get a(n) _____ thrill from the achievements of Olympic athletes.

7. His endless talk about himself and his interests produces _____ in others.

8. Although the _____ were defeated by the government's forces, a small group escaped into the mountains, where it kept the spirit of rebellion alive.

9. I welcome honest criticism, but I deeply resented their _____ on my sincerity and good faith.

10. Since she had always been quiet and retiring, we were amazed when she stood up at the meeting and _____ the chairperson for failing to give everyone a chance to speak.

Synonyms

*Choose the word or form of the word from this Unit that is the same or most nearly the same in meaning as the **boldface** word or expression in the phrase. Write that word on the line. Use a dictionary if necessary.*

1. trying to **limit** our imaginations _____
2. **wheedled** into doing the dishes _____
3. had **outlandish** ideas _____
4. behaves in such a **curt** manner _____
5. **unchangeable** laws of nature _____
6. the cleverest plan we could **devise** _____
7. **abominable** treatment of prisoners of war _____
8. the fear-mongering of an **agitator** _____
9. wish to **rebuke** the vandals _____
10. **set straight** his mistaken belief _____
11. the disposition of a **radical** _____
12. the **self-regard** of power brokers _____
13. **transform** solids into liquids _____
14. awarded a **cushy job** for being related to the boss _____
15. an unwarranted **disparagement** against my friend _____

Antonyms

*Choose the word or form of the word from this Unit that is most nearly opposite in meaning to the **boldface** word or expression in the phrase. Write that word on the line. Use a dictionary if necessary.*

1. experienced **genuine** thrills at the race _____
2. made a **conspicuous** entrance _____
3. the outcome for those who **obey** the rules _____
4. the **normal** behavior of a pack of wolves _____
5. trips resulting in **enthusiasm** _____

Writing: Words in Action

In a brief essay, describe an ancient civilization you would like to visit, its landmarks, and the experts you would like to consult to learn more about the aspects of that civilization. Use examples from your studies, observations, and the reading (refer to pages 80–81). Use three or more words from this Unit.

Vocabulary in Context

*Some of the words you have studied in this Unit appear in **boldface** type. Read the passage below, and then circle the letter of the correct answer for each word as it is used in context.*

One hot, steamy day in 1925, Percy Fawcett wrote his wife a **brusque** letter and headed into the Amazon forest with his son Jack and Jack's best friend, Raleigh Rimell. They would never return. Fawcett and his small party were searching for what he called the City of Z, a highly sophisticated yet undiscovered civilization deep within the jungle. Fawcett was not, of course, the first to embark on such a quest. Almost 400 years earlier, Gonzalo Pizarro, a Spanish conquistador and **demagogue**, led his own ill-fated Amazonian expedition in search of the legendary city of El Dorado. Contemporaries of Fawcett surely believed the man suffered **megalomania** for making such an audacious venture with such a small party, but his was no **insurgent** expedition. Colonel Fawcett (he had served in the Royal Artillery in Ceylon) was an experienced explorer, backed by London's Royal Geographical Society.

Neither Fawcett's remains nor the City of Z were ever found. As the decades passed and the Amazon forest was explored, exploited, and felled, the idea of an undiscovered civilization became increasingly improbable. Modern scientists seemingly provided the legend's death knell. The Amazon, they said, with its poor soils, could never have supported the agriculture necessary for an advanced society.

Fawcett, however, may be proven correct after all, for satellite images and forest clearing have recently revealed a series of giant earthen structures covering more than 100 miles of Amazonian jungle. An ancient people—estimated by scientists to number at least 60,000—was somehow able to **contrive** to build an impressive array of monuments, connected by a network of straight roadways. Here, finally, is evidence to **disabuse** the harshest skeptics. Percy Fawcett was no foolish dreamer but a man ahead of his time.

---

1. A **brusque** letter is
  a. short
  b. loving
  c. without formalities
  d. carefully worded

2. A **demagogue** is someone who
  a. exploits popular prejudices
  b. is elected democratically
  c. threatens violence
  d. corrupts local leaders

3. A person with **megalomania** is
  a. deluded
  b. unwise
  c. larger than life
  d. courageous

4. An expedition that is **insurgent** is
  a. defeated
  b. successful
  c. supported
  d. revolutionary

5. The word **contrive** most nearly means to
  a. construct
  b. bring about
  c. attempt
  d. have the skills to

6. To **disabuse** skeptics, evidence must
  a. be free from error
  b. establish the facts
  c. be persuasive
  d. be conclusive

Vocabulary for Comprehension
Part 1

*Read this passage, which contains words in **boldface** that appear in Units 4–6. Then choose the best answer to each question based on what is stated or implied in the passage. You may refer to the passage as often as necessary.*

Questions 1–10 are based on the following passage.

Ever since Jane Goodall began observing wild chimpanzees in Tanganyika in the 1960s, humans have had to get used to the idea that other species can
(5) also make and use tools. By now, the list of animals with documented toolmaking capacity has expanded to include orangutans, dolphins, elephants, and even otters. But as ingenious as these fellow
(10) toolmakers are, their various implements are generally primitive and **immutable**—one-offs to perform a certain task, then discarded. Genuine toolmaking culture—the ability to improve a tool and share the
(15) improvements with other individuals in a population—seemed quite beyond the reach of our animal cousins. Not so fast. Scientists working on the South Pacific island of New Caledonia can now
(20) **disabuse** us of the idea that toolmaking culture is a uniquely human achievement.

New Caledonian crow, *Corvus moneduloides*, is intelligent, curious, and **sedulous**, qualities that have allowed it to
(25) develop a surprising range of tools. What's more, this **insular** species seems to innovate. The birds may start with one of several tool **archetypes** in mind, say a twig stripped of leaves with a hook at one end.
(30) But the crows can then modify the design to improve its functionality—and teach their offspring how to fabricate the new, improved version. So the innovation does not die with its inventor, but rather is passed
(35) down from one generation to the next.

New Caledonian crows use the tough leaves of the pandanus tree to make three related kinds of tool. Employing a craft

technique that involves a series of careful
(40) snips and tears, the birds **contrive** to fashion narrow, wide, and saw-toothed probes. (All of the tools, of course, are used by the crows to **extricate** delectable morsels such as slugs and beetle larvae
(45) from crannies that would otherwise be out of reach.) Researchers figured out a clever way of studying the crows' tool use. Instead of trying to follow the birds through the forest, scientists found thousands of
(50) "imprints" of the pandanus tools—exact outlines of the tools cut from pandanus leaves, which were still attached to the trees. By analyzing the distribution of different tool designs, the scientists were
(55) able to determine that different crow groups favored different styles of tools and passed that knowledge—including incremental improvements—down to succeeding generations. The tools are
(60) prized possessions. Although the pandanus probes are **unwieldy**, crows were frequently observed carrying them between foraging areas and even safeguarding them for later use. The
(65) New Caledonian crow, in other words, has evolved a complex tool culture.

The tools are difficult to make, but these crows have developed a social structure that gives young birds time to hone their
(70) skills. New Caledonian crows form close-knit nuclear families, and youngsters stay with their parents for two years or more. This long apprenticeship provides young birds plenty of opportunity to observe
(75) how the tools are made and the benefits conferred on tool users. Parents, report field biologists, are admirably patient. Young birds' first attempts at toolmaking do

not amount to much, and few grubs
(80) are procured. Before frustration sets in,
a nearby parent offers encouragement,
another demonstration, and a **salutary**
cockroach treat.

1. The main purpose of the passage is to
   A) examine the evidence that New
   Caledonian crows make and use tools.
   B) argue that New Caledonian crows
   have a toolmaking culture.
   C) give details of the natural history of
   New Caledonian crows.
   D) prove that humans are not the only
   toolmakers.

2. According to the author, animals such as
chimpanzees do not have a toolmaking
culture because they
   A) only make primitive tools.
   B) are not intelligent or curious enough.
   C) do not improve tools and then pass the
   improvements to the next generation.
   D) do not have the right materials.

3. As it is used in line 11, "immutable"
most nearly means
   A) limited in function.
   B) disposable.
   C) unsophisticated.
   D) not subject to change.

4. The second paragraph (lines 22–35)
summarizes
   A) how New Caledonian crows make tools.
   B) the argument that New Caledonian
   crows have a toolmaking culture.
   C) the importance of tools for New
   Caledonian crows.
   D) the key traits of New Caledonian crows.

5. As it is used in line 28, "archetypes"
most nearly means
   A) models that serve as a pattern.
   B) rough drafts.
   C) architectural models.
   D) versions.

6. The author includes the third paragraph
(lines 36–66) in order to
   A) explain the importance of leaves to
   New Caledonian crows.
   B) detail the work of scientists studying
   New Caledonian crows.
   C) explain the toolmaking culture of
   New Caledonian crows.
   D) describe how New Caledonian crows
   make tools from pandanus leaves.

7. Which choice provides the best evidence
for the answer to the previous question?
   A) Lines 36–38 ("New Caledonian. . . tool")
   B) Lines 38–42 ("Employing. . . probes")
   C) Lines 46–47 ("Researchers. . . use")
   D) Lines 53–59 ("By. . . generations")

8. According to the third paragraph
(lines 36–66), what evidence led field
researchers to infer that the pandanus
tools are valuable?
   A) The tools are not easy to carry, but
   crows frequently travel with them.
   B) The tools are effective for
   gathering food.
   C) Crows put a lot of work into
   making the tools.
   D) Crows leave behind an outline of
   their tool-crafting technique.

9. What point does the author make by
including the last paragraph?
   A) Pandanus tools are difficult to make.
   B) New Caledonian crows have a
   family structure that allows for
   extended learning.
   C) Young crows have an extended
   adolescence.
   D) Parent birds teach their young how
   to make pandanus tools.

10. As it is used in line 82, "salutary" most
nearly means
   A) rewarding.
   B) large.
   C) related to greetings.
   D) wholesome.

Vocabulary for Comprehension
Part 2

Read these passages, which contain words in **boldface** that appear in Units 4–6. Then choose the best answer to each question based on what is stated or implied in the passage(s). You may refer to the passages as often as necessary.

Questions 1–10 are based on the following passages.

Passage 1

At a New York documentary film festival, viewers could see a movie chronicling a community's fight over water privatization. Or they could watch a film exploring the
(5) implications of America's love affair with lawns. A San Francisco documentary festival offered a more diverse lineup. Attendees could see a movie about the rise, fall, and resurrection of a band of
(10) African American punk rockers in Los Angeles or a history of the U.S. atomic weapons program.

As these examples illustrate, documentaries allow people to **transgress**
(15) the constraints of their lives, opening new vistas into the panorama of human reality. A well-made documentary educates and enlightens. It provides insights—good and bad—that **reverberate** in viewers' minds,
(20) helping them understand their position in relation to others in the world.

On the other hand, telenovelas, the Latin American version of soap operas, offer viewers little more than escapism. Maids
(25) who once were heiresses, ranch hands who marry millionaires, —telenovelas **blazon** fantastic storylines and implausible characters across the nation's television sets every night. As pure entertainment,
(30) telenovelas may have their worth (though the more **vapid** shows seem to lack even that merit). But no one can argue that the **sleazy** genre represents reality.

Passage 2

Erudite fans of documentary films
(35) have much to discuss, for the history of documentaries is grand and deep. From Robert Flaherty's early masterpiece of Inuit life, *Nanook of the North*, to Barbara Kopple's stunning portrayal of a coal
(40) miners' strike, *Harlan County, U.S.A.*, documentaries give viewers glimpses of reality that inform and enlighten. But even unabashed partisans of documentaries must offer a **caveat**—this esteemed genre
(45) of filmmaking often gets it wrong. One merely has to watch a couple of nature documentaries, with their impossibly perfect "hunt" scenes, to realize that much in the documentary world is staged. So
(50) there is hardly **equitable** for documentary aficionados to criticize the popular genre of telenovelas as unrealistic fantasy, a low and sleazy form of entertainment.

Some of the most **scathing** critics of
(55) telenovelas miss an important point—these Latin American soaps may not approach reality straight on, but they are grounded in the real world. Viewers understand this. A colorful Brazilian telenovela about the life
(60) of Moses may appear melodramatic and over-the-top. But Moses was incorruptible, and viewers naturally see the contrast between the television character and their political leaders. The show is fantastic, but
(65) its feet are firmly planted in the audience's reality. Similarly, a Mexican telenovela about ultra-rich architects, shady politicians, and their various offspring may strike some observers as ridiculous escapism. But

(70) Mexican viewers know who represents whom, and thus they feel **vicarious** satisfaction when the hardworking hero or heroine finally vanquishes the villain.

1. The author of Passage 1 describes several documentary films to
   A) compare the lineups of two film festivals.
   B) show how documentaries expose viewers to a variety of new experiences.
   C) explain why people like documentaries.
   D) argue that documentaries are more realistic than telenovelas.

2. As it is used in line 14, "transgress" most nearly means
   A) go beyond a limit.
   B) overcome an obstacle.
   C) break a law.
   D) transfer.

3. As it is used in line 19, "reverberate" most nearly means
   A) transform.
   B) endure.
   C) reflected repeatedly.
   D) change completely.

4. The central claim of Passage 2 is that documentaries are informative but
   A) telenovelas are more entertaining.
   B) telenovelas are also grounded in reality.
   C) documentary fans misunderstand telenovelas.
   D) documentaries and telenovelas are more similar than some people want to admit.

5. As it is used in line 34, "erudite" most nearly means
   A) uninterested.
   B) conspicuous.
   C) boastful.
   D) well read.

6. As it is used in line 44, "caveat" most nearly means
   A) excuse.
   B) revelation.
   C) admonition.
   D) scheme.

7. The author of Passage 2 would most likely respond to the assertion in Passage 1 that documentaries "educate and enlighten" (lines 17–18) by
   A) pointing out that some documentaries include staged scenes.
   B) exposing the hypocrisy of some fans of documentary films.
   C) arguing that telenovelas portray reality.
   D) agreeing with the author of Passage 1.

8. Which choice provides the best evidence for the answer to the previous question?
   A) Lines 36–42 ("From . . enlighten")
   B) Lines 45–49 ("One merely . . . staged")
   C) Lines 49–53 ("So . . . entertainment")
   D) Lines 54–58 ("Some of . . . world")

9. The author of Passage 1 would most likely respond to the discussion of the Mexican telenovela in Passage 2 (lines 66–73) by stating that the show
   A) is poor entertainment.
   B) mainly provides escapism to viewers.
   C) has realistic and fantastic elements.
   D) may be entertaining but is unrealistic.

10. Which statement best describes the overall relationship between Passage 1 and Passage 2?
   A) Passage 2 agrees with part of the argument in Passage 1 and disagrees with another part.
   B) Passage 2 offers factual support for its argument, while Passage 1 expresses opinions in support of its argument.
   C) Passage 1 refutes the argument of Passage 2.
   D) Passage 1 ignores the argument of Passage 2.

Synonyms

*From the word bank below, choose the word that has the same or nearly the same meaning as the **boldface** word in each sentence and write it on the line. You will not use all of the words.*

aggrandize	contraband	megalomania	scourge
amnesty	demagogue	precept	sinecure
aspersion	fetter	remonstrate	soporific
castigate	insurgent	salutary	unwieldy

1. The medical evidence for the **curative** effects of a Mediterranean diet is extensive and convincing. _____

2. Ants are commonly portrayed as the main **bane** of an outdoor picnic, but wasps and flies can be just as troublesome. _____

3. The teachers did not want to **hamper** the young children's creativity by telling them to write about a particular topic. _____

4. It's true that the governor has the power to grant a **reprieve** to the prisoner, but there is no guarantee that he will do so. _____

5. When I have trouble falling asleep, I listen to a recording of the sound of ocean waves because it always has a soothing and **anesthetic** effect on me. _____

6. In *Hamlet*, Polonius advises Laertes to follow this **principle** above all: "To thine own self be true." _____

7. The **mutinous** rebels were surrounded, arrested, and put on trial. _____

8. That kayak is much too heavy and **bulky** for you to carry by yourself. _____

9. The customs officers at the airport are assisted by dogs trained to sniff out narcotics and other **unlawful** goods. _____

10. A judge can be expected to **censure** any attorney who does not follow accepted procedures. _____

11. The addition of new warships will significantly **augment** the queen's fleet. _____

12. Because she has never run for or held public office before, there is not even a hint of **innuendo** surrounding her political conduct. _____

Two-Word Completions

Select the pair of words that best completes the meaning of each of the following sentences.

1. Rubber's remarkable _____ to resume its original shape makes it one of the world's most _____ materials.
   a. propensity . . . resilient
   b. autonomy . . . erudite
   c. ennui . . . gossamer
   d. aura . . . fractious

2. Only the sound of my footsteps _____ through the empty hallway disturbed the _____ silence in which the deserted office building was enveloped. "It's as quiet as a tomb in here at night," I thought as I made my way to the exit.
   a. reverberating . . . sepulchral
   b. transmuting . . . bizarre
   c. transgressing . . . gossamer
   d. filching. . . anomalous

3. He is usually so courteous and _____ that I was completely taken aback by his unaccountably _____ and surly reply to my question.
   a. equitable . . . erudite
   b. straitlaced . . . querulous
   c. fractious . . . scurrilous
   d. affable . . . brusque

4. "The American legal system is not _____, nor are our laws _____," the Chief Justice observed. "Like everything else in this fluid world of ours, they change and develop over time."
   a. transient . . . resilient
   b. anomalous . . . autonomous
   c. axiomatic . . . inscrutable
   d. immutable . . . irrevocable

5. "It took months of _____ effort and astute planning on my part to _____ this company from the mess in which I found it," the new owner smugly boasted. "If I hadn't worked like a dog, the firm would still be in financial hot water."
   a. sedulous . . . extricate
   b. irrevocable . . . disabuse
   c. amorphous . . . cajole
   d. immutable . . . contrive

6. She led such a(n) _____ life among her books and papers that her first outing in many years caused her to experience dismay at how _____ the neighborhood had become.
   a. bizarre . . . heinous
   b. querulous . . . resilient
   c. insular . . . sleazy
   d. straitlaced . . . transmuted

7. When I returned from lunch earlier than I had planned, I surprised a thief _____ attempting to _____ a few dollars from the petty cash drawer.
   a. querulously . . . cajole
   b. surreptitiously . . . filch
   c. irrevocably . . . flout
   d. brusquely . . . repudiate

Denotation and Connotation

A dictionary definition provides the **denotation** of a word. The denotation is the word's objective, formal meaning. The **connotation** of a word is its implied or informal meaning, which includes positive or negative emotional associations.

Suppose you were writing an article about the cat family. To describe lions, you might use words such as *ferocious* or *majestic*. If you were writing about a pet cat, you would more likely choose words such as *frisky* or *cuddly*.

Consider these synonyms for the neutral word *sedulous*:

industrious   *persistent*   *insistent*   *pushy*

Industrious and *persistent* have positive connotations, whereas *insistent* and *pushy* have negative connotations.

Look at these examples of words. Notice how the connotation of each word varies.

NEUTRAL	POSITIVE	NEGATIVE
flexible	resilient	spongy
warning	caveat	alarm
increase	amplify	aggrandize

Expressing the Connotation

Read each sentence. Select the word in parentheses that expresses the connotation (positive, negative, or neutral) given at the beginning of the sentence.

neutral
1. People who are (**firm, immutable**) in their beliefs tend to resist progress, even when the entire community would benefit.

positive
2. My parents do not approve when I fail to live up to certain expectations, but at least their reprimands are (**impersonal, equitable**).

negative
3. It never ceases to amaze me that (**sleazy, disreputable**) politicians often avoid getting caught.

negative
4. David is usually polite, so when he spoke to the reporters in such a (**brusque, firm**) manner, people assumed something was wrong.

positive
5. I just read a biography about Salvador Dalí and his (**bizarre, fantastic**) art.

positive
6. My (**refined, straitlaced**) mother does not approve of the language that comedians use on late-night television.

negative
7. Details about the (**heinous, grave**) crime were censored as the detectives searched for a suspect.

neutral
8. Our old ice chest was too (**large, unwieldy**) to carry down to the beach, so we decided to purchase one that has wheels.

Classical Roots

grad, gress—to step, walk

The root *gress* appears in **transgress** (page 87). The literal meaning is "to step beyond." The word now means "to go beyond a limit or bound" or "to violate a command or law." Some other words based on the same root are listed below.

aggressive	digress	gradient	regress
congress	egress	gradualism	retrograde

From the list of words above, choose the one that corresponds to each of the brief definitions below. Write the word in the blank space in the illustrative sentence below the definition. Use a dictionary if necessary.

1. a policy of approaching a desired end by slight degrees
The moderates advocate a policy of_____.

2. to turn aside, get off the main topic (*"to step away"*)
She tried not to _____ from her speech.

3. an exit; a going out (*"walking out"*)
We could not find a means of _____.

4. to move backward; to decline, grow worse
Their reading skills will _____ if they do not study over the summer.

5. a part (*as of a road or path*) that slopes upward or downward
The climbers struggled up the dangerously steep _____.

6. a meeting (*especially of persons or minds*)
We were invited to attend a(n) _____ of medical workers.

7. moving backward, contrary to the usual or normal order; tending toward a worse state
They resisted the _____ tendencies of the small but vocal faction.

8. attacking, taking the first step in an attack or quarrel; energetic, forceful (*"walking toward"*)
Most wild animals are not _____ toward humans.

*Read the following passage, taking note of the **boldface** words and their contexts. These words are among those you will be studying in Unit 7. It may help you to complete the exercises in this Unit if you refer to the way the words are used below.*

An Overlooked Exploration
\<Informational Essay\>

The USS *Vincennes* in Antarctica, 1840

On May 18, 1836, the U.S. Congress authorized an expedition to explore the Pacific Ocean and the South Seas. Its aim was to extend "the bounds of science and to promote knowledge." The four-year voyage achieved both goals, covering 87,000 miles between 1838 and 1842. However, this important journey remains relatively unknown today compared with Lewis and Clark's comparatively modest two-year, 8,000-mile expedition to the Pacific Coast.

Congress did not need to **concoct** a **grandiose** justification for authorizing $300,000 for the Ex. Ex., as the U.S. South Seas Exploring Expedition was called. The promise of information about newly discovered lands and unfamiliar peoples captivated curious readers across the nation. To military leaders, such information would be both useful and strategic. A third, and not **inconsequential**, factor was economic: New lands meant new opportunities for American businesses. Notable support came from New

England's wealthy whalers, whose industry—one of the most important and powerful at that time—faced growing demand for whale products and now sought new hunting territory. To **mitigate** the decline of their quarry, whalers had begun sending ships into the unfamiliar Antarctic waters. These **vulnerable** vessels often foundered on unknown hazards, causing shipwrecks. Such disasters meant both a loss of life and (**crass** as it may seem to point out) a loss of profits as well. Thus, there was great support in the United States for a voyage that would tell Americans more about faraway lands and waters

The six ships of the Ex. Ex. sailed from Virginia on August 18, 1838, under the command of Charles Wilkes (1798–1877), the head of the Navy's strategic information-gathering Department of Charts and Instruments. The flotilla headed down to South America, rounded Cape Horn, and made a side trip to the Antarctic. From there, it sailed up the west coast of South America, then over to Tahiti, the Fiji Islands, and Australia. The squad went on to the Hawaiian Islands, continuing east to the Pacific Northwest, then sailed home to New York via Manila, Singapore, and Cape Town. It was a circuitous route that might **disconcert** all but the most skillful navigators. However, the route proved productive: The **stalwart** seafarers produced 241 navigational charts, mapped 1,500 desolate, rocky miles of **austere** Antarctic coast (a landmass they named), and explored some 200 Pacific islands. In addition, the team charted the Northwest coastline, boosting American claims to the Oregon Territory, the Columbia River, Puget Sound, and the San Francisco Bay.

The officers and the civilian experts were **punctilious** about their scientific duties. As the Navy required, the crew filled journals with observations and maps, and it gathered thousands of natural specimens and ethnographic objects—plants and animals, corals and fossils, baskets and weapons—that the vast trove led to the founding, in 1846, of the Smithsonian Institution in Washington, D.C. Despite these many treasures, misery marked the mission. Wilkes was a **redoubtable** leader with great scientific talent, yet he was arrogant and later proved cruel as well. Before setting sail, Wilkes attempted to dismiss civilian experts in the belief that nonmilitary men would **debase** the Navy's noble endeavor. At sea, he pushed

both himself and crew members hard, often **reproving** those he thought laggards.

He showed little mercy. In 1840, Pacific Islanders slaughtered two **cadaverous** sailors who had gone ashore in search of food to augment their scant rations. Wilkes offered the killers no opportunity to make **restitution**. Instead, the expedition attacked, leading to the deaths of 80 people. In Wilkes's defense, his men did not, in further retribution, **desecrate** holy places or **pillage** villages. On the whole, however, his **beneficent** acts were few. Although Wilkes named geographical features after crew members, this gesture failed to offset the brutal floggings he ordered for minor **infractions** of Naval regulations.

Captain Charles Wilkes

When the expedition arrived in New York City on June 10, 1842, Wilkes got his just deserts. Brought to court, he faced a court-martial but was acquitted of all charges except that of ordering illegally harsh punishments. It was a tumultuous trial and a sad ending to a spectacular expedition. With the advent of the Civil War, the triumphs of the Ex. Ex. soon drifted from contemporary consciousness. Yet the horrors of the expedition live on in fiction. Herman Melville used accounts of Wilkes's dictatorial conduct when he created the character of Ahab, the tyrannical captain in his 1851 novel *Moby-Dick*.

Audio

For iWords and audio passages, go to SadlierConnect.com

The Smithsonian Institution, circa 1847–1865

Definitions

Note the spelling, pronunciation, part(s) of speech, and definition(s) of each of the following words. Then write the appropriate form of the word in the blank space in the illustrative sentence(s) following.

1. **beneficent**
   (bə nef′ ə sənt)

   (*adj.*) performing acts of kindness or charity; conferring benefits, doing good

   From them I learned that purely _____ acts can require as much hard work as a nine-to-five job.

2. **concoct**
   (kän käkt′)

   (*v.*) to prepare by combining ingredients, make up (as a dish); to devise, invent, fabricate

   He _____ a savory stew with fresh herbs and vegetables from the garden.

3. **crass**
   (kras)

   (*adj.*) coarse, unfeeling; stupid

   We feel that the positions of our representative show a _____ indifference to our problems.

4. **desecrate**
   (des′ ə krāt)

   (*v.*) to commit sacrilege upon, treat irreverently; to contaminate, pollute

   The search continues for the vandals who _____ the cemetery.

5. **infraction**
   (in frak′ shən)

   (*n.*) a breaking of a law or obligation

   His uncle paid a fine for his _____ of the local recycling regulations.

6. **pillage**
   (pil′ ij)

   (*v.*) to rob of goods by open force (as in war), plunder; (*n.*) the act of looting; booty

   The commanding officer warned his troops not to _____ the conquered city.

   In Europe during the Dark Ages, _____ and murder became facts of life.

7. **prate**
   (prāt)

   (*v.*) to talk a great deal in a foolish or aimless fashion

   He would _____ endlessly about the past but say nothing useful about our present dilemma.

8. **punctilious**
   (pəŋk til′ ē əs)

   (*adj.*) very careful and exact, attentive to fine points of etiquette

   The clerk was so _____ in obeying court rules that I had to remind him why I was there.

9. redoubtable
(ri daŭ' tə bəl)

(*adj.*) inspiring fear or awe; illustrious, eminent

As a ruler he was _____, but, like all such rulers, he was not much loved.

10. vulnerable
(vəl' nər ə bəl)

(*adj.*) open to attack; capable of being wounded or damaged; unprotected

Those brave enough to have opposed the dictator's rise now found themselves in a _____ position.

Using Context

*For each item, determine whether the **boldface** word from pages 102–103 makes sense in the context of the sentence. Circle the item numbers next to the six sentences in which the words are used correctly.*

1. The delicious smells of the dishes that the chefs **concoct** permeate the air.

2. I try to **desecrate** our planet by recycling, taking public transportation, and growing my own vegetables.

3. Your story of meeting the famous movie star in the middle of nowhere is so **redoubtable** that no one will believe a word you say.

4. The lawyer makes **beneficent** contributions to society by taking on cases at no cost for those who cannot afford legal representation.

5. With the impending hurricane, many people were at the grocery store to **pillage** enough food to sustain them through the storm.

6. People with a fair complexion are most **vulnerable** to sunburn, and therefore, they should always apply sunscreen when they are outdoors.

7. I enjoy reunions of all kinds, even if it means listening to people **prate** about matters that don't pertain to me.

8. The **infraction** he suffered after forgetting his lines during the play was enough to make him give up acting for good.

9. Your **crass** dismissal of my feelings shows how little respect you have for me.

10. She is so **punctilious** about taking notes during class that she needed a new notebook after only one lecture.

Choosing the Right Word

*Select the **boldface** word that better completes each sentence. You might refer to the passage on pages 100–101 to see how most of these words are used in context. Note that the choices might be related forms of the Unit words.*

1. It is a (**desecration, pillage**) of the memory of Susan B. Anthony to neglect to go to the polls on election day.

2. He is so (**punctilious, redoubtable**) about every detail that it is said he irons his shoelaces before wearing them.

3. In her clumsy efforts to be recognized as an "intellectual," she (**desecrates, prates**) endlessly about matters she does not really understand.

4. Her self-confidence is so unshakeable that she is simply not (**punctilious, vulnerable**) to "put-down" remarks that would annoy other people.

5. Whenever I go to a concert, I seem to spend half my time shushing the (**crass, vulnerable**) boors who chitchat while the orchestra is playing.

6. Andrew (**desecrated, prated**) incessantly for an hour but made few insightful points.

7. The sale of so many great works of art to foreign collectors is, in my eyes, little more than (**pillage, infraction**) of our cultural heritage.

8. She is such a (**redoubtable, crass**) foe of the trite phrase that her students tremble lest her wrath descend on them for using a cliché.

9. The master chef has (**desecrated, concocted**) a dessert so rich that it will be a menace to weight watchers throughout the country.

10. The woman is known and loved throughout the community for her many (**redoubtable, beneficent**) acts on behalf of all types of unfortunates.

11. Although his conduct may not have violated any law, I consider it a gross (**pillage, infraction**) of conventional ethical standards.

12. The families who lost their homes in the fire were grateful for the (**beneficence, desecration**) shown by their neighbors, who offered shelter and clothing.

Completing the Sentence

Choose the word from the word bank that best completes each of the following sentences. Write the correct word or form of the word in the space provided.

beneficent	crass	infraction	prate	redoubtable
concoct	desecrate	pillage	punctilious	vulnerable

1. Whenever she serves as chairperson, she is so _____ that she insists on observing every fine point of parliamentary procedure.

2. Our democracy, I believe, is more _____ to decay from within than it is to attack from the outside.

3. Before they arrived home from the party, they _____ an elaborate story that they hoped would excuse their being two hours late.

4. We are, I trust, long past the time when it was considered quite "natural" for newly elected officials to _____ the city treasury.

5. I became desperately tired of listening to him _____ about how important he was, how much money he had, and so forth.

6. They _____ the funeral service by talking loudly during the ceremonies, laughing, and generally showing a complete lack of respect.

7. It is hard to forgive the _____ selfishness with which they took most of the food supplies for their own use.

8. Even a so-called minor _____ of the traffic laws may lead to a serious accident.

9. Though most of our players were the equals of theirs, the large size of their _____ team intimidated us.

10. His work on behalf of the homeless was merely the latest in a long line of _____ undertakings.

Definitions

Note the spelling, pronunciation, part(s) of speech, and definition(s) of each of the following words. Then write the appropriate form of the word in the blank space in the illustrative sentence(s) following.

1. austere
(ô stēr′)

(*adj.*) severe or stern in manner; without adornment or luxury, simple, plain; harsh or sour in flavor

The _____ clothing and conduct of the Puritans expressed their humility.

2. cadaverous
(kə dav′ ər əs)

(*adj.*) pale, gaunt, resembling a corpse

The rescued captives were weak from hunger and _____ in appearance.

3. debase
(di bās′)

(*v.*) to lower in character, quality, or value; to degrade, adulterate; to cause to deteriorate

Every time a new rule is introduced in a popular sport, there are fans who say it will _____ the game.

4. disconcert
(dis kən sərt′)

(*v.*) to confuse; to disturb the composure of

They had hoped to _____ him with an unexpected question, but he was well prepared.

5. grandiose
(gran′ dē ōs)

(*adj.*) grand in an impressive or stately way; marked by pompous affectation or grandeur, absurdly exaggerated

In how many stories, I wonder, does an ambitious villain become the victim of _____ plans?

6. inconsequential
(in kän sə kwen′ shəl)

(*adj.*) trifling, unimportant

Feel free to ignore the _____ details, provided that you know exactly which ones they are.

7. mitigate
(mit′ ə gāt)

(*v.*) to make milder or softer, to moderate in force or intensity

I had hoped to _____ her anger by offering an apology.

8. reprove
(ri prüv′)

(*v.*) to find fault with, scold, rebuke

She _____ her staff for having followed orders blindly.

9. **restitution**
(res tə tü' shən)

(*n.*) the act of restoring someone or something to the rightful owner or to a former state or position; making good on a loss or damage

They made _____ for the damage to the car but never fully regained the friendship of its owner.

10. **stalwart**
(stôl' wərt)

(*adj.*) strong and sturdy; brave; resolute; (*n.*) a brave, strong person; a strong supporter; one who takes an uncompromising position

She became as _____ on the basketball court as she was quick at mathematical puzzles.

The enemy had broken through the line but was repulsed by the _____ defending the gates.

Using Context

*For each item, determine whether the **boldface** word from pages 106–107 makes sense in the context of the sentence. Circle the item numbers next to the six sentences in which the words are used correctly.*

1. She cares more about being an entrepreneur than about making a huge amount of money, so she will not **debase** herself by selling her startup company to the highest bidder.

2. The billionaire viewed his car being destroyed in a hurricane as an **inconsequential** event, as he had seven more vehicles at home.

3. Her style is so **austere** that she always looks as though she is bursting with color.

4. I want to **reprove** your opinion of me by apologizing for the bad first impression I made.

5. The company makes such **grandiose** promises about how their product will change people's lives that I can't imagine it actually works.

6. After the rush of final exams, when I had hardly any time to eat or sleep, I looked at the **cadaverous** figure reflected in the mirror and resolved to have a good meal and a long nap.

7. You won't **disconcert** his nerves if you ask him these questions.

8. I offered **restitution** for ruining her glasses, but said she was buying a new pair anyway.

9. I tried to **mitigate** the pain but nothing would stop the pounding in my head.

10. Your ideas about the business we could build are too **stalwart** to be accomplished.

Choosing the Right Word

*Select the **boldface** word that better completes each sentence. You might refer to the passage on pages 100–101 to see how most of these words are used in context. Note that the choices might be related forms of the Unit words.*

1. All the power of Great Britain could not shake the American colonists in their (**stalwart, inconsequential**) opposition to measures that they considered unfair and tyrannical.

2. By concentrating on personal gain, he has (**debased, disconcerted**) both himself and the high office to which he was elected.

3. That sum may seem (**grandiose, inconsequential**) to you, but to me it is a great deal of money.

4. I have met few people who enjoy living an (**inconsequential, austere**) life of plain food, few possessions, and little sleep.

5. Her (**grandiose, cadaverous**) schemes for world conquest collapsed in a nightmare of military defeat and internal revolt.

6. The starving drought victims looked more like (**cadavers, stalwarts**) than living people.

7. As (**restitution, stalwart**) for the damage he had caused to the family car, Phil promised to clean and polish it regularly for a full year.

8. The fact that she did everything possible to help the poor child after the accident tends to (**mitigate, reprove**) her responsibility for the tragedy.

9. Tommy had (**grandiose, stalwart**) plans to build a stately mansion.

10. Some people find Francisco Goya's later works, known as the Black Paintings, (**disconcerting, inconsequential**) because of their horrific, gloomy nature.

11. The principal (**disconcerted, reproved**) the entire student body for its discourteous behavior toward the guest speaker at the school assembly.

12. When we were children, my brother always got to play the role of the showy superhero, while I would take the part of the (**austere, stalwart**) and faithful sidekick.

Completing the Sentence

Choose the word from the word bank that best completes each of the following sentences. Write the correct word or form of the word in the space provided.

austere	debase	grandiose	mitigate	restitution
cadaverous	disconcert	inconsequential	reprove	stalwart

1. I found that beneath his rather _____ manner and appearance there was a warm, sympathetic person.

2. An official who is responsible for shaping vital national policies should not waste time and energy on such _____ matters.

3. Though she looked rather frail, her _____ spirit made her a tireless crusader for women's rights.

4. I'm telling you this not to _____ you for having made a mistake but to prevent the mistake from being repeated.

5. Who can ever forget those pictures showing the _____ faces of the people who had been in concentration camps!

6. Fond remembrances of happy days of family life intensified rather than _____ her grief.

7. At a time when we need a modest, low-cost housing program, how can we be expected to accept such a(n) _____ scheme?

8. Is there any way that we can make _____ for the terrible wrong we have done them?

9. She has _____ her considerable talents by writing books that are designed to appeal to the lowest tastes.

10. He went right on with his speech, refusing to be _____ by the heckling of a few loudmouths.

Synonyms

*Choose the word or form of the word from this Unit that is the same or most nearly the same in meaning as the **boldface** word or expression in the phrase. Write that word on the line. Use a dictionary if necessary.*

1. **intrepid** explorers of the new lands _____
2. a **breach** of our agreement _____
3. to **chatter** tediously about the weather _____
4. **raid** the museum of valuables _____
5. **diminish** the severity of the punishment _____
6. appeared **pallid** after an illness _____
7. exaggerating **minor** flaws _____
8. **vulgar** appeal for money _____
9. **exposed** to wind and high water _____
10. **compensation** for his loss _____
11. **chastise** the misbehaving students _____
12. supports **charitable** institutions _____
13. **lower** the currency's value _____
14. not **perturbed** by the noise _____
15. **devised** a silly excuse _____

Antonyms

*Choose the word or form of the word from this Unit that is most nearly opposite in meaning to the **boldface** word or expression in the phrase. Write that word on the line. Use a dictionary if necessary.*

1. her **unaffected** delivery of Shakespeare's lines _____
2. **unimpressive** as a challenger _____
3. **honor** this tribal ritual _____
4. wore **flamboyant** clothing _____
5. **negligent** in filling out the form _____

Writing: Words in Action

Suppose that you are a news reporter in 1842, the year Wilkes returned from his expedition. Write an editorial in which you explain and support your opinion about Wilkes's expedition and his role as a leader. Use at least two details from the passage (pages 100–101) and three or more words from this Unit.

Vocabulary in Context

*Some of the words you have studied in this Unit appear in **boldface** type. Read the passage below, and then circle the letter of the correct answer for each word as it is used in context.*

Since ancient times, a mariner who has "sailed the Seven Seas" has sailed the world. The **stalwart** Phoenicians used the phrase more than 3,000 years ago. The world they knew bordered the Mediterranean, and their Seven Seas—Alboran, Balearic, Ligurian, Tyrrhenian, Ionian, Adriatic and Aegean—were all part of the Mediterranean.

The Greeks dominated the region during the first millennium BCE, and their Seven Seas suggest an expanding world. The Aegean and the Adriatic remained seas and the Mediterranean became one of the seven, while the addition of the Black Sea, the Caspian Sea, the Red Sea, and the Persian Gulf show the growth of the Greek Empire under the **redoubtable** Alexander the Great (356–323 BCE).

As the Romans succeeded the Greeks as masters of the Mediterranean and beyond, the Aegean lost its status as a "sea." The addition of the Arabian Sea reflects the expansion of Roman trade to the south and east. To the **punctilious** Romans, the Mediterranean was the *Mare Internum*, the "inner sea"—which implies an understanding of a *Mare Externum*, or "outer sea."

To medieval mariners, the Seven Seas were usually the North Sea, the Baltic, the Atlantic, the Mediterranean, and the Black, Red, and Arabian Seas. After the discovery of the New World, mariners knew the Seven Seas as the Arctic, Atlantic, Pacific and Indian Oceans, the Mediterranean and Caribbean Seas, and the Gulf of Mexico.

Today's Seven Seas are all oceans: the Arctic, North Atlantic, South Atlantic, North Pacific, South Pacific, Indian, and Southern Oceans, and they express geographical fact and demarcation. Modern mariners, however, have more in common with the Phoenicians than with **austere** modern cartographers. When they say they have sailed the Seven Seas, they do not **prate** of geographical areas and **crass** subdivisions. Their claim still carries something of the ancient mystery and magic of having sailed beyond every horizon.

---

1. A person that is **stalwart** is
- **a.** brave and resolute
- **b.** strong and swashbuckling
- **c.** adventurous and pioneering
- **d.** optimistic and persevering

2. If a king is **redoubtable**, he is
- **a.** dubious
- **b.** illustrious
- **c.** infamous
- **d.** truthful

3. The word **punctilious** most nearly means
- **a.** timely
- **b.** ruthless
- **c.** ambitious
- **d.** meticulous

4. Someone who is **austere** is
- **a.** accurate
- **b.** unimaginative
- **c.** hardworking
- **d.** strict

5. People who **prate**
- **a.** complain
- **b.** boast
- **c.** talk aimlessly
- **d.** sing

6. The word **crass** most nearly means
- **a.** clear
- **b.** crude
- **c.** blundering
- **d.** precise

Read the following passage, taking note of the **boldface** words and their contexts. These words are among those you will be studying in Unit 8. It may help you to complete the exercises in this Unit if you refer to the way the words are used below.

Mythical Journeys
<Humorous Essay>

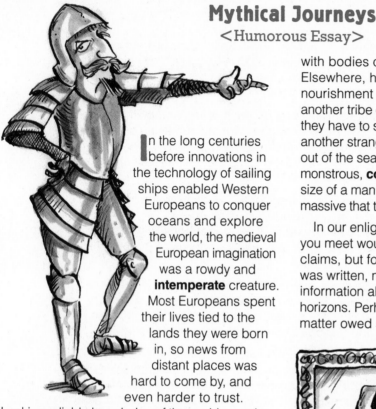

In the long centuries before innovations in the technology of sailing ships enabled Western Europeans to conquer oceans and explore the world, the medieval European imagination was a rowdy and **intemperate** creature. Most Europeans spent their lives tied to the lands they were born in, so news from distant places was hard to come by, and even harder to trust. Lacking reliable knowledge of the world, people were **susceptible** to all manner of fantastic belief. Calm, **dispassionate** thinking was **relegated** to the background while imagination ran full throttle. Careful judgment was **subservient** to superstition and shaky **hypothetical** claims. Fables about foreign lands were frequently accepted as facts.

A notorious example of fiction erroneously taken for fact in those superstitious times is *The Travels of Sir John Mandeville*. Written in the fourteenth century, the book recounts the journeys of an English knight who leaves England and travels through the East. Along the way, so the story goes, Sir John stumbles across an island of *cynocephalus*— creatures with bodies of humans and heads of dogs. Elsewhere, he finds one tribe that relies for nourishment on the very smell of apples, and another tribe of tiny folks with mouths so small they have to slurp their meals through reeds. In another strange land, he discovers fish leaping out of the sea to offer themselves up as food; monstrous, **corpulent** worms with heads the size of a man's thigh; and humongous snails so massive that the locals use their shells for homes.

In our enlightened times, practically anyone you meet would **disavow** belief in such fanciful claims, but for over a century after the book was written, many took it for a trusty source of information about the world beyond Europe's horizons. Perhaps the lack of **dissension** in this matter owed something to the fact that, along

with all the tales of fabulous creatures and peoples, the book is full of accurate geographical accounts, which, incredibly, would have made it useful to travelers of the day. Indeed, with so many medieval sources blending fact and fiction, it would take centuries before explorers and geographers learned to **expurgate** the fables from the record of history.

Consider the plight of Christopher Columbus, the most celebrated voyager ever to have taken up the **gauntlet** and accepted the challenge of exploration. In a letter to his Spanish patrons, we find a befuddled Columbus reporting that, to his **consternation**, he hasn't encountered a single monster during his voyage. He even apologizes, afraid this shortcoming might **impugn** his reputation. As far as old Columbus was concerned, part of his job was to track down the dog-headed men, one-eyed giants, and other fabulous creatures the travelers of his day took for granted—thanks, in part, to the wondrous tales of Sir John Mandeville. But try as he might… well, the fact is Columbus never found them.

Superstitious belief in the tall tales of legendary travelers began to **dissipate** in the seventeenth and eighteenth centuries. In

the end, the air of **odium** that eventually came to surround such beliefs probably resulted from increased familiarity with our planet Earth, as much as it might have been caused by any change in the intellectual climate. As exploration gradually covered the entire globe, it just turned out that there weren't any dog-headed men after all, and nothing cuts down superstition like a long, hard look at the facts.

For iWords and audio passages, go to SadlierConnect.com.

Definitions

Note the spelling, pronunciation, part(s) of speech, and definition(s) of each of the following words. Then write the appropriate form of the word in the blank space in the illustrative sentence(s) following.

---

1. acrimonious
(ak rə mō′ nē əs)

(*adj.*) stinging, bitter in temper or tone
She whirled to face me when I spoke, and her answer startled me by its _____ intensity.

---

2. consternation
(kän stər nā′ shən)

(*n.*) dismay, confusion
His father looked at the mess with _____, hardly knowing what to say first.

---

3. dispassionate
(dis pash′ ə nət)

(*adj.*) impartial; calm, free from emotion
Being a neighbor but not quite a family friend, he was called in to give a _____ view of our plan.

---

4. dissipate
(dis′ ə pāt)

(*v.*) to cause to disappear; to scatter, dispel; to spend foolishly, squander; to be extravagant in pursuit of pleasure
As chairman he is fair and open, but he _____ his energies on trivial things.

---

5. expurgate
(ek′ spər gāt)

(*v.*) to remove objectionable passages or words from a written text; to cleanse, purify
According to the unwritten law of journalism, the editor alone has the right to _____ the article.

---

6. hypothetical
(hī pə thet′ ə kəl)

(*adj.*) based on an assumption or guess; used as a provisional or tentative idea to guide or direct investigation
Science is not based on _____ assumptions, but on proven facts.

---

7. intemperate
(in tem′ pər ət)

(*adj.*) immoderate, lacking in self-control; inclement
Experience taught her to control her _____ outbursts of anger.

---

8. odium
(ō′ dē əm)

(*n.*) hatred, contempt; disgrace or infamy resulting from hateful conduct
Those eager to heap _____ on the fallen tyrant learned that he had escaped in the night.

---

9. relegate
(rel' ə gāt)

(v.) to place in a lower position; to assign, refer, turn over; to banish

Even if they _____ him to a mere clerical job, he is determined to make his presence felt.

10. susceptible
(sə sep' tə bəl)

(adj.) open to; easily influenced; lacking in resistance

The trouble with being _____ to flattery is that you can never be sure that the flatterer is sincere.

Using Context

*For each item, determine whether the **boldface** word from pages 114–115 makes sense in the context of the sentence. Circle the item numbers next to the six sentences in which the words are used correctly.*

1. I was thrilled to **relegate** the goalie to the varsity soccer team from JV after he impressed me with his athletic skills.

2. When auditioning for the school play, the judges had us sing from behind a curtain so that they could remain **dispassionate** when choosing the most talented students.

3. The editor was advised to **expurgate** so many scenes from the movie to show it on television that it was an hour shorter than the original version.

4. To prepare for the debate, we created a list of **hypothetical** arguments the opposing team might make and crafted a response to each.

5. It is important to instill confidence and self-respect in all young people so that they are not **susceptible** to peer pressure.

6. To be eligible to run for president of the student council, I had to **dissipate** at least twenty signatures from my classmates.

7. Their conversation went from a well-mannered debate to an **acrimonious** argument so quickly that I couldn't tell which comment had made them so hostile toward each other.

8. We were lucky to have such **intemperate** weather for my cousin's outdoor wedding.

9. Although the suspect was proven innocent, he could not escape the **odium** of some local residents who faulted him for having been involved in the incident.

10. Our coach's **consternation** of the foul that was called against our team was so loud that we could hear her arguing above the jeering of the fans.

Choosing the Right Word

*Select the **boldface** word that better completes each sentence. You might refer to the passage on pages 112–113 to see how most of these words are used in context. Note that the choices might be related forms of the Unit words.*

1. If we are going to be required to perform a(n) (**relegated, expurgated**) version of *Romeo and Juliet*, then I think it is not worth doing.

2. Imagine our (**consternation, odium**) when the brakes failed, and we headed full speed toward the busy intersection!

3. Try your best to subdue your natural reluctance and make a (**hypothetical, dispassionate**) decision that will be in your son's best interests.

4. The immediate success of my book caused great (**odium, consternation**) to my sister, who thinks she is the writer in the family.

5. After the sun set, red and purple hues lingered in the sky for several minutes before the colors (**relegated, dissipated**).

6. Students who have been well trained in the social sciences should not be (**susceptible, acrimonious**) to the cheap fallacies of racism.

7. There is often a thin line between the kind of debate that is spirited and useful and that which is (**acrimonious, hypothetical**) and nonproductive.

8. Though I was annoyed by the child's behavior, the father's outburst of anger seemed to me deplorably (**intemperate, dispassionate**).

9. My Spanish friend finds it hard to understand the (**odium, consternation**) attached to bullfighting in most non-Hispanic countries.

10. When Mr. Krummer saw my pathetically inept efforts to prepare a banana split, I was (**dissipated, relegated**) to the ranks of the unemployed.

11. By reference to (**susceptible, hypothetical**) cases, you may be able to clarify the difference between "murder" and "manslaughter" for the law students.

12. The estate he had inherited from his father was (**dissipated, expurgated**) in a long series of impractical and/or mismanaged business enterprises.

Completing the Sentence

Choose the word from the word bank that best completes each of the following sentences. Write the correct word or form of the word in the space provided.

acrimonious	dispassionate	expurgate	intemperate	relegate
consternation	dissipate	hypothetical	odium	susceptible

1. We have had enough of high-powered, excited oratory; what we need now is a(n) _____ examination of the facts.

2. He is so _____ to flattery that with a few complimentary words I can get him to do almost anything I want.

3. Our discussion that day was a(n) _____ one, based on the possibility— still far from definite—that I would take the job.

4. To the _____ of the people in the stands, the lion leaped out of the cage and bounded toward the exit.

5. Vigorous debate is fine, but is there any real need for such unrestrained and _____ name-calling?

6. Thomas Bowdler _____ certain words from Shakespeare's plays because he felt that they were unfit to "be read aloud in a family."

7. The _____ for this tragic failure does not belong to any individual or small group but to the community as a whole.

8. The job of cleaning up the field and the stands after the big game was _____ to the freshmen.

9. Though her overall position seemed to be sensible, her language was so unrestrained and _____ that people wouldn't support her.

10. Instead of using all their forces in one concerted attack on the enemy, they _____ their strength in minor engagements.

Definitions

Note the spelling, pronunciation, part(s) of speech, and definition(s) of each of the following words. Then write the appropriate form of the word in the blank space in the illustrative sentence(s) following.

1. bovine
(bō′ vīn)

(*adj.*) resembling a cow or ox; sluggish, unresponsive
After I told him what had happened, he sat there with a
_____ expression and said nothing.

2. corpulent
(kôr′ pyə lənt)

(*adj.*) fat; having a large, bulky body
Though she had grown _____ with
the years, the opera singer's voice and her way with a
song were the same.

3. disavow
(dis ə vau′)

(*v.*) to deny responsibility for or connection with
The suspect stubbornly continued to
_____ any part in the kidnapping plot.

4. dissension
(di sen′ shən)

(*n.*) disagreement, sharp difference of opinion
The political party was torn by _____
and finally split into two wings.

5. gauntlet
(gônt′ lət)

(*n.*) an armored or protective glove; a challenge; two
lines of men armed with weapons with which to beat
a person forced to run between them; an ordeal
In the Middle Ages, a knight threw down his
_____ as a challenge, and
another knight picked it up only if he accepted.

6. ignoble
(ig nō′ bəl)

(*adj.*) mean, low, base
Most people will agree that a noble purpose does
not justify _____ means.

7. impugn
(im pyün′)

(*v.*) to call into question; to attack as false
You can _____ the senator's facts, but
you cannot accuse her of concealing her intentions.

8. perfidy
(pər′ fə dē)

(*n.*) faithlessness, treachery
Rulers in Shakespeare's plays often find themselves
armed against enemies but not against the
_____ of their friends.

9. squeamish
(skwē′ mish)

(*adj.*) inclined to nausea; easily shocked or upset; excessively fastidious or refined

If I am called _____ for disliking the horror movie, what do we call those who say that they liked it?

10. subservient
(səb sər′ vē ənt)

(*adj.*) subordinate in capacity or role; submissively obedient; serving to promote some end

The officers were taught to be respectful of but not blindly _____ to their superior's wishes.

Using Context

*For each item, determine whether the **boldface** word from pages 118–119 makes sense in the context of the sentence. Circle the item numbers next to the six sentences in which the words are used correctly.*

1. My sister is so **corpulent** and light on her feet from years of dancing that I can't even hear her footsteps when she walks around the house.

2. He will make a great teacher because of his **ignoble** temperament, which is necessary in a profession that requires such patience.

3. Despite the **dissension** within the band, they tried to present themselves as being the best of friends in interviews.

4. I must **impugn** you to tell me where you got your jacket, because I plan to head straight there and buy the same one.

5. In my new job, I plan to do as my superiors say so that I can learn from them, but I do not want to come across as so **subservient** that it appears I cannot think for myself.

6. The **gauntlet** between the two families is so old that no one even knows what started it.

7. We were shocked by the lazy applause and **bovine** enthusiasm of the crowd, especially after their team hit a homerun.

8. I was amazed at the level of **perfidy** some so-called best friends would sink to when they were all competing for the title of best performer.

9. Aspiring medical students who dream of becoming doctors should first make sure that they do not get **squeamish** around severe injuries.

10. I tried to **disavow** the notion that I deserved any credit in the creation of the new play, as my best friend had written it while I had simply acted in it, but fans kept bestowing praise on me.

Choosing the Right Word

*Select the **boldface** word that better completes each sentence. You might refer to the passage on pages 112–113 to see how most of these words are used in context. Note that the choices might be related forms of the Unit words.*

1. The (**gauntlet, dissension**) between Athena and Poseidon led to a contest between the two immortals, in which they bestowed gifts to the Athenians.

2. Not too long ago in our society, a (**corpulent, bovine**) body was generally admired as a sign of prosperity and physical vigor.

3. I am not ordinarily a (**corpulent, squeamish**) person, but the sight of that terrible automobile accident haunted me for weeks.

4. Aren't you going a little far when you accuse me of (**gauntlet, perfidy**) because I didn't vote for you in the beauty contest?

5. Far from being (**ignoble, subservient**), her failure after making a valiant effort may serve as an inspiration to young people.

6. It is not for me to (**disavow, impugn**) his motives, but how could anyone, except an overambitious scoundrel, have misled his friends in that way?

7. I refuse to ride a roller coaster; fast rides make me (**squeamish, subservient**).

8. A certain amount of disagreement is healthy in any organization, but in our club (**dissension, perfidy**) has almost become a way of life.

9. I noticed with some distaste how her usually overbearing manner became (**ignoble, subservient**) when our employer joined the group.

10. The prisoner attempted to (**disavow, impugn**) his confession on the grounds that he had not been informed of his legal rights.

11. Their (**bovine, squeamish**) stares and obvious inability to understand the seriousness of the situation made me doubt their mental capacity.

12. The retiring coach said he no longer had the stomach to run the (**gauntlet, perfidy**) of critics who assailed him after every loss.

Completing the Sentence

Choose the word from the word bank that best completes each of the following sentences. Write the correct word or form of the word in the space provided.

bovine	disavow	gauntlet	impugn	squeamish
corpulent	dissension	ignoble	perfidy	subservient

1. She is a person of such fine moral standards that she seems incapable of a(n) _____ act.

2. Because Vidkun Quisling cooperated with the Nazis, his name has become a symbol of _____ in his home country of Norway.

3. The bold candidate threw down the _____ and dared her opponent to face her in a televised debate.

4. Now that these ugly facts about his business dealings have come to light, I must _____ my support of his candidacy.

5. People with a tendency toward being _____ must wage a lifelong struggle against rich foods.

6. Anyone as _____ as that trainee will have trouble accustoming himself or herself to the sights, sounds, and smells of hospital work.

7. Although she seems rather plodding in her behavior and rarely becomes excited, I think it is unfair to call her "_____."

8. Far from presenting a unified front, the party is torn by all kinds of strife and _____.

9. I am not trying to _____ his truthfulness, but I still do not see how the facts support his claims.

10. Under the American form of government, all branches of the military are clearly _____ to the civilian authority.

Synonyms

*Choose the word or form of the word from this Unit that is the same or most nearly the same in meaning as the **boldface** word or expression in the phrase. Write that word on the line. Use a dictionary if necessary.*

1. not a hint of **duplicity** in him _____

2. **downgraded** to coach seating _____

3. caused **strife** within the department _____

4. after the fumes **dispersed** _____

5. **purged** the offensive parts of the speech _____

6. stared in **bewilderment** _____

7. his **caustic** way of speaking _____

8. to **disown** any credit for herself _____

9. **take issue with** his credentials _____

10. a **dishonorable** end to a shadowy life _____

11. feeling **woozy** at the very thought _____

12. setting aside her **conjectural** motive _____

13. the brutal **contest** he endured _____

14. **secondary** to the group's interests _____

15. their **mindless**, faithful devotion _____

Antonyms

*Choose the word or form of the word from this Unit that is most nearly opposite in meaning to the **boldface** word or expression in the phrase. Write that word on the line. Use a dictionary if necessary.*

1. had a **slender** physique _____

2. used **moderate** language in the debate _____

3. **admiration** heaped on the outsider _____

4. **resistant** to the virus _____

5. an **engaged** observer _____

Writing: Words in Action

As Columbus, write a letter to your patrons in Spain expressing your disappointment that you have not come across any evidence of strange creatures. Reassure your patrons that your voyage still has value for other reasons. Use examples from the passage (pages 112–113) and three or more words from this Unit.

Vocabulary in Context

*Some of the words you have studied in this Unit appear in **boldface** type. Read the passage below, and then circle the letter of the correct answer for each word as it is used in context.*

Robinson Crusoe, so rumor is rife,
Came from Lower Largo, Fife . . .

The old rhyme refers to Alexander Selkirk (1676-1721), the Scottish sea captain whose experiences led Daniel Defoe to write *The Life and Strange Surprizing Adventures of Robinson Crusoe of York, Mariner: Who Lived Eight and Twenty Years, all alone in an un-inhabited Island on the Coast of America, near the Mouth of the Great River of Oroonoque; Having been cast on Shore by Shipwreck, wherein all the Men perished but himself. With An Account how he was at last as strangely deliver'd by Pyrates. Written by Himself* (1719).

The title page of Defoe's best seller neatly summarizes the adventures of Alexander Selkirk. Young Selkirk was the captain of a privateer—pirate ships with permission to attack the king's enemies—and it was not a career for the **squeamish**. Selkirk became sailing master of the Cinque Ports, where he had an **acrimonious** relationship with the captain, Stradling, who tolerated no **dissension**. Captain Stradling's sea battles had left the ship so leaky that Selkirk advised returning to port, and when the **bovine** Stradling refused, Selkirk demanded to be put ashore on an uninhabited island in the South Pacific. Selkirk remained there for over four years and, like Crusoe, he survived on goat meat and crawfish.

Daniel Defoe never traveled much, but he was an avid reader of travel books. William Dampier's *A New Voyage Round the World* (1697) records the rescue in 1684 of a crewman from a South Pacific island—the same island that Selkirk would be abandoned on twenty years later and describe in his memoirs. That Defoe read Dampier's and Selkirk's accounts and used them as the basis of his book is indisputable. His intentions were not to be **ignoble** or as an expression of **perfidy**, though, and his book brought to life the adventures of two men whom history might otherwise have forgotten.

---

1. **Squeamish** people are
   a. fastidious
   b. timid
   c. easily shocked
   d. law-abiding

2. When a discussion becomes **acrimonious**, it gets
   a. rancorous
   b. long-winded
   c. one-sided
   d. cordial

3. The word **dissension** most nearly means
   a. disagreement
   b. compromise
   c. insubordination
   d. revolt

4. People described as **bovine** are likely to be
   a. bad-tempered
   b. vegetarian
   c. strong-willed
   d. unresponsive

5. **Ignoble** intentions are
   a. worthwhile
   b. dishonorable
   c. incompetent
   d. incomplete

6. **Perfidy** most nearly means
   a. treachery
   b. thoughtlessness
   c. forethought
   d. benevolence

Read the following passage, taking note of the **boldface** words and their contexts. These words are among those you will be studying in Unit 9. It may help you to complete the exercises in this Unit if you refer to the way the words are used below.

The Swedish Nightingale
<Narrative Nonfiction>

The Swedish singer Jenny Lind (1820–1887) was just a **novice** when she made her operatic debut in Stockholm at the age of eighteen. But fame and fortune soon followed, as she quickly went on to enjoy the **adulation** of audiences throughout Europe and, eventually, across the globe. Given that she was one of the first international celebrities, with a major career that lasted for decades and made her a very rich woman, it seems almost **egregious** that few people today have ever heard of Jenny Lind. Yet, as so many celebrated names prove over time, fame is fleeting.

Jenny Lind

Lind possessed a voice so beautiful, and a name so recognizable in Europe, that wherever she performed concert halls quickly sold out. Thus it was not surprising that, after hearing of her many triumphs abroad, the legendary American showman P. T. Barnum proposed to Lind that she tour the United States. Lind did not **equivocate**, for such a tour would provide the opportunity to fund her many charities. However, the singer was as wise as she was talented, and negotiated a contract on terms that were as favorable to her as to Barnum: For 150 concerts over an eighteen-month period, Lind wanted $250,000— a huge sum for the time (about $5 million today). The tour made Lind very wealthy, but despite such earnings, her name was never associated with **avarice**; for Lind devoted much of her accumulated wealth to philanthropic causes, particularly schools, hospitals, and orphanages. Given the singer's generosity, no one would entertain the **supposition** that Lind was **torpid** in aiding the less fortunate. She had not been born into **penury**, yet she had an intuitive sympathy for the poor.

Before her marriage in 1852, Lind was linked romantically to some of the most celebrated figures in the art circles of her day, including the composers Frédéric Chopin and Felix Mendelssohn, as well as the writer Hans Christian Andersen, who wrote a fairy tale called "The Nightingale" that was inspired by

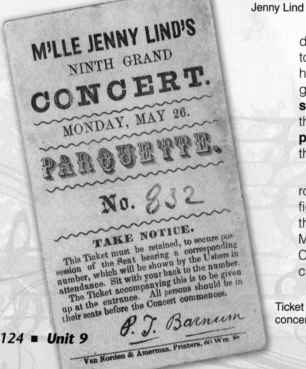

M'LLE JENNY LIND'S
NINTH GRAND
CONCERT.
MONDAY, MAY 26.
PARQUETTE.
No. 832

TAKE NOTICE.
This Ticket must be retained, to secure possession of the Seat bearing a corresponding number, which will be shown by the Ushers in attendance. Sit with your back to the number.
The Ticket accompanying this is to be given up at the entrance. All persons should be in their seats before the Concert commences.
P. T. Barnum

Van Norden & Amerman, Printers, 60 Wm St.

Ticket for Jenny Lind's New York concert on May 26, 1851

the singer. Thereafter, Lind was often called "the Swedish Nightingale." She also inspired one of Mendelssohn's masterpieces, the oratorio *Elijah*. Despite such tributes and great fame, Lind was not **pretentious**, arrogant, or conceited; no one who met her could say she was **culpable** of such boorish behavior.

As for P.T. Barnum's role in Lind's career, it had some notable twists and turns. A prodigiously talented showman, Barnum was the mastermind behind a wide range of events, including concerts, museum exhibitions, and the circuses that still bear his name. Gifted with a masterful sense of public relations, he recognized a fantastic money-making opportunity in Jenny Lind: The Swedish Nightingale would help **resuscitate** Barnum's fortunes. But Lind's representative in the contract negotiations was **astute**: He demanded a large advance payment for the American tour. The idea was **anathema** to Barnum, who was accustomed to dealing with his clients on a pay-as-you-go basis. The showman was hard-pressed to raise the funds, but by nature never **dilatory** when it came to making money, Barnum soon found investors and the tour went forward.

Before the tour, few Americans had heard of Lind. However, Barnum's advertisements spread the word about this "gift from Heaven" so shrewdly that by the time the singer arrived by steamship in New York, Lind had become a household name on this side of the Atlantic, too. A crowd of 40,000 people gathered in lower Manhattan to welcome her. Any misgivings in Barnum's mind that Lind's fame in America would prove **evanescent** must have vanished that day. On tour, Lind performed in a broad variety of venues, ranging from the grand halls of Washington, D.C., before members of the Supreme Court, to Mammoth Cave in central Kentucky. Wherever she went, the enthusiasm for the singer did not **abate**; if anything, it increased in intensity.

Every biographer who has told the story of the Swedish Nightingale **recapitulates** the many achievements of this nineteenth-century celebrity phenomenon. They all agree that part of Lind's appeal was the extraordinary agility, power, and range of her singing voice. But they point out that Lind's musical talent was enhanced even more by her aura of propriety and refinement. In an era of conservative mores, such a public image was a decided plus for a celebrity performer, and Barnum took full advantage of Lind's squeaky-clean reputation. But with or without Barnum, there was never anything **nebulous** about her fame: From the day she first walked onstage, Jenny Lind had "star power."

Hans Christian Andersen

Audio

For ¡Words and audio passages, go to SadlierConnect.com.

Definitions

Note the spelling, pronunciation, part(s) of speech, and definition(s) of each of the following words. Then write the appropriate form of the word in the blank space in the illustrative sentence(s) following.

1. **adulation**
   (aj ə lā′ shən)

   (*n.*) praise or flattery that is excessive
   Athletes have little choice but to enjoy the sometimes puzzling _____ of their fans.

2. **astute**
   (ə stüt′)

   (*adj.*) shrewd, crafty, showing practical wisdom
   The _____ management of money is a valuable skill but may not by itself make a good executive.

3. **dilatory**
   (dil′ ə tôr ē)

   (*adj.*) tending to delay or procrastinate; not prompt; intended to delay or postpone
   She hired an assistant because, on her own, she was always _____ in paying her bills.

4. **equivocate**
   (i kwiv′ ə kāt)

   (*v.*) to speak or act in a way that allows for more than one interpretation; to be deliberately vague or ambiguous
   I won't soon give my vote to a candidate who shows such a marked tendency to _____.

5. **irresolute**
   (ir ez′ ə lüt)

   (*adj.*) unable to make up one's mind, hesitating
   In *Hamlet*, the prince is _____ about whether to obey his father's ghost or to go on as if nothing has happened.

6. **nebulous**
   (neb′ yə ləs)

   (*adj.*) cloudlike, resembling a cloud; cloudy in color, not transparent; vague, confused, indistinct
   By the time everyone had expressed an opinion, the original idea had become somewhat _____.

7. **penury**
   (pen′ yə rē)

   (*n.*) extreme poverty; barrenness, insufficiency
   We never seem to tire of stories of people who go from _____ to sudden wealth.

8. **recapitulate**
   (rē ka pich′ ə lāt)

   (*v.*) to review a series of facts; to sum up
   Don't bother to _____ the plot of the book; instead, tell me if you liked it.

9. **slovenly**
(sləv' ən lē)

(*adj.*) untidy, dirty, careless

Her room was in a _____ state, and it took her an entire Saturday to clean it.

10. **supposition**
(səp ə zish' ən)

(*n.*) something that is assumed or taken for granted without conclusive evidence

Guided by a _____ that turned out to be false, they made some disastrous decisions.

Using Context

*For each item, determine whether the **boldface** word from pages 126–127 makes sense in the context of the sentence. Circle the item numbers next to the six sentences in which the words are used correctly.*

1. From the middle of the **dilatory** lake you can't even make out the shore.

2. Whenever there is a big event in the news, I always appreciate my parents' ability to **equivocate** by explaining what happened and treating me as an adult.

3. Since I had to take a call during the first act of the play, I asked my friend to **recapitulate** the parts that I missed before the second act.

4. The **astute** reviews of my part in the play left me with questions about how well or poorly I performed.

5. Although she keeps her house in immaculate condition, her car is always in such a **slovenly** state that I'm reluctant to ride with her.

6. After starring in the biggest movie of the year, the young actress went from being virtually unknown to receiving **adulation** everywhere she went.

7. He lives a life of such **penury** that we all wonder why he bothers to work, but his passion for helping those less fortunate is not about the money.

8. I have a great idea for an ending to my novel, but the details of how I can craft the story to reach that point are still **nebulous**.

9. I have received so much unsolicited advice about whether or not to take the job that I am more **irresolute** now than when I first got the offer.

10. Your **supposition** that I was the one who left the mysterious message is based more on gut feeling than on fact.

Choosing the Right Word

*Select the **boldface** word that better completes each sentence. You might refer to the passage on pages 124–125 to see how most of these words are used in context. Note that the choices might be related forms of the Unit words.*

1. In playing chess, she deliberately uses (**dilatory, nebulous**) tactics to make her opponent impatient and tense.

2. Sportswriters attribute the success of the pennant-winning team largely to the (**astute, irresolute**) managing of old Buck Coakley.

3. As a result of (**irresolution, penury**) when that novel was first submitted, the publishing house lost the biggest best seller of the year.

4. Biologists have a theory that every plant or animal in the course of its development (**equivocates, recapitulates**) all the stages of its evolution.

5. In the densely populated and underdeveloped countries we visited, we saw the depths to which people can be reduced by (**penury, adulation**).

6. Sheila was feeling insecure after experiencing a (**slovenly, nebulous**) sense of dread that something terrible was going to happen during her speech.

7. In everyone's life, a situation may arise that calls for a basic moral choice to be made, without compromise or (**supposition, equivocation**).

8. Since my mother is such a(n) (**astute, dilatory**) manager, she was the perfect choice to run the children's museum in our community.

9. The (**slovenly, astute**) physical appearance of the report was matched by its careless writing and disorganized content.

10. What she calls her "philosophy of life" seems to me a hodgepodge of childish fallacies and (**dilatory, nebulous**) generalizations.

11. Is it any wonder that a 17-year-old star athlete becomes smug when she receives such (**recapitulation, adulation**) from the entire school?

12. You may be right in your belief that she won't let us use her car, but remember that this is still only a (**penury, supposition**).

Completing the Sentence

Choose the word from the word bank that best completes each of the following sentences. Write the correct word or form of the word in the space provided.

adulation	dilatory	irresolute	penury	slovenly
astute	equivocate	nebulous	recapitulate	supposition

1. Although she tried to _____, we insisted on a simple "yes" or "no" answer.

2. He holds forth in great detail on what is wrong with our city government, but the remedies he suggests are exceedingly _____.

3. When you are _____ in returning a book to the library, you are preventing someone else from using it.

4. Your brilliant plan is based on one false _____ that I am willing to work without pay.

5. After giving us extremely detailed instructions for more than an hour, she briefly _____ and then sent us out on our assignments.

6. I was impressed by the _____ way our hostess guided the conversation away from topics that might be embarrassing to her guests.

7. The _____ she had experienced in her childhood and youth made her keenly aware of the value of money.

8. It will mean more to him to gain the approval of the few people who can appreciate his work than to receive the _____ of the crowd.

9. I was so _____ about whether to go out for basketball or for swimming that I ended up going out for neither.

10. I told my friend that dress for the party was casual, but he showed up looking, in my opinion, just plain _____.

Definitions

Note the spelling, pronunciation, part(s) of speech, and definition(s) of each of the following words. Then write the appropriate form of the word in the blank space in the illustrative sentence(s) following.

1. abate
(ə bāt′)

(*v.*) to make less in amount, degree, etc.; to subside, become less; to nullify; to deduct, omit

We stood on the dock on that moonless night, waiting for the storm to _____.

2. anathema
(ə nath′ ə mə)

(*n.*) an object of intense dislike; a curse or strong denunciation (often used adjectivally without the article)

The author's views on bringing up children are _____ to my dad but a delight to my mother.

3. avarice
(av′ ər is)

(*n.*) a greedy desire, particularly for wealth

Her career exhibited both the miser's ever-growing _____ and the miser's diminishing charm.

4. culpable
(kəl′ pə bəl)

(*adj.*) deserving blame, worthy of condemnation

It was the inspectors' _____ neglect of duty that left such old buses in service.

5. egregious
(i grē′ jəs)

(*adj.*) conspicuous, standing out from the mass (used particularly in an unfavorable sense)

Whoever allowed that man on a stage is guilty of an _____ blunder.

6. evanescent
(ev ə nes′ ənt)

(*adj.*) vanishing, soon passing away; light and airy

Looking back, I see that the magic of that summer was _____.

7. novice
(näv′ is)

(*n.*) one who is just a beginner at some activity requiring skill and experience (also used adjectivally)

You must be patient and realize that all his mistakes are typical of a _____ in this line of work.

8. pretentious
(prē ten′ shəs)

(*adj.*) done for show, striving to make a big impression; claiming merit or position unjustifiably; ambitious

Talking about one's wealth is thought to be _____ and in poor taste.

9. **resuscitate**
   (ri səs' ə tāt)

   (*v.*) to revive, bring back to consciousness or existence
   We need someone who can _____
   our neighborhood's community spirit.

10. **torpid**
    (tôr' pid)

    (*adj.*) inactive, sluggish, dull
    We all felt _____ after that long,
    dull lecture.

Using Context

*For each item, determine whether the **boldface** word from pages 130–131 makes sense in the context of the sentence. Circle the item numbers next to the six sentences in which the words are used correctly.*

1. The **anathema** I feel for my hometown is so strong that I plan on moving back there as soon as I am able.

2. The newly elected mayor promised to **resuscitate** the city's environmentally conscious plans, which her predecessor had started and neglected many years before.

3. After a day of lazing around, I should have felt refreshed and energized, but I felt more **torpid** than when I first woke up.

4. Because I saw the crime happen and did nothing to stop it, I consider myself just as **culpable** as the actual perpetrator.

5. The actor was sure that everyone noticed him fumble his lines in the second act, but it was not a mistake **egregious** enough for anyone who did not know the play by heart to perceive.

6. I will **abate** the rules set for the trivia game and refrain from using my cell phone, but I can't say the same for all the other participants.

7. When I won the board game three times in a row, all my friends accused me of lying when I claimed to be a **novice**.

8. "You've shown such **avarice** in your studies this year that we would like you to tutor some of the students who are falling behind," the principal said to me.

9. She often brings up names of obscure novels in conversation to impress us with her education, but she just ends up sounding **pretentious**.

10. Since my best friend and I live in different parts of the country, I comfort myself by looking up at the **evanescent** stars in the sky and knowing that she can see them too.

Choosing the Right Word

Select the **boldface** word that better completes each sentence. You might refer to the passage on pages 124–125 to see how most of these words are used in context. Note that the choices might be related forms of the Unit words.

1. Before becoming a successful writer, Jack London was a (**torpid, novice**) prospector, searching for gold in Alaska.

2. Since he is known to be a multimillionaire, it seems almost (**culpable, pretentious**) of him, in an inverted sense, to drive around in a small, battered, inexpensive car.

3. The glory of this perfect spring day seems to be all the more precious because it is so (**torpid, evanescent**).

4. When the results of her mistakes became public knowledge, she gained a well-deserved reputation for being a(n) (**pretentious, egregious**) blunderer.

5. As the election drew nearer, the candidates went from reasonable discussion to quarrelsomeness to (**anathematizing, resuscitating**) each other.

6. They say that school spirit at Central High is dead, but I am confident that it can be (**resuscitated, abated**) if the right methods are used.

7. What do you think of the concept that when a crime is committed, society is often as (**culpable, pretentious**) as the criminal?

8. The heat in the room, the quiet drone of the fly at the window, and the bright sunlight put me into a (**torpid, culpable**) state.

9. I was absolutely stunned when I reviewed my bank statement, not realizing I had made an (**evanescent, egregious**) error in accounting.

10. As soon as the hurricane (**abated, resuscitated**), rescue teams rushed out to help people in the devastated area.

11. She is completely indifferent to wealth and luxurious living; her (**anathema, avarice**) is directed instead toward fame and prestige.

12. Only a(n) (**anathema, novice**) at golf would have tried to use a driver when hitting into such a strong wind.

Completing the Sentence

Choose the word from the word bank that best completes each of the following sentences. Write the correct word or form of the word in the space provided.

abate	avarice	egregious	novice	resuscitate
anathema	culpable	evanescent	pretentious	torpid

1. Sure, it's great to be a big-league ballplayer, but bear in mind that the years of stardom are brief and _____.

2. How can you consider her _____ when a landslide that no one could have foreseen or prevented caused the accident?

3. The study of history teaches us that a hunger for land, like other kinds of _____, is the cause of a great many wars.

4. I don't think I'd call such a(n) _____ grammatical mistake a minor "slip of the pen."

5. Using the most up-to-date equipment, the firefighters worked tirelessly to _____ the victim of smoke inhalation.

6. Does he use all those quotations as a means of clarifying his meaning, or simply as a(n) _____ display of his learning?

7. Since I truly loathe people who think they are "above the common herd," any form of snobbery is absolutely _____ to me.

8. As her anger slowly _____, she realized that such childish outbursts of emotion would do nothing to help solve her problems.

9. Since he was a(n) _____ at the game, the three veteran players hoped to find someone more suitable to play on their team.

10. Her mind, _____ as a result of hours of exposure to the bitter cold, was not alert enough to sense the impending danger.

Synonyms

*Choose the word or form of the word from this Unit that is the same or most nearly the same in meaning as the **boldface** word or expression in the phrase. Write that word on the line. Use a dictionary if necessary.*

1. a muttered **execration**   _____
2. earned the crowd's **adoration**   _____
3. **prevaricated** about the true amount   _____
4. a maddeningly **murky** explanation   _____
5. **breathe new life into** the dull party   _____
6. a **showy** way of speaking   _____
7. made an **assumption** based on past behavior   _____
8. ashamed of a **slipshod** job   _____
9. a delicate and **fleeting** beauty   _____
10. **restate** your requirements   _____
11. used **stalling** tactics   _____
12. **dithering** over a choice   _____
13. an **insightful** observer of world affairs   _____
14. made **listless** by the heat   _____
15. guilty of **brazen** rudeness   _____

Antonyms

*Choose the word or form of the word from this Unit that is most nearly opposite in meaning to the **boldface** word or expression in the phrase. Write that word on the line. Use a dictionary if necessary.*

1. **innocent** of the crime   _____
2. an **expert** chess player   _____
3. driven by **generosity**   _____
4. lived in extreme **affluence**   _____
5. caused the flood to **intensify**   _____

Writing: Words in Action

Suppose you have been hired by P. T. Barnum to promote an upcoming concert by Jenny Lind in a major American city. Write a press release to persuade people to attend the event. Use at least two details from the passage (pages 124–125) and three or more words from this Unit.

Vocabulary in Context

*Some of the words you have studied in this Unit appear in **boldface** type. Read the passage below, and then circle the letter of the correct answer for each word as it is used in context.*

From 1730 onward, when the first performance of a Shakespearean play was staged on the American continent, "the Bard," has been a staple of the American theater. Since 1932, the world's largest Shakespeare archive, the Folger Shakespeare Library, has graced Washington, D.C. Abraham Lincoln revered Shakespeare and displayed his **adulation** by declaiming speeches from the plays from memory. Ironically, his assassin, John Wilkes Booth, was born into a renowned acting family whose members included his British-born father, Junius Brutus Booth, and his brother, Edwin Booth. From 1864–1865, the latter played Hamlet, a character known for being **irresolute**, for one hundred consecutive nights. Not surprisingly, he became identified with the part.

Audiences did not **equivocate** about their favorite Shakespearean actors. In the mid-nineteenth century, probably the keenest rivalry flared between William Charles Macready, a British theatrical star, and Edwin Forrest, born and raised in Philadelphia. Forrest, whom some detractors scorned for his **slovenly** appearance, is said to have hissed Macready at a performance of *Hamlet* in England. From this moment on, the feud grew increasingly bitter. The two thespians became **anathema** to each other, and their fans became increasingly hostile. When Macready toured the United States in 1849, Forrest trailed him, booking theaters to play the same parts as the British star. At a performance of *Macbeth* in New York at the Astor Place Opera House, Forrest's supporters stormed the theater, committing an **egregious** act. Macready made a narrow escape, but more than twenty people were killed in the ensuing melee. The Astor Place Riot remains one of the bloodiest episodes in the city's history.

---

1. **Adulation** is
   a. favoritism
   b. derision
   c. idolization
   d. respect

2. An **irresolute** individual is typically
   a. disrespectful
   b. indecisive
   c. taciturn
   d. enigmatic

3. To **equivocate** is to
   a. hedge
   b. elaborate
   c. portend
   d. recapitulate

4. A **slovenly** appearance might also be described as
   a. pretentious
   b. meticulous
   c. unkempt
   d. affluent

5. **Anathema** most nearly means
   a. intense dislike
   b. anguished foreboding
   c. bitter harangue
   d. pitiful complaint

6. An **egregious** act is
   a. flagrant
   b. congenial
   c. stubborn
   d. paltry

Vocabulary for Comprehension
Part 1

*Read this passage, which contains words in **boldface** that appear in Units 7–9. Then choose the best answer to each question based on what is stated or implied in the passage. You may refer to the passage as often as necessary.*

Questions 1–10 are based on the following passage.

This passage is adapted from *Green Mansions: A Romance of the Tropical Forest* by William Henry Hudson. Originally published in 1916.

Next day I returned to the forest of evil report, which had now an even greater charm—the fascination of the unknown and the mysterious, but still, the **austere**

(5) warning I had received **disconcerted** me, and I could not help thinking about it. What, then, prevented the locals from visiting this particular wood? The question troubled me not a little, and, **irresolute** as

(10) I was, I became ashamed of the feeling, while I fought against it. In the end I made my way to the same sequestered spot where I had rested on my previous visit.

In this place I witnessed a new thing.

(15) Sitting under the shade of a large tree, I began to hear a confused noise as of a coming tempest of wind mixed with shrill calls and cries. Nearer it came, and at last a flock of birds, mostly small, appeared in

(20) sight swarming in a **grandiose** fashion through the trees, some running on the trunks and larger branches, others flitting through the foliage. Many now hovering and now darting this way or that. They

(25) were all busily pursuing insects, moving on at the same time, and as soon as they had finished examining the trees near me, the flight **dissipated**. Not satisfied with what I had witnessed, I had the **intemperate**

(30) impulse to jump up and rush after the flock. All my caution and all recollection of what the Native Indians had said about the supposed wooded **anathema** was now forgot, so great was my interest in this

(35) bird-army, but they quickly left me behind, as I was stopped by an impenetrable tangle of vegetation. In the midst of this leafy labyrinth I sat down on a projecting root to cool my blood before attempting to

(40) make my way back to my former position. After that tempest of motion and confused noises the silence of the forest seemed very profound; but before long it was broken by a low strain of exquisite bird-

(45) melody, wonderfully pure and expressive, unlike any musical sound I had ever heard before. It seemed to issue from a thick cluster of broad leaves a few yards away. With my eyes fixed on this green hiding-

(50) place I waited with suspended breath for its repetition.

It was a voice purified and brightened to something almost angelic. Imagine, then, my deep **consternation** when it was not

(55) repeated! I rose very reluctantly and slowly began making my way back; but when I had progressed about thirty yards, again the sweet voice sounded just behind me, and turning quickly, I stood still and waited.

(60) The same voice, but not the same song— the notes were more varied and rapidly enunciated, as if the singer had been more excited. The blood rushed to my heart as I listened and my nerves tingled with a

(65) new delight produced by such mysterious music. Before many moments I heard it again, now warbling another **evanescent** song, lower than at first, infinitely sweet and tender, sinking to sounds that soon ceased

(70) to be audible; the whole having lasted as long as it would take me to repeat a sentence of a dozen words. This seemed the singer's farewell to me, for I waited in vain to hear it repeated once more!

1. According to the first paragraph, the narrator feels
   A) uncertain about entering the forest, as he was told of its dangers.
   B) excited to revisit the forest, as he is hoping to uncover its dangers.
   C) desperate to enter the forest, as he is not concerned with the warnings he received.
   D) hesitant about returning to the forest, because of what he had witnessed.

2. As it is used in line 5, the word "disconcerted" most nearly means
   A) worried.
   B) pacified.
   C) annoyed.
   D) rattled.

3. As it is used in line 29, the word "intemperate" most nearly means
   A) modest.
   B) uncontrolled.
   C) sudden.
   D) instinctive.

4. The "supposed wooded anathema" (line 33) refers to
   A) the large flock of birds eating all of the insects.
   B) a frightening mystery believed about the forest.
   C) the overwhelming greenery that impedes the narrator's path.
   D) a song in the woods that lures people into a trap.

5. Which of the following sentences is supported by the second paragraph?
   A) As the narrator enters the forest, he calmly witnesses an animated flock of birds pursuing insects.
   B) As the narrator sits under the shade of a large tree, he remembers the Native Americans's warnings about the forest.
   C) As the narrator recovers from chasing a flight of swarming birds, he is intrigued by the sound of an unexpected song.
   D) As the narrator listens to a bird-melody, he notes the contrast between the noise of the flock and the serenity of the song.

6. In the second and third paragraphs, what was the narrator's reaction after hearing the first mysterious song?
   A) Surprise, as he was expecting to hear the birds from earlier
   B) Displeasure, as the song was not what he expected to hear
   C) Disappointment, as he was hoping to hear the song again
   D) Joy, as the song was much more beautiful than the sound of the earlier flock

7. Which choice provides the best evidence for the answer to the previous question?
   A) Lines 47–48 ("It seemed. . . away")
   B) Lines 49–51 ("With. . . repetition")
   C) Lines 52–53 ("It was a voice. . . angelic")
   D) Lines 53–55 ("Imagine. . . repeated")

8. As it is used in line 67, the word "evanescent" most nearly means
   A) intricate.
   B) eternal.
   C) heavenly.
   D) fleeting.

9. It can reasonably be inferred from the passage that the narrator
   A) is not accustomed to the forest, and therefore sees nature as a mystery.
   B) studies birds for a living, as he is fascinated by them.
   C) has lived in a rural area his whole life, as he is very comfortable in the forest.
   D) is a musician, since he is searching for melodies in the forest.

10. Which of the following sentences best summarizes the passage?
    A) The narrator returns to a mysterious forest and is captivated by a bird song.
    B) The narrator enters a forest and is captivated by the sound and movement of a large flock of birds.
    C) The narrator leaves a forest because of the noisy birds in its interior.
    D) The narrator visits a forest to hear the sound of a rare bird that is known to hide in low bushes.

Vocabulary for Comprehension
Part 2

*Read this passage, which contains words in **boldface** that appear in Units 7–9. Then choose the best answer to each question based on what is stated or implied in the passage. You may refer to the passage as often as necessary.*

Questions 1–10 are based on the following passage.

This passage is adapted from the short story *The Squirrels that Live in a House* by Harriet Beecher Stowe. Originally published in 1897.

Once upon a time a gentleman went out into a great forest, and cut away the trees, to build a nice little cottage. It was low to the ground, and so much of it was glass

(5) that one could look out on every side and see the happenings of the forest. You could see the shadows of the ferns, and the spots of sunshine that fell through their branches. You could see the **punctilious** robins and

(10) bluebirds neatly building their nests, and watch them daily as they raised their young. You could also see red and gray squirrels, and little striped chipmunks, as they would dart about, here and there, and **prate**

(15) about the goings-on of the woods.

You may be sure that such an **egregious** thing as a house for humans did not come into this wild wood without making quite a stir among the original inhabitants. As the

(20) **redoubtable** structure went up, there was a great commotion in all the woods. There wasn't even a cricket that did not have his own **supposition** about it, and did not express to the others just what he thought

(25) the world was coming to.

Old Ms. Rabbit declared that the hammering made her nervous. "Depend upon it, children," she said to her long-eared family, "no good will come to us from

(30) this establishment. I am not **susceptible** to such change, for where man is, there comes always trouble for us rabbits."

The old chestnut tree drew a great sigh which shook his leaves, and expressed it

(35) as his conviction that no good would ever

come of it, while the squirrels talked together of the **hypothetical** state of things that would ensue. "Why!" said the old gray squirrel, "it's evident that Nature made the

(40) nuts for us, but one of these humans feasts upon what would keep a hundred squirrel families in comfort." Mr. Ground-mole said it did not require sharp eyes to see into the future, and it would bring down the price

(45) of real estate in the whole vicinity, so that every quadruped would be obliged to move away. The bluebirds took more **dispassionate** views on the matter, but Ms. Ground-mole observed that they were

(50) a flighty set, who spent half their time in the Southern States, and could not be expected to have any attachment to their native soil.

"Man," said the old chestnut-tree, "is

(55) never ceasing in its warfare on Nature. In our forest how peacefully has everything gone on! No matter how hard has been the winter and how high the snow-banks have piled, all has come right again in spring.

(60) We have storms that threaten to shake everything to pieces! The thunder roars, the lightning flashes, and the winds howl! But they eventually **abate**, and everything comes out better and brighter than before.

(65) Not a bird is harmed, not the frailest flower destroyed, but man comes, and in one day he will make a desolation that centuries cannot repair. The noble oak, that has been cut away to build this contemptible

(70) human dwelling, had a life older and wiser than that of any man. It was a fresh young tree when Shakespeare was born; it was growing while those whom they call the wisest and strongest lived, and died,

(75) and yet it had outlived them all."

1. The main purpose of the passage is to
   A) give a fictional account of a man building a cottage in the woods.
   B) provide a comical view of the impact of humans on nature.
   C) prove that animals and trees have more of a right to the forest than humans do.
   D) show the impact of humans on nature, from the perspective of nature itself.

2. As it is used in line 9, "punctilious" most nearly means
   A) jovial.
   B) reckless.
   C) meticulous.
   D) polite.

3. Which of the following statements about the cottage, as seen by the forest inhabitants, is supported by the passage?
   A) The dwelling is the first of its kind and represents the arrival of new neighbors.
   B) The large structure stands out and incites fear in the animals and trees.
   C) The imposing building is the envy of the squirrels, while the birds prefer nests.
   D) The quaint house invades the privacy of the squirrels and birds.

4. According to the second paragraph (lines 16–25), the animals view the cottage as a
   A) sign of terrible things to come for the forest and its inhabitants.
   B) strange structure that does not belong.
   C) new home that will bring positive changes to the forest.
   D) beautiful place to live, with a great view.

5. Based on lines 19–25, it can reasonably be inferred that
   A) the crickets usually do not have an opinion, but in this case they did.
   B) the crickets did not get involved with the commotion about this matter.
   C) all the forest creatures, even the crickets, had beliefs about this matter.
   D) all the crickets were hesitant to express their opinion about this matter.

6. As it is used in line 30, "susceptible" most nearly means
   A) receptive.
   B) helpless.
   C) oblivious.
   D) resistant.

7. In the third and fourth paragraphs (lines 26–53), the only forest creatures who do not express a negative view about the arrival of humans in the forest are the
   A) gray squirrels.
   B) rabbits.
   C) ground-moles.
   D) bluebirds.

8. Which choice provides the best evidence for the answer to the previous question?
   A) Lines 26–27 ("Old. . . nervous")
   B) Lines 38–42 (""Why!' . . . comfort")
   C) Lines 42–47 ("Mr. Ground-mole . . . away")
   D) Lines 47–48 ("The bluebirds . . . matter)

9. As it is used in line 63, "abate" most nearly means
   A) persist.
   B) intensify.
   C) cease.
   D) subside.

10. The purpose of the last paragraph is to
    A) marvel at the wonders of nature and point out the ability of humans to destroy it in an instant.
    B) refute the idea that the endeavors of humans have a positive impact on the world.
    C) reaffirm nature's power over all of humankind.
    D) convey to the reader that every living thing is negatively effected by the actions of humans.

Synonyms

*From the word bank below, choose the word that has the same or nearly the same meaning as the **boldface** word in each sentence and write it on the line. You will not use all of the words.*

adulation	dilatory	hypothetical	prate
austere	dispassionate	ignoble	reprove
bovine	evanescent	irresolute	subservient
crass	gauntlet	nebulous	torpid

1. When she continued to **prattle** about trivialities the first three hours of the car trip, I finally had to ask for some peace and quiet. _____

2. The referee was supposed to be an **unbiased** moderator of the game, but everyone suspected that he wanted the visiting team to win. _____

3. I am still **vacillating** about which college I will attend, but I remain certain that I want to go somewhere out of state. _____

4. The weekend at the beach seemed as **fleeting** as a dream, and before I knew it, I was back at work, feeling as if I'd never left. _____

5. He claims that his tendency to speak honestly is a good quality, but I see it as a problem when his remarks come across as **crude** insults. _____

6. Everyone agreed that the famous actor's actions were so **sordid** that he would never be cast in a movie again. _____

7. Rather than energizing me, running in the morning makes me so **lethargic** for the rest of the day that I can barely keep my eyes open. _____

8. The bride's friends and family all knew to act **servile** on the day of the wedding and to fulfill even the most ridiculous of requests. _____

9. Her tendency to be late is not because she is a slow driver, but because she is **laggard** in leaving the house. _____

10. My understanding of the topic is **fuzzy** at best, but if we study it together, perhaps we will both comprehend it better. _____

11. I feared that my parents would **chastise** me for my less-than-stellar grades, but instead they sat down with me and helped me make a study plan for the future. _____

12. His **slow** and plodding movements made me suspect his injury from last week was still bothering him. _____

Two-Word Completions

Select the pair of words that best completes the meaning of each of the following sentences.

1. For a minor _____ of the rules of a hockey game, the offending player is _____ to the penalty box, or "sin bin," for two minutes. For a more serious violation, he is put there for five.
   a. supposition . . . disavowed
   b. dissension . . . debased
   c. anathema . . . recapitulated
   d. infraction . . . relegated

2. His kindness may have been a(n) _____ act, performed in a moment of distraction, but its _____ impact on the young orphans caused them to grow up and pursue careers as social workers.
   a. susceptible . . . intemperate
   b. inconsequential . . . beneficent
   c. pretentious . . . egregious
   d. vulnerable . . . astute

3. In AD 267, a band of barbarous Heruli raided the ancient Greek religious center at Delphi. For several days they _____ the town and _____ its temples. Then they rode off, laden with plunder.
   a. resuscitated . . . debased
   b. relegated . . . dissipated
   c. disconcerted . . . expurgated
   d. pillaged . . . desecrated

4. A person has to have a strong stomach to work in a funeral parlor or morgue. Handling _____ is definitely not a job for the _____.
   a. cadavers . . . squeamish
   b. stalwarts . . . slovenly
   c. concoctions . . . acrimonious
   d. novices . . . redoubtable

5. "Those who circumvent the law are often as _____ as those who actually break it," the lawyer remarked. "The seriousness of such an offense is rarely _____ by the fact that, technically, no crime has been committed."
   a. vulnerable . . . impugned
   b. culpable . . . mitigated
   c. susceptible . . . disavowed
   d. corpulent . . . abated

6. The _____ of history forever attaches itself to the name of Benedict Arnold for his villainous act of _____ during the American Revolution.
   a. consternation . . . equivocation
   b. acrimony . . . beneficence
   c. anathema . . . restitution
   d. odium . . . perfidy

7. Though a few lucky "haves" are able to provide themselves with all the comforts of life on a truly _____ scale, the bulk of the people in many third-world countries seem to live like paupers in the most extreme state of _____ and neglect.
   a. punctilious . . . dissension
   b. egregious . . . avarice
   c. redoubtable . . . perfidy
   d. grandiose . . . penury

WORD STUDY

Idioms

In the essay "An Overlooked Exploration" (see pages 100–101), the author states that Charles Wilkes "got his just deserts" when he returned from his expedition. To get one's "just deserts" (*deserts* is pronounced like *desserts* but means "a reward or punishment that is deserved") means to receive retribution for one's actions.

Phrases such as "just deserts" are idioms. **Idioms** are phrases or expressions that usually have a meaning different from the one that the individual words suggest. Idioms are figures of speech, expressions that are not to be taken literally. Many idioms are clever and colorful, and people say them so often that they do not even realize they are using them. Though the meaning of some idioms can be determined from context clues, others are not quite as obvious and have to be learned.

Choosing the Right Idiom

Read each sentence. Use context clues to figure out the meaning of each idiom in **boldface***. Then write the letter of the definition for the idiom in the sentence.*

1. Bob has been campaigning for Senator Jones, but I think he is **backing the wrong horse**. _____

2. We decided to ask Leroy to join our team because he is great at **thinking on his feet**. _____

3. I'm so glad the president kept her speech **short and sweet**. _____

4. Tomas will be in for **a rude awakening** when he gets his own apartment and has to cook and clean for himself! _____

5. The new song I'm learning is **a piece of cake**, so I should be able to play it tomorrow. _____

6. You left too early and missed the amazing encore. The band **brought the house down**! _____

7. I'm not surprised your company went bankrupt after you told me they had been **cooking the books**. _____

8. My mother sent me out **on a wild goose chase** to find decorations for my sister's birthday party. _____

9. I wouldn't trust Megan; she is pretty good at using **crocodile tears** to get her way. _____

10. I wish Dad would just **cut to the chase** and tell me if I can borrow the car or not. _____

a. a wasted effort looking for something that is difficult to find or nonexistent

b. an unpleasant understanding or revelation

c. something easy; a task that can be completed without much effort

d. fake sadness used to manipulate people

e. supporting the wrong or losing side

f. brief yet meaningful; direct and to the point

g. put on a successful performance

h. leave out the details and get to the point

i. manipulating financial figures

j. making decisions with little effort or prior planning

Classical Roots

mor—form, shape;
the—to put or place

The root *mor* appears in **amorphous** (page 58), "shapeless, without definite form." The root *the* appears in **anathema** (page 130), meaning "an object of intense dislike." Some other words based on these roots are listed below.

anthropomorphic	metamorphosis	parenthetical	theme
epithet	morphology	pseudomorph	thesis

From the list of words above, choose the one that corresponds to each of the brief definitions below. Write the word in the blank space in the illustrative sentence below the definition. Use an online or print dictionary if necessary.

1. a topic of discourse or discussion; an idea, point of view
   The _____ of the essay was the misuse of technology.

2. a marked change, a transformation
   The child was amazed by the _____ of the caterpillar.

3. characterized by the attribution of human qualities to nonhuman phenomena
   Giving pets human names is a common _____ practice.

4. contained in parenthesis; qualifying or explanatory
   She made a few _____ remarks before starting her speech.

5. the study of form and structure
   Students of biological _____ analyze animal forms.

6. a term used to characterize the nature of a person or thing
   "The King" is the _____ used by Elvis fans for their hero.

7. a proposition that is put forth for argument
   The professor offered evidence in support of her _____.

8. a false, deceptive, or irregular form
   Scientists are seldom fooled by a(n) _____.

*Read the following passage, taking note of the **boldface** words and their contexts. These words are among those you will be studying in Unit 10. It may help you to complete the exercises in this Unit if you refer to the way the words are used below.*

Sinking Nation
<Magazine Article>

It sounds like a tropical paradise, with a **munificent** bounty of natural attractions: sun-bleached beaches, turquoise waters, swaying coconut palm trees, breathtaking sunsets. But the tiny South Pacific nation of Tuvalu is sinking, and its inhabitants are threatened and cannot afford to **procrastinate**: Unless drastic measures are taken, climate experts predict that Tuvalu could disappear in under fifty years.

Located halfway between Australia and Hawaii, Tuvalu is an archipelago made up of nine small, low-lying reef islands and atolls. A former British protectorate, it gained independence in 1978 and United Nations membership in 2000. With a population of about 10,000 and encompassing a total land area of ten square miles, Tuvalu is the fourth-smallest country in the world (only Monaco, Vatican City, and Tuvalu's South Pacific neighbor, Nauru, are smaller).

Over time, earthquakes, tsunamis, cyclones, and hurricanes have caused erosion and taken a toll. But the more recent—and dangerous—sea-level rise is attributed to the catastrophic effects of global warming. The islands and atolls of Tuvalu offer no **coverts** where people can escape the sea.

The world first became aware of the scope of the crisis at the 1997 Kyoto Conference, which was convened to address climate change. The timing of the conference was **fortuitous**. Before then, Tuvaluans had viewed the issue with **equanimity**; they adjusted to rising sea levels by moving farther and farther inland. Naysayers who deny climate change is to blame assert that the **provocative** claims of the islanders are overblown. And facts and figures may seem **recondite**, but one fact is clear: The land mass is getting significantly smaller each year, and Tuvalu is being reclaimed by the sea.

The narrow island nation of Tuvalu, in the Pacific Ocean, as seen from the air

Pacific Island leaders meet at the Pacific Islands Forum.

Tuvaluan leaders are hoping to avoid the **bedlam** that their nation faces by finding the most **efficacious** means of solving their problem. So they talk to officials from the United States, Australia, and other major nations and plead for cooperation in capping greenhouse-gas emissions. (Tuvaluan leaders have, at times, received **gratuitous**, even **imperious**, responses. Some insensitive government representatives claim the islanders are to blame for the flooding because of their own poor environmental management.) But actions speak louder than words, and Tuvalu cannot wait.

The people of Tuvalu are poor and lack the financial resources to mount much of a "Save Tuvalu" campaign. The nation is too remote to attract many tourists. Per-capita income is negligible; the islanders survive mostly by fishing and farming the little land they have. (One interesting **annotation**, or side note, to this story: Tuvalu is resorting to Internet Age solutions. Besides publicizing this pressing threat to its existence, the nation has **accrued** significant revenue by leasing the marketing rights to its ".tv" Internet domain name. The deal has brought in millions of dollars that can be invested in projects aimed at alleviating the country's problems.)

Each year, approximately seventy-five natives resettle in New Zealand, and leaders are in talks with other South Pacific nations to take in more people. This slow relocation provokes thorny legal and human-rights issues: Does a country still exist if all its inhabitants leave, deciding that they cannot remain **sedentary** in the face of the encroaching sea? Will Tuvaluans still be Tuvaluans if the ocean swallows their homeland? Can they still be represented at the UN? Can they continue to claim fishing and other ocean rights that bring in much-needed income? The **gist** of the problem is this: Without a man-made miracle, the Tuvaluans' tiny homeland will sink without a trace—thus making it a modern-day Atlantis.

Schoolchildren in Tuvalu

Definitions

Note the spelling, pronunciation, part(s) of speech, and definition(s) of each of the following words. Then write the appropriate form of the word in the blank space in the illustrative sentence(s) following.

---

1. accrue
(ə krü′)

(*v.*) to grow or accumulate over time; to happen as a natural result

We allowed the interest to _____ on the account until it turned into a small fortune.

---

2. bedlam
(bed′ ləm)

(*n.*) a state or scene of uproar and confusion

Is this the same band that caused mob scenes and virtual _____ on its first tour?

---

3. covert
(kō′ vert)
(ko′ vert)

(*adj.*) hidden, disguised, purposefully kept secret; sheltered, secluded; (*n.*) a sheltered place, a hiding place

Napoleon was an expert at making _____ preparations to attack unsuspecting opponents.

The bear made a lunge from her _____ before we realized she was nearby.

---

4. efficacious
(ef ə kā′ shəs)

(*adj.*) effective, producing results

Not the most charming of senators, he nevertheless wielded the most _____ knowledge of statecraft.

---

5. equanimity
(ek wə nim′ ə tē)

(*n.*) calmness, composure, refusal to panic

Injustice always sent him into a rage, but he could endure misfortune with _____.

---

6. gratuitous
(grə tü′ ə təs)

(*adj.*) freely given; not called for by circumstances, unwarranted

Though she had hoped to leave the lecture early, several members of the audience asked _____ questions, delaying her by an hour.

---

7. invective
(in vek′ tiv)

(*n.*) a strong denunciation or condemnation; abusive language; (*adj.*) abusive, vituperative

He let loose his usual hail of _____, a furious shower that left the air a bit clearer.

As _____ speeches go, this one displayed originality, vigor, and, here and there, some wit.

---

8. munificent
(myü nif′ ə sənt)

(*adj.*) extremely generous, lavish

Nothing the volunteers said could save the program until our anonymous friend donated a _____ sum.

| **9. procrastinate** (prə kras′ tə nāt) | (*v.*) to delay, put off until later We all want to _____ when a task is no fun, but some people make delaying a way of life. |
| **10. recondite** (rek′ ən dīt) | (*adj.*) exceeding ordinary knowledge and understanding The theories of relativity can seem _____, even for people who are well versed in the sciences. |

Using Context

*For each item, determine whether the **boldface** word from pages 146–147 makes sense in the context of the sentence. Circle the item numbers next to the six sentences in which the words are used correctly.*

1. I would have enjoyed the film had it not been for the scenes of **gratuitous** violence, which seemed to only exist for the shock value.

2. The private investigator's methods were not as **covert** as he thought, since the suspect always seemed to know his plans well enough to stay one step ahead.

3. The dog clearly had a blast tearing up the carpet, but looked so **recondite** after I scolded him that I couldn't remain angry for long.

4. The library is named after the **munificent** family who donated money to pay for the construction of the magnificent building.

5. We all admire her ability to face a crisis with **equanimity** and to focus on finding solutions instead of bemoaning the situation.

6. A thick layer of dust would **accrue** on every surface when we returned to the summer house after many months away.

7. When the weather got warmer and students lingered outside before classes, the principal issued an **invective** reminding students of the consequences of being late.

8. The guidance counselor advised me to complete my college application weeks before the due date and not **procrastinate**.

9. Her **efficacious** personality is so infectious that I'm always in a good mood for the rest of the day after talking with her.

10. The campgrounds are normally so noisy and crowded that I wake up early to savor the **bedlam** and watch the sun rise before everyone else is up.

Choosing the Right Word

*Select the **boldface** word that better completes each sentence. You might refer to the passage on pages 144–145 to see how most of these words are used in context. Note that the choices might be related forms of the Unit words.*

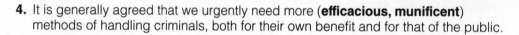

1. I am convinced that some substantial advantages will surely (**accrue, procrastinate**) to me if I complete my college education.

2. To bear evils with (**invective, equanimity**) doesn't mean that you should make no effort to correct them.

3. My sad story is that after working in the yard for three hours in the hot sun cleaning up the yard, I received the hardly (**gratuitous, munificent**) sum of $5.50.

4. It is generally agreed that we urgently need more (**efficacious, munificent**) methods of handling criminals, both for their own benefit and for that of the public.

5. The proverb "Make haste slowly" endorses prudence—not (**invective, procrastination**).

6. We appreciated the services he furnished (**gratuitously, covertly**), but we soon came to see that it would have been cheaper to pay for a really professional job.

7. When my sister arrived at my tiny apartment with two very excited dogs, the place was thrown into absolute (**bedlam, equanimity**).

8. After working for a year at the same job, I was hoping that I had (**procrastinated, accrued**) enough vacation days to take a week off and travel to California.

9. He tried to make it appear that he was speaking in a friendly spirit, but I detected the (**recondite, covert**) malice beneath his "harmless" remarks.

10. Instead of that highly involved and (**recondite, efficacious**) discussion of the nation's energy needs, why don't you simply tell us what we can do to help solve the problem?

11. Why do you (**procrastinate, accrue**) whenever you have to write an essay?

12. Instead of relying on facts and logic, she used all kinds of rhetorical tricks and slashing (**invective, equanimity**) to attack her opponent.

Completing the Sentence

Choose the word from the word bank that best completes each of the following sentences. Write the correct word or form of the word in the space provided.

accrue	covert	equanimity	invective	procrastinate
bedlam	efficacious	gratuitous	munificent	recondite

1. Think of the great advantages that will _____ for all of us if we can carry out a truly effective program to conserve and maintain our natural resources.

2. In view of the fact that I have been driving for many years without having a single accident, his advice on how to handle a car seemed entirely _____.

3. This research program is entirely devoted to developing a drug that will be _____ in the treatment of arthritis.

4. My opponent's last speech was filled with such acrimonious language and bitter _____ that I walked out of the room without even trying to reply.

5. Anyone who _____ when the opportunity to make a very profitable deal presents itself is not going to be notably successful in the business world.

6. The _____ gift of the Mellon family made it possible to set up the National Gallery of Art in Washington, D.C.

7. We have seen her accept victory with grace; now can she face defeat with _____?

8. It is up to the courts to decide how far police authorities may go in making use of _____ means of surveillance to catch criminals.

9. _____ broke out in the meeting hall as the speaker tried vainly to be heard over the angry shouting of the audience.

10. The kinds of books I enjoy reading range from light and airy comedies to _____ studies of social and philosophical problems.

Definitions

Note the spelling, pronunciation, part(s) of speech, and definition(s) of each of the following words. Then write the appropriate form of the word in the blank space in the illustrative sentence(s) following.

1. annotation
(an ə tā′ shən)

(n.) a critical or explanatory note or comment, especially for a literary work

Laurence Sterne's novel *Tristram Shandy* has almost as many _____ as lines of text.

2. debonair
(deb ə nâr′)

(adj.) pleasant, courteous, lighthearted; smooth and polished in manner and appearance

Quite a few _____ young men asked my cousin to dance.

3. dun
(dən)

(v.) to demand insistently, especially in payment of a debt; (n.) a creditor; (adj.) dark, dull, drab, dingy

Many of Dickens's characters are _____ by creditors because of their large debts.

4. fortuitous
(fôr tü′ ə təs)

(adj.) accidental, occurring by a happy chance

Due to a _____ drop in oil prices, the shipping company showed healthy profits for the year.

5. gist
(jist)

(n.) the essential part, main point, or essence

Would the talented fellow who keeps the back row in stitches please repeat the _____ of what I said?

6. imperious
(im pir′ ē əs)

(adj.) overbearing, arrogant; seeking to dominate; pressing, compelling

The Wizard of Oz's _____ manner masked the reality that he was a fussy little man behind a curtain.

7. motley
(mät′ lē)

(adj.) showing great variety; composed of different elements or many colors; (n.) a jester's costume; a jester

Tall and short, thick and thin, old and young, we share the family name but are a _____ bunch indeed.

To "put on _____" is to say what only a king's jester would dare to say.

8. provocative
(prə väk′ ə tiv)

(adj.) tending to produce a strong feeling or response; arousing desire or appetite; irritating, annoying

The ideas presented in the film were so _____ that I thought about them for days.

9. **reprobate**
(rep′ rə bāt)

(*n.*) a depraved, vicious, or unprincipled person, scoundrel; (*adj.*) corrupt or unprincipled; (*v.*) to disapprove of, condemn

_____ are usually more charming, funny, or thrilling in fiction than they are in life.

10. **sedentary**
(sed′ ən ter ē)

(*adj.*) characterized by or calling for continued sitting; remaining in one place

She exchanged her _____ job for a position as a swimming instructor.

Using Context

*For each item, determine whether the **boldface** word from pages 150–151 makes sense in the context of the sentence. Circle the item numbers next to the six sentences in which the words are used correctly.*

1. It will be interesting to see that actor play the part of the **debonair** spy, since we are used to seeing him in roles where he is moody and reclusive.

2. The first draft of the article was so well done that the editor only had to make one **annotation**, suggesting that it be longer.

3. His behavior has been so **imperious** lately that none of us know what could have caused such a change from his usual domineering self.

4. Since she runs every morning, is on her feet all day at her job as a nurse, and then walks her dog when she gets home, you could hardly describe her lifestyle as **sedentary**.

5. I may not be able to repeat the speech word for word, but I can tell you the **gist** of it.

6. If you continue to **dun** my reputation to my friends and family, I will have no choice but to reveal your true character to them.

7. After being rejected for another summer job, I had a **fortuitous** encounter with an overwhelmed mother who was looking for a babysitter.

8. The new book is a surprisingly **provocative** read, especially considering it comes from an author best known for writing formulaic thrillers.

9. She is known as a **reprobate** in our local community, as she volunteers at the nursing home, the animal shelter, and the children's hospital.

10. The members of the **motley** group all had similar childhoods, education and work experiences, and career goals.

Choosing the Right Word

*Select the **boldface** word that better completes each sentence. You might refer to the passage on pages 144–145 to see how most of these words are used in context. Note that the choices might be related forms of the Unit words.*

1. The scholars who compiled the notes and (**annotations, provocations**) for my portable edition of Chaucer did a superb job of clarifying obscure or puzzling words and passages.

2. His tone of voice was so (**motley, imperious**) that I wasn't sure if he was asking me for a loan or demanding payment of tribute.

3. Although they claimed that their summary gave us the (**annotation, gist**) of the resolution, the fact is that it omitted important details.

4. The queen strode into the chamber and (**imperiously, fortuitously**) commanded her subjects to be silent.

5. During the war, soldiers assigned to desk jobs were sometimes sarcastically called the "chairbound infantry" or the "(**sedentary, provocative**) commandos."

6. It was quite (**fortuitous, debonair**) that we met the studio owner, since she was looking for a new artist to feature in her gallery.

7. This new book is a(n) (**imperious, provocative**) examination of our school system that may upset some of your most cherished ideas about higher education.

8. The crass and (**reprobate, fortuitous**) conduct of those responsible for the scandal deserved public censure.

9. Research shows that those who lead a (**debonair, sedentary**) lifestyle are more prone to chronic medical conditions, such as heart disease and diabetes.

10. The difficult stage part called for an actor to gradually change during the course of the play from a morose introvert to a(n) (**debonair, imperious**) charmer.

11. Only a genius could have converted such a (**motley, sedentary**) group of individuals, drawn from all walks of life, into a disciplined and efficient organization.

12. What good will it do you to (**dun, reprobate**) me so mercilessly when you know that I am flat broke?

Completing the Sentence

Choose the word from the word bank that best completes each of the following sentences. Write the correct word or form of the word in the space provided.

| annotation | dun | gist | motley | reprobate |
| debonair | fortuitous | imperious | provocative | sedentary |

1. Although their language was deliberately _____, I did not allow it to cause me to lose my self-control.

2. Daily exercise is recommended particularly for people whose occupations are, for the most part, _____.

3. No sooner had the incorrigible old _____ gotten out of jail than he returned to the wicked ways that had landed him there in the first place.

4. If you resent being _____ by tradespeople, why not try paying your bills on time?

5. It will be helpful if you can state the _____ of your arguments in a few sentences.

6. She is a leader who can command loyalty and instant obedience without resorting to abusive language, threats, or a(n) _____ manner.

7. His elegant appearance was matched by the _____ ease and polish of his manners.

8. As the British writer W. Somerset Maugham once observed, human nature is a(n) _____ collection of strengths and weaknesses, foibles and follies.

9. Our meeting seemed at the time to be entirely _____, but I learned later that it was the result of a careful plan.

10. The instructor returned my thesis with a number of comments, queries, and other _____ penciled in the margin.

Synonyms

*Choose the word or form of the word from this Unit that is the same or most nearly the same in meaning as the **boldface** word or expression in the phrase. Write that word on the line. Use a dictionary if necessary.*

1. a film with **unnecessary** scenes of violence _____
2. **accumulate** vacation time at work _____
3. a **bounteous** donation _____
4. accepted the decision with **composure** _____
5. an explanation too **esoteric** to follow _____
6. added **commentary** to the text _____
7. **lucky** in choosing the right teammate _____
8. a **suave** greeting from our host _____
9. the **general picture** of his story _____
10. an angry **diatribe** _____
11. **pestering** her for overdue payments _____
12. became **idle** during retirement _____
13. another excuse to **postpone** the assignment _____
14. a **miscreant** in her business methods _____
15. an **assorted** crew of teens _____

Antonyms

*Choose the word or form of the word from this Unit that is most nearly opposite in meaning to the **boldface** word or expression in the phrase. Write that word on the line. Use a dictionary if necessary.*

1. **tranquility** before the storm _____
2. spoke in an **unassuming** tone _____
3. an **unstimulating** question _____
4. an **open** meeting _____
5. a highly **ineffective** medicine _____

Writing: Words in Action

Suppose you are a Tuvaluan who wants to relocate with your fellow citizens. You all want to maintain your identity as a people and a culture. Write a persuasive letter to the United Nations, stating your case. Use at least two details from the passage (pages 144–145) and three or more words from this Unit.

Vocabulary in Context

*Some of the words you have studied in this Unit appear in **boldface** type. Read the passage below, and then circle the letter of the correct answer for each word as it is used in context.*

Miami, a **motley** city whose residents seem to share only one trait, a professed desire to live in "paradise," is experiencing yet another building boom. Cranes shadow the landscape, skyscrapers sprout upward, and a new wave of arrivals elbows its way in. Water should not be a problem for this growing metropolis. Sitting above the abundant Biscayne aquifer—and getting upward of sixty inches of rain each year—Miami would appear to have plenty of fresh water. Climate change, however, is rapidly undermining the city's water situation in ways that few South Floridians want to consider. A warming climate means rising sea levels, and Miami, which is built as close to the Atlantic Ocean as is physically possible, cannot avoid the consequences.

Here in South Florida, any discussion of climate change by public officials is likely to be met by **invective**. Property owners are inclined to view public officials as **reprobates** when they speak of costly adaptations or, more seriously, retreat from the coastline. Many of these owners have sunk their life savings into their homes and businesses. For them, government warnings about rising sea levels are simply an excuse for city government to further **dun** taxpayers.

But, explains a soft-spoken and **debonair** geology professor, Miami does indeed face a water problem—*underground* flooding. Underlying the city is a vast formation of porous limestone, through which seawater flows freely. Because saltwater is denser than freshwater, the ocean water does not disturb the aquifer above. Unfortunately, as sea levels rise, the layer of saltwater in the limestone does, too. The **gist** of the professor's argument is that Miami's network of municipal wells—the source of drinking water for millions of residents—will one day become salty and unusable.

---

1. The population of a **motley** city shows
   a. uniformity
   b. poverty
   c. vibrant growth
   d. great variety

2. The word **invective** most nearly means
   a. rejection
   b. strong denunciation
   c. investigation
   d. clever rebuttal

3. A **reprobate** is a
   a. real estate agent
   b. coast guard
   c. speaker
   d. scoundrel

4. To **dun** taxpayers is to
   a. demand payment
   b. raise tax rates
   c. anger them
   d. fool them

5. A **debonair** professor is
   a. intelligent
   b. courteous
   c. forward-thinking
   d. deceptive

6. The **gist** of an argument is its
   a. conclusion
   b. theme
   c. essential part
   d. summary

*Read the following passage, taking note of the **boldface** words and their contexts. These words are among those you will be studying in Unit 11. It may help you to complete the exercises in this Unit if you refer to the way the words are used below.*

Oyez! Oyez!: The Evolution of News
<Informational Essay>

It has long been said that bad news travels fast, but nowadays it might be said that all news travels fast. The ability of human societies to **disseminate** information over great distances has improved immensely over the centuries, spurred by the advance of technology.

In ancient times, people sent messages from a distance using drums, smoke, and fire as signals. While these techniques served a purpose, the range of information they delivered was limited, and most news spread by word of mouth. Communicating across distances was **contingent** on travel, and the speed of delivery was limited by the pace of the messenger. Ancient civilizations built networks of roads and relay stations to promote communication. Foot runners entrusted with delivering urgent official news were selected from among the strongest and most **abstemious** young men, who were considered the most responsible. The Royal Road constructed by the Persian Empire

Persian messenger,
fourteenth century

The Smoke Signal, by
Frederic Remington

stretched over 1,500 miles and had over 100 stations where riders exchanged their tired horses for fresh mounts. Riding day and night, Persian messengers could cross the Empire in seven days. Ancient communication also benefited from the invention of writing and related technologies, such as paper and papyrus. Town criers with loud voices, expressive gestures, and **florid** outfits provided news to town **denizens**. Their cries of "Oyez! Oyez!" (Hear ye! Hear ye!) notified listeners of news to follow.

During the European Renaissance, merchants circulated handwritten newsletters containing information about international trade and foreign customs. Printed news pamphlets, made possible by the invention of the printing press, were a **salient** part of the fifteenth century. The first real newspapers appeared in Western Europe in the seventeenth century. At the time, European governments sought to use the newspapers to **inculcate** their own policies, imposing harsh penalties on publishers of political or religious **heresies**. Popular resistance to censorship gradually achieved increased freedom of the press. By the late nineteenth century, newspapers had become familiar throughout the world. News bureaus sprang up in cities across the globe to facilitate the collection of news, benefiting from the invention of the electric telegraph and telephone. News became a big business, and journalism became an important profession. Many newspapers published "yellow journalism," **foisting** poorly researched stories, **specious** rhetoric, and sensational scandals on their readers. To correct these **censurable** practices, a new breed of journalists, led by Joseph Pulitzer, attempted to impose professional standards in the industry. They emphasized unbiased reporting, research, and fact-checking to **corroborate** information.

The newspaper industry began to decline during the twentieth century as new technologies emerged. Newspaper circulation dropped as radio and television broadcast news directly into homes, providing instantaneous reports on the latest events. Since the 1990s, the Internet has become an increasingly important source of news. Thousands of Web sites offer news today, ranging from official government sites, to professional news organizations, to aimless, **discursive** blogs. Internet access, social media, and mobile devices enable people all over the world to capture photographs and video of events and publish them online for a global audience.

An electronic tablet, 2010

Some critics claim that the internet has **pernicious** effects on the news industry, eroding standards of journalism and spreading rumors and opinions instead of facts. Others applaud the Internet's contribution to the industry and to democratic debate. While the argument rages on, **perceptive** audiences learn to tell fact from fiction, and the steady churn of technology prepares the way for the future course of the evolution of the news.

Printing press, circa 1960

Audio

For iWords and audio passages, go to SadlierConnect.com.

Definitions

Note the spelling, pronunciation, part(s) of speech, and definition(s) of each of the following words. Then write the appropriate form of the word in the blank space in the illustrative sentence(s) following.

1. censurable
(sen' shər ə bəl)

(*adj.*) deserving of blame or correction
Because he was unaware of what he had done, we decided that his behavior was not _____.

2. corroborate
(kə räb' ə rāt)

(*v.*) to confirm, make more certain, bolster, substantiate, verify
He could tell the court where I was and for how long, but he needed a witness to _____ his statements.

3. denizen
(den' ə zən)

(*n.*) an inhabitant, resident; one who frequents a place
A lover of marine life, she knew the names of all the scaly _____ of our lake.

4. discursive
(dis kər' siv)

(*adj.*) passing aimlessly from one place or subject to another, rambling, roving, nomadic
Within the _____ account of his life, there was a fairly complete history of the whole village.

5. florid
(flär' id)

(*adj.*) highly colored, reddish; excessively ornate, showy
The _____ style of architecture in the old part of town was a welcome change from the grim, newer blocks we had seen.

6. gauche
(gōsh)

(*adj.*) awkward, lacking in social graces, tactless, clumsy
Though he was sincere when he thanked his guest for having stayed an extra week, his comment was considered _____.

7. inculcate
(in' kəl kāt)

(*v.*) to impress on the mind by repetition, teach persistently and earnestly
It is important to _____ a healthy respect for authority into army recruits.

8. perceptive
(pər sep' tiv)

(*adj.*) having sympathetic insight or understanding, capable of keen appreciation
Her _____ eye took in the roomful of noisy children and settled on the one child who was ill at ease.

9. salient
(sāl′ yənt)

(*adj.*) leaping, jumping, or springing forth; prominent, standing out, conspicuous; (*n.*) a projection or bulge, a land form that projects upward or outward

I think the most _____ feature of the new plan is its similarity to the old plan.

Our forces occupied a _____ that was extremely vulnerable to attack.

10. sear
(sir)

(*v.*) to make or become dry and withered; to char or scorch the surface of; to harden or make unfeeling; to parch, singe

We wanted to serve grilled vegetables, but I _____ them, and they tasted like leather.

Using Context

*For each item, determine whether the **boldface** word from pages 158–159 makes sense in the context of the sentence. Circle the item numbers next to the six sentences in which the words are used correctly.*

1. I love the beach but cannot stand the crowds, so I try to go early in the morning or around sunset when the mood is **florid** and I can relax.

2. The professor was an expert in political science, but his **discursive** lectures often veered off into some of his other areas of interest.

3. Many things may escape my notice, but I'm **perceptive** enough to know that when someone insists that everything is okay, they often mean just the opposite.

4. Critics all agreed that the film is **censurable** enough to earn awards in every category.

5. Her dry sense of humor fell flat with the rest of the group, and they assumed her attempts at jokes were merely **gauche** comments.

6. In order for any alibi to pass muster, someone else must be able to **corroborate** the story.

7. According to the chef, the best way to cook the fish is to **sear** it on both sides in a pan over medium-high heat, and then put it in a moderately hot oven to complete the cooking.

8. Every **denizen** of this community must vote in local elections to ensure all voices are heard.

9. The guard's **salient** pose would not break, even when people tried to make him laugh.

10. Despite the evidence in her favor, the jury decided to **inculcate** the defendant based on the fact that she was the last known person to visit the scene of the crime.

Choosing the Right Word

*Select the **boldface** word that better completes each sentence. You might refer to the passage on pages 156–157 to see how most of these words are used in context. Note that the choices might be related forms of the Unit words.*

1. In a series of (**searing, florid**) attacks now known as the *Philippics,* Cicero launched his entire battery of political invectives against the hapless Mark Anthony.

2. Children are often remarkably (**discursive, perceptive**) in understanding how adults feel about them.

3. No doubt her efforts to advance her own interests were (**florid, censurable**), but let's try to keep a sense of proportion and not condemn her too much.

4. Out of the endless flow of dull verbiage in that long lecture, we could recognize only two or three (**gauche, salient**) points.

5. Although the essays are highly (**discursive, gauche**), covering a wide range of topics, they are written with such clarity and grace that they are easy to follow.

6. Her (**perceptive, florid**) writing style, abounding in adjectives and fancy metaphors, is far from suitable for factual newspaper stories.

7. The most tragic aspect of a forest fire is its destructive effects on the innumerable plant and animal (**salients, denizens**) of that environment.

8. He thought he was being witty and charming, but I regard his conduct at the party as altogether (**perceptive, gauche**).

9. Before we (**inculcate, corroborate**) certain principles in young people, let's be sure that these principles are truly desirable for them and their society.

10. All the available evidence (**corroborates, sears**) my theory that the theft was planned by someone familiar with the layout of the house.

11. The attorney argued that the corporation's failure to compensate the worker for projects not in his contract was (**censurable, salient**) behavior.

12. This folk song is eight minutes of (**perceptive, discursive**) lyrics covering everything from world wars to civil rights to the lives of iconic musicians, but it has become a cult favorite.

Completing the Sentence

Choose the word from the word bank that best completes each of the following sentences. Write the correct word or form of the word in the space provided.

censurable	denizen	florid	inculcate	salient
corroborate	discursive	gauche	perceptive	sear

1. Among all those pale and sallow people, her highly _____ complexion stood out like a beacon.

2. It is hard to believe that people coming from such a refined social milieu could actually be so _____ and boorish.

3. His talk on world affairs was so disorganized and _____ that it left us more confused than ever.

4. The old fellow did indeed look like a typical _____ of the racetrack, as described in Damon Runyon's famous stories.

5. Unless you can produce witnesses to _____ your claim that you stopped at the red light, the mere assertion will have little or no effect on the jury.

6. Psychologists tell us that the years of early childhood are the best time to _____ basic concepts of right and wrong.

7. If you wish to seal in the juices and bring out the flavor of your pot roast, _____ it briefly in a hot pan before you put it in the oven.

8. I don't like to criticize your behavior, but I feel obliged to tell you that your discourtesy to that confused tourist was highly _____.

9. Eudora Welty is considered one of the most _____ and insightful American writers of her time.

10. A(n) _____ characteristic of every great athlete is the ability to perform at maximum efficiency under extreme pressure.

Definitions

Note the spelling, pronunciation, part(s) of speech, and definition(s) of each of the following words. Then write the appropriate form of the word in the blank space in the illustrative sentence(s) following.

1. abstemious
(ab stē′ mē əs)

(*adj.*) moderate, sparing (as in eating and drinking); characterized by abstinence and self-discipline
She came from a long line of quiet, thrifty, and _____ farming folk.

2. contingent
(kən tin′ jənt)

(*adj.*) likely but not certain to happen, possible; dependent on uncertain events or conditions; happening by chance; (*n.*) a representative group forming part of a larger body
_____ on our parents' approval, we plan to take a trip through Alaska next summer.
The meeting was delayed due to the late arrival of the California _____.

3. disseminate
(di sem′ ə nāt)

(*v.*) to scatter or spread widely
I decided that it was a bad idea to use my position in order to _____ my personal views.

4. dowdy
(dau′ dē)

(*adj.*) poorly dressed, shabby; lacking smartness and good taste
The actor wore _____ clothing and sunglasses so that no one would recognize him.

5. foist
(foist)

(*v.*) to impose by fraud; to pass off as worthy or genuine; to bring about by stealth, dishonesty, or coercion
During the nineteenth century the unscrupulous Jay Gould _____ thousands of worthless railroad shares on an unsuspecting public.

6. heresy
(her′ ə sē)

(*n.*) an opinion different from accepted belief; the denial of an idea that is generally held sacred
Saving money to accumulate interest seems to be a form of _____ in these days of instant credit.

7. palpable
(pal′ pə bəl)

(*adj.*) capable of being touched or felt; easily seen, heard, or recognized
The energy and excitement in the stands was almost _____ during the football game.

8. pernicious
(per nish′ əs)

(*adj.*) extremely harmful; deadly, fatal
Night air was once thought to have a _____ effect on infants who were in poor health.

9. satiate
(v., sā′ shē āt;
adj., sā′ shē it)

(v.) to satisfy completely; to fill to excess; (adj.) full, satisfied
Nothing will _____ my hunger.
The _____ brown bear had a good
sleep after raiding the honey-laden beehives.

10. specious
(spē′ shəs)

(adj.) deceptive, apparently good or valid but lacking real merit
Though her résumé looked very impressive, her claims of
vast experience in the field were _____.

Using Context

*For each item, determine whether the **boldface** word from pages 162–163 makes sense in the context of the sentence. Circle the item numbers next to the six sentences in which the words are used correctly.*

1. We would like to extend to you an offer of employment with this company, **contingent** on your passing a background check.

2. Although I had been excited about our trip to the mountains, the long drive seemed to **satiate** all my energy, and I could barely keep my eyes open when we arrived.

3. The headmistress had such an **abstemious** presence that even the rowdiest children would become well-behaved as soon as they saw her coming down the hall.

4. My parents tried to **disseminate** the notion that they were taking us on a surprise trip during winter break by talking about all the things they had planned at home, but I had already seen the plane tickets.

5. The store's promise of a refund for a return within 10 days of purchase of a product a customer is not satisfied with turned out to be **specious**.

6. Her **dowdy** appearance lately shows how overworked and tired she is, as she normally spends a great deal of time putting trendy outfits together.

7. Never underestimate the **pernicious** powers of having a good laugh when you're in a sour mood.

8. As the group around me discussed the latest episode of the hit television show, I refrained from stating my dislike of the program for fear of being accused of **heresy**.

9. As the contestants waited to hear who had won the award for Best Picture, the suspense in the room was almost **palpable**.

10. My coworker tried to **foist** yet another one of his assignments on me by claiming he had enough on his plate already, and I finally called him out on his laziness.

Choosing the Right Word

*Select the **boldface** word that better completes each sentence. You might refer to the passage on pages 156–157 to see how most of these words are used in context. Note that the choices might be related forms of the Unit words.*

1. Disguised as an old hag, the wicked queen gave Snow White a (**palpable, pernicious**) apple, which trapped the young heroine into a prolonged, death-like sleep.

2. During times of extreme economic hardship and war, families often eat (**dowdily, abstemiously**).

3. Although the Declaration of Independence was framed only to justify a revolution in the British colonies in North America, its ideas and ideals have been (**disseminated, satiated**) throughout the world.

4. Though I rather like the better television game shows, I find that after a certain point, I'm (**satiated, foisted**) and ready for more substantial fare.

5. The study of history teaches us that many ideas regarded as (**heresies, disseminations**) by one generation are accepted as sound and orthodox by the next.

6. A passing grade is (**pernicious, contingent**) on your participation in class.

7. Modern nutritionists emphasize that there is a(n) (**palpable, abstemious**) difference between "eating to live" and "living to eat."

8. As the Scottish poet Robert Burns aptly suggests, even the best-laid plans are often entirely (**palpable, contingent**) on events we cannot control.

9. The more we studied the drug problem, the more we became aware of its (**contingent, pernicious**) influence on the American people today.

10. Don't you get tired of glossy advertisements that try to (**foist, satiate**) short-lived and sometimes absurd fashion trends on the consumer?

11. Some English rulers were strikingly elegant and imposing figures; others were somewhat (**specious, dowdy**) and unprepossessing.

12. We are most likely to fall victim to (**abstemious, specious**) reasoning when we have an emotional desire to believe what we are being told.

Completing the Sentence

Choose the word from the word bank that best completes each of the following sentences. Write the correct word or form of the word in the space provided.

abstemious	disseminate	foist	palpable	satiate
contingent	dowdy	heresy	pernicious	specious

1. When I referred to her favorite singer as an "untalented, overpaid, and conceited lout," she looked at me in shock, as though I were guilty of _____.

2. Though this may not be the most stylish blouse I own, I thought to myself, at least it doesn't make me look _____!

3. Her good health in old age is due in large part to the _____ habits of her younger years.

4. No honest mechanic will try to _____ inferior replacement parts on his customers.

5. The stubborn refusal to give me a chance to compete for the scholarship on the same basis as everyone else is a(n) _____ injustice to the whole idea of fair play.

6. Since we wished to have some say in the town council's final decision, we sent a small _____ of our most persuasive speakers to the hearings.

7. Is there any need for me to describe at length the _____ effects of smoking?

8. If I had the time, I could point out many flaws in the _____ arguments you find so impressive.

9. The purpose of this program is to _____ throughout the community information about job-training opportunities for young people.

10. After the long summer vacation, I was _____ with loafing and eager to return to school!

Synonyms

*Choose the word or form of the word from this Unit that is the same or most nearly the same in meaning as the **boldface** word or expression in the phrase. Write that word on the line. Use a dictionary if necessary.*

1. **broadcast** the news _____

2. **instill** the importance of good hygiene _____

3. **dependent** on passing the test _____

4. **gratify** the appetite for gossip _____

5. a **tangible** change in the mood of the crowd _____

6. a form of **dissent** _____

7. a **native** of the high country _____

8. **impose** their ideas on the public _____

9. **authenticate** a silly rumor _____

10. take care not to **burn** your hand _____

11. not tolerating **vulgar** behavior _____

12. their **discriminating** remarks _____

13. a **flowery** introduction _____

14. a long and **digressive** novel _____

15. **tacky** window decorations _____

Antonyms

*Choose the word or form of the word from this Unit that is most nearly opposite in meaning to the **boldface** word or expression in the phrase. Write that word on the line. Use a dictionary if necessary.*

1. a **laudable** track record on policy _____

2. an **intemperate** lifestyle _____

3. a **minor** point in the presentation _____

4. a **valid** argument _____

5. **beneficial** effects of the product _____

Writing: Words in Action

Has the availability of "instant news" changed our lives for the better, or has it had negative effects? Support your essay with specific details, your observations and studies, and the reading (refer to pages 156–157). Write at least three paragraphs, and use three or more words from this Unit.

Vocabulary in Context

*Some of the words you have studied in this Unit appear in **boldface** type. Read the passage below, and then circle the letter of the correct answer for each word as it is used in context.*

From the time of the *New-England Courant,* founded in Boston by Ben Franklin's older brother James in 1721, American newspapers have always been a highly competitive business. Rivalry among news organizations reached one of its peaks in the late nineteenth century when two newspaper magnates, Joseph Pulitzer and William Randolph Hearst, competed fiercely for readers in New York City. Pulitzer and Hearst epitomized a style that came to be called "yellow journalism."

The term originated in a popular cartoon series in Pulitzer's paper, the *New York World,* called "The Yellow Kid." When Hearst bought the *New York Journal* in 1895, he lured away the cartoonist, Richard F. Outcault. The dueling cartoon strips in the two papers were not all that interested readers, however. Reporting became increasingly sensationalistic, and no subject was too **gauche** for the papers to handle. No amount of scandal appeared to **satiate** the reading public, and by the late 1890s, the periodicals of the previous generation seemed positively **dowdy** by comparison.

Pulitzer and Hearst had an almost **palpable** interest in Cuba, where a struggle for independence from Spain intensified in the mid-1890s. The newspapers carried **searing** accounts of Spanish oppression, some of them later exposed to be **specious**. In early 1898, when the American battleship *Maine* exploded and sank in Havana Harbor, Hearst and Pulitzer both published pernicious rumors of plots to sink the ship. Less than three months later, the Spanish-American War began. Although it is inaccurate to claim that yellow journalism caused the conflict, the historical record makes clear that the press wielded significant influence on public opinion about international issues.

---

1. A **gauche** remark or situation is

  a. repetitive   **c.** elegant
  b. pompous   **d.** awkward

2. To **satiate** is to

  a. satisfy   **c.** undermine
  b. languish   **d.** recall

3. The word **dowdy** most nearly means

  a. chic   **c.** shoddy
  b. pale   **d.** proper

4. Something **palpable** can be

  a. dragged   **c.** touched
  b. framed   **d.** planned

5. A **searing** report might also be described as

  a. concise   **c.** equivocal
  b. insightful   **d.** scorching

6. A **specious** statement is

  a. deceptive   **c.** revelatory
  b. exceptional   **d.** authentic

UNIT 12

*Read the following passage, taking note of the **boldface** words and their contexts. These words are among those you will be studying in Unit 12. It may help you to complete the exercises in this Unit if you refer to the way the words are used below.*

The Facts in the Case of the Greatest Mystery Writer
<Debate>

After his class read two Edgar Allan Poe stories, "The Murders in the Rue Morgue" (1841) and "The Purloined Letter" (1844), Mr. Shippen asked: *While Edgar Allan Poe deserves credit for inventing the modern detective story, are his stories the best examples of the genre?* A lively discussion between two students followed.

Nate: Poe's brilliant detective stories are rightly praised as **scintillating** forerunners of this genre in fiction. Poe's sharp, **incisive** style and his ability to establish and then **enhance** suspense fully justify his reputation as the master of the modern detective story. "The Murders in the Rue Morgue" and "The Purloined Letter" exhibit features that became standard in later detective fiction: A crime is committed, an investigation ensues, and an unexpected solution is discovered by the brilliant mental gymnastics of the detective.

Kyra: I strongly disagree with Nate's appraisal of Poe's detective stories. Let's begin with Poe's style. It is difficult to **absolve** Poe of the offenses of pomposity and digression. The opening of "The Murders in the Rue Morgue" consists of lengthy, abstract discussions of the concept of "analysis," and Poe's efforts to distinguish between analysis and ingenuity are **deleterious** to storytelling. Moreover, his style is more **prosaic** than evocative, more **redundant** than concise. Take the story's first sentence: "The mental features discoursed of as the analytical, are, in themselves, but little susceptible of analysis." Spare us, Edgar!

Nate: In detective stories, the character of the detective is paramount, and Poe invented a figure who became a **paragon** for the genre: the brilliant but idiosyncratic C. Auguste Dupin—the ancestor of Sherlock Holmes, Hercule Poirot, Miss Marple, and other fictional detectives. His powers of observation and deduction **enthrall** the reader, while he is seldom arrogant or **ostentatious**, except when he dryly mocks the limitations of the Paris police—thus establishing another common character in detectives stories, the inept local policeman.

Kyra: Dupin is not nearly as impressive as Conan Doyle's Sherlock Holmes. In the "Rue Morgue," Poe violates what many readers

Illustration from "The Raven," 1864

Above: Basil Rathbone and Nigel Bruce in "Sherlock Holmes Faces Death," 1943

would regard as a compact between author and reader by making the murderer an escaped orangutan! Dupin releases the animal's owner of any responsibility—an action with which many readers disagree.

Nate: Look before you leap, Kyra! Since you referred to Sherlock Holmes, it's worth observing that in his detective tales, Poe establishes a first-person narrator who is the detective's close personal friend. Conan Doyle followed exactly this pattern with Sherlock Holmes and Dr. Watson, and Conan Doyle himself credits Poe as his inspiration.

As for the story's plot in "Rue Morgue," a central part of the puzzle is a **clangor** of shrieks and cries heard by witnesses. From the evidence, Dupin discerns an **implicit** conclusion: one participant in the crime was a human, while the other was not. This conclusion is supported by the issue of motive, and the fact that a large amount of money was left untouched suggests that the murders were not the result of **cupidity**. In "The Purloined Letter," furthermore, Dupin shows himself to be a master of **politic** behavior

as he subtly disarms a powerful government minister who has resorted to blackmail.

Kyra: I'm sorry, Nate, but "The Purloined Letter" does little to **extenuate** Poe's clumsiness in this genre. The two-dimensional dialogue often descends to **caricature**, and the plot depends on a twofold substitution of a duplicate for the stolen letter. Such repetition is awkward and **inimical** to credibility. However **winsome** Dupin may be, I don't believe that the detective could have tricked the villain with the same device that the blackmailer himself employed to obtain the letter in the first place.

Mr. Shippen: We will have to agree to disagree, as the class period ended five minutes ago!

Audio

For iWords and audio passages, go to SadlierConnect.com

Definitions

Note the spelling, pronunciation, part(s) of speech, and definition(s) of each of the following words. Then write the appropriate form of the word in the blank space in the illustrative sentence(s) following.

1. **clangor**
   (klang′ ər)

   (*n.*) a loud ringing sound; (*v.*) to make a loud ringing noise
   For more than a century, American grade schools summoned children to school with the _____ of a bell.

2. **contiguous**
   (kən tig′ yü əs)

   (*adj.*) side by side, touching; near; adjacent in time
   Trouble arose over who should control the weeds and bushes that rioted in the lot _____ to ours.

3. **enhance**
   (en hans′)

   (*v.*) to raise to a higher degree; to increase the value or desirability of
   She sanded and varnished the old table in order to _____ its appearance and value.

4. **extenuate**
   (ek sten′ yü āt)

   (*v.*) to lessen the seriousness or magnitude of an offense by making partial excuses
   "Do not _____ the circumstances!" my mom said when I explained I had been studying rather than cleaning my room.

5. **implicit**
   (im plis′ it)

   (*adj.*) implied or understood though unexpressed; without doubts or reservations, unquestioning; potentially contained in
   She never said so, but it was _____ that she did not like conversations before her morning coffee.

6. **ostentatious**
   (äs ten tā′ shəs)

   (*adj.*) marked by conspicuous or pretentious display, showy
   The restaurant's interior was so _____ that the meager meal, when it came, seemed an afterthought.

7. **paragon**
   (par′ ə gän)

   (*n.*) a model of excellence or perfection
   I may not be a _____ of scholarship, but I do try my best.

8. **prosaic**
   (prō zā′ ik)

   (*adj.*) dull, lacking in distinction and originality; matter-of-fact, straightforward; characteristic of prose, not poetic
   I remember his singing voice as being on key and clear but also _____.

9. **scintillating**
   (sin' tə lāt iŋ)

   (*adj., part.*) sparkling, twinkling, exceptionally brilliant (applied to mental or personal qualities)
   She was known for her _____ conversation.

10. **winsome**
    (win' səm)

    (*adj.*) charming, attractive, pleasing (often suggesting a childlike charm and innocence)
    When my little brother wanted something badly, he became as _____ as a puppy.

Using Context

*For each item, determine whether the **boldface** word from pages 170–171 makes sense in the context of the sentence. Circle the item numbers next to the six sentences in which the words are used correctly.*

1. Our class was reluctant to end the **scintillating** conversation about the novel even as the bell started to ring and the next class began entering the room.

2. The **contiguous** path leading out of the dense woods took us back to the visitor's center where our hike began.

3. Sprinkling some salt on watermelon may sound unappetizing, but apparently it will **enhance** the flavor of the sweet and juicy fruit.

4. Although you did not actually say I could borrow your car, I thought you were giving me **implicit** permission by leaving the keys on the kitchen table.

5. The **clangor** of a fire alarm startled me from a deep sleep and caused my ears to ring so loudly that I could not fall back asleep.

6. As president of the student council, head cheerleader, and planner of the latest fundraiser, she is the **paragon** of school spirit.

7. His travels throughout the world have given him a **winsome** edge, and he acts as if he is more informed than anyone he meets.

8. When I learned about tonight's airing of a two-hour special of my favorite TV show, I asked my mother if she would **extenuate** my allotted TV time.

9. All of the speeches given at the retirement party were **prosaic** enough to leave the guest of honor in tears of gratitude.

10. The party planners clearly thought they had organized a classy event, but to the guests it seemed to be nothing more than an **ostentatious** display of wealth.

Choosing the Right Word

Select the **boldface** word that better completes each sentence. You might refer to the passage on pages 168–169 to see how most of these words are used in context. Note that the choices might be related forms of the Unit words.

1. The commander expected (**ostentatious, implicit**) obedience from his troops.

2. My parents portrayed my older brother as such a (**clangor, paragon**) that I despaired of ever being able to follow in his footsteps.

3. She delivered her lines with such artistry and verve that she made the rather commonplace dialogue seem (**scintillating, prosaic**).

4. I realized I was being kept awake not by the (**paragon, clangor**) of the city traffic but by a gnawing fear that I had done the wrong thing.

5. The aspiring salesperson stood in front of the mirror for hours, practicing a (**winsome, contiguous**) smile.

6. My five-year-old niece enjoys telling (**implicit, ostentatious**) stories about her travels to strange lands in a giant balloon.

7. I've heard that if you sprinkle cinnamon in coffee, it (**extenuates, enhances**) the flavor and diminishes the bitterness.

8. The proposed advertisement was supposed to be "dynamic" and a "real eye-catcher," but I found it utterly (**winsome, prosaic**).

9. I will try to tell the story in a balanced way, without either exaggerating or (**scintillating, extenuating**) his responsibility for those sad events.

10. We thought it best to buy a house that was close to my parents' home, but not (**prosaic, contiguous**) to it.

11. A fresh coat of paint and some attention to the lawn would greatly (**enhance, extenuate**) the appearance of our bungalow.

12. Broccoli, considered by dietitians to be a (**clangor, paragon**) among vegetables, is packed with calcium and antioxidants.

Completing the Sentence

Choose the word from the word bank that best completes each of the following sentences. Write the correct word or form of the word in the space provided.

clangor	enhance	implicit	paragon	scintillating
contiguous	extenuate	ostentatious	prosaic	winsome

1. In most contracts, there are _____ duties and obligations that must be fulfilled even though they aren't expressed in so many words.

2. Because we had been told the new series was original and witty, we were disappointed by the obvious and _____ situation comedy that unfolded on our screen.

3. She did her work so quietly that it took us time to realize that she was a veritable _____ of efficiency and diligence.

4. The fact that he had hungry children at home does not justify what he did, but it does _____ his crime.

5. Until she rose to speak, the meeting had been dull, but she immediately enlivened it with her _____ wit.

6. The _____ of the fire bells as they echoed through the night filled our hearts with terror.

7. "Evening dress is far too _____ for such an informal occasion," I thought to myself as I tried to decide what to wear that night.

8. Because the gym is _____ to the library, it is easy for me to shift from academic to athletic activities.

9. His new haircut greatly _____ his appearance.

10. Marie's appealing personality and endearing manner make her quite _____ and engaging.

Definitions

Note the spelling, pronunciation, part(s) of speech, and definition(s) of each of the following words. Then write the appropriate form of the word in the blank space in the illustrative sentence(s) following.

1. absolve
(ab zälv')

(*v.*) to clear from blame, responsibility, or guilt
They assumed that their alibi would _____ them of suspicion.

2. caricature
(kar' i kə chür)

(*n.*) a representation, such as a drawing, that exaggerates a subject's characteristic features; (*v.*) to present someone or something in a deliberately distorted way
What began as a hasty newspaper _____ soon turned up on coffee mugs, T-shirts, and sweatshirts.
The satirical television program _____ the movie star and made him seem clumsier than he really was.

3. cupidity
(kyü pid' ə tē)

(*n.*) an eager desire for something; greed
You say that these catalogue prices show the quality of the goods, but I say they show the seller's _____.

4. deleterious
(del ə tir' ē əs)

(*adj.*) harmful, injurious
Wishing can give zest and purpose to anyone's life, but wishful thinking can have a _____ effect.

5. enthrall
(en thrôl')

(*v.*) to captivate, charm, hold spellbound; to enslave; to imprison
All the critics were _____ by the performance and wrote rave reviews.

6. incisive
(in sī' siv)

(*adj.*) sharp, keen, penetrating (with a suggestion of decisiveness and effectiveness)
I am truly thankful for your _____ remarks about my report.

7. inimical
(in im'i kəl)

(*adj.*) tending to cause harm or obstruct developments; being oppositional or adverse
Several _____ groups have tried to create chaos and undermine democratic principles.

8. politic
(päl' ə tik)

(*adj.*) prudent, shrewdly conceived and developed; artful, expedient
In your angry state I think it would be _____ to say nothing, at least until you have calmed down.

9. redundant
(ri dən' dənt)

(*adj.*) extra, excess, more than is needed; wordy, repetitive; profuse, lush

Some _____ expressions, such as "hollow tubing," are acceptable in the English language.

10. sanctimonious
(saŋk tə mō' nē əs)

(*adj.*) making a show of virtue or righteousness; hypocritically moralistic or pious, self-righteous, canting, holier-than-thou

Cautionary tales that take on a _____ tone often achieve the opposite of the desired result.

Using Context

*For each item, determine whether the **boldface** word from pages 174–175 makes sense in the context of the sentence. Circle the item numbers next to the six sentences in which the words are used correctly.*

1. The impact of the arguments in your essay was diminished by your use of **redundant** phrases such as "absolutely sure" and "false pretense."

2. She is proud of the money that she works hard to earn, but she also shows her **cupidity** by donating as much as she can to causes she supports.

3. The arrogant billionaire was outraged when an insulting **caricature** of him made the rounds on all of the late-night TV shows.

4. While it is important to get your vitamins in order to be healthy, taking some in excessive amounts could actually be **deleterious** to your health.

5. The telemarketer's **sanctimonious** tone was so sincere and heartfelt, I felt compelled to listen and hear what she had to say.

6. I try not to let my friends **absolve** me in their drama, but sometimes I can't help but take sides.

7. An actor would not find at all helpful a critic's **incisive** review of his or her performance.

8. He refuses to accept any responsibility for things that go wrong in his life, and instead claims that there are some **inimical** forces working against him.

9. The new play promised to **enthrall** its audience, but the only aspect we found impressive was how the actor could fill up so much time with so little to say.

10. No one expected such **politic** remarks during the class discussion from the girl who normally sat silently in the back of the room.

Choosing the Right Word

*Select the **boldface** word that better completes each sentence. You might refer to the passage on pages 168–169 to see how most of these words are used in context. Note that the choices might be related forms of the Unit words.*

1. In the Lincoln-Douglas debates, Lincoln asked a few (**incisive, redundant**) questions that exposed the fatal weaknesses in his opponent's position.

2. Any conduct that is (**inimical, sanctimonious**) to school policy, including violation of state laws, is grounds for immediate dismissal.

3. Isn't it logical to conclude that because poor eating habits have a (**politic, deleterious**) effect on one's health, you should not make snack foods the cornerstone of your diet?

4. When she demanded that I immediately "return back" the money I owed her, I found her not merely unpleasant, but also (**redundant, deleterious**).

5. Our astute professor gave an (**incisive, inimical**) lecture on literary symbolism.

6. What we do now to remedy the evils in our society will determine whether or not we are to be (**absolved, enthralled**) of blame for the injustices of the past.

7. Words about "tolerance" are empty and (**sanctimonious, incisive**) when they come from one who has shown no concern about civil liberties.

8. The severe drought and locust infestation proved to have a (**deleterious, sanctimonious**) effect on the harvest.

9. Rumors of "easy money" and "lush profits" to be made in the stock market aroused the (**caricature, cupidity**) of many small investors.

10. "In seeking to discredit me," I replied, "my opponent has deliberately (**absolved, caricatured**) my ideas, making them seem simplistic and unrealistic."

11. It is hardly (**politic, inimical**) for someone who hopes to win a popularity contest to go about making such brutally frank remarks.

12. As long as we are (**enthralled, absolved**) by the idea that it is possible to get something for nothing, we will not be able to come up with a sound economic program.

Completing the Sentence

Choose the word from the word bank that best completes each of the following sentences. Write the correct word or form of the word in the space provided.

absolve	cupidity	enthrall	inimical	redundant
caricature	deleterious	incisive	politic	sanctimonious

1. With that one _____ comment, she brought an end to all the aimless talk and directed our attention to the real problem facing us.

2. Though ranking officials on both sides hoped to reach a truce and prepare a peace treaty, fringe groups refused to suspend their _____ activities.

3. To characterize the literary style of Edgar Allan Poe as "unique and one of a kind" is certainly _____.

4. His long nose and prominent teeth give the candidate the kind of face that cartoonists love to _____.

5. The jury may have found her not guilty, but the "court of public opinion" will never _____ her of responsibility for the crime.

6. Detective stories seem to _____ him to such a degree that he reads virtually nothing else.

7. Over the years, her normal desire for financial security was gradually distorted into a boundless _____.

8. We resented his _____ self-assurance that he was morally superior to everyone else.

9. How can anyone be so foolish as to develop a smoking habit when it has been proven that cigarettes are _____ to health?

10. There are some situations in life when it is _____ to remain quiet and wait for a better opportunity to assert oneself.

Synonyms

Choose the word or form of the word from this Unit that is the same or most nearly the same in meaning as the **boldface** word or expression in the phrase. Write that word on the line. Use a dictionary if necessary.

1. a **trenchant** report _____
2. **vindicated** of wrongdoing _____
3. a **parody** of his behavior _____
4. a book with the power to **enchant** _____
5. the investor's ever-growing **avarice** _____
6. had **tacit** consent to proceed _____
7. an **engaging** smile _____
8. bought lots that were **adjoining** _____
9. the **peal** of the tower bell _____
10. a **lively** play of wit _____
11. to **intensify** the taste of the sauce _____
12. a **smug** accusation _____
13. the **commonplace** routines of housework _____
14. **excuse** our misdeeds _____
15. an **exemplar** of team spirit _____

Antonyms

Choose the word or form of the word from this Unit that is most nearly opposite in meaning to the **boldface** word or expression in the phrase. Write that word on the line. Use a dictionary if necessary.

1. issued **succinct** instructions _____
2. **beneficial** to the environment _____
3. a **modest** house _____
4. a **friendly** gaze _____
5. **imprudent** to give my opinion _____

Writing: Words in Action

Suppose you are one of Mr. Shippen's students. You have to persuade the class who the better mystery writer is—Poe or Doyle. Write an argument in favor of one writer. Use at least two details from the passage (pages 168–169) and three or more words from the Unit.

Vocabulary in Context

*Some of the words you have studied in this Unit appear in **boldface** type. Read the passage below, and then circle the letter of the correct answer for each word as it is used in context.*

Bleak House is a rich and complex novel by Charles Dickens. On one level it is a satire on the law, but on another level, it is an impassioned plea on behalf of the London poor and an examination of personal philanthropy and public responsibility in which every human life is in some way **contiguous** with every other.

At its core, *Bleak House* is a mystery thriller. It is certainly the earliest true detective story in English, and in Inspector Bucket the novel features the earliest true police detective. Edgar Allan Poe's C. Auguste Dupin is more of a magician than a master of detection. He seems to exist solely as a demonstration of his oddly **sanctimonious** creator's theories of "analysis," where the reader is invited to marvel at Dupin's "preternatural" gifts but not to understand the character who exercises them. He is a virtual **caricature**. In the figure of Inspector Bucket, Dickens not only creates a prodigiously gifted analyst of evidence, but a detective to whom the evidence is a reflection of what it is to be human.

Bucket, like Dickens himself, is an **incisive** observer of people. Bucket is fascinated by every single character that contributes to the vast tidal wave of humanity that tumbles through the hundreds of pages of *Bleak House*. There is nothing **ostentatious** about Bucket, and he is **enthralled** by procedure and technique—by the actual job of solving a crime. And unlike many detectives who follow in his wake, Bucket never loses his affection for humanity, despite his acquaintance with the darker side of life.

---

1. If two things are **contiguous**, they are
   a. touching
   b. opposed
   c. aligned
   d. unrelated

2. A **sanctimonious** person is
   a. wise
   b. religious
   c. highly educated
   d. hypocritically moralistic

3. A **caricature** of a person is a representation that
   a. is comical
   b. looks silly
   c. is two-dimensional
   d. exaggerates a certain trait

4. If a speech is **incisive**, it is
   a. acute and penetrating
   b. cutting and satirical
   c. critical and argumentative
   d. hostile and destructive

5. To be **ostentatious** is to be
   a. pretentious
   b. outstanding
   c. flashy
   d. colorful

6. The word **enthralled** most nearly means
   a. preoccupied
   b. busy
   c. disenchanted
   d. riveted

Vocabulary for Comprehension

Part 1

*Read this passage, which contains words in **boldface** that appear in Units 10–12. Then choose the best answer to each question based on what is stated or implied in the passage. You may refer to the passage as often as necessary.*

Questions 1–10 are based on the following passage.

In the early eighteenth century, books were rare and expensive commodities that were only available to the extremely wealthy and to members of the clergy.
(5) In 1731, Benjamin Franklin noticed this **palpable** dearth of access to reading material. An organization called the Junto was also in existence at this time. The Junto explored many divergent ideas,
(10) ranging from issues in society to those in political science, yet its members were not wealthy enough to possess the required books for their studies. The Junto discovered that if its members merged
(15) their resources, all could have access to the **motley** collection of books. Thus, Franklin, along with members of the Junto, composed the "Articles of Agreement" to establish a library. The first library
(20) originated when fifty Junto members invested forty shillings each to **accrue** enough books so that each member could benefit from this collection; each year, Junto members invested an additional
(25) ten shillings each to buy extra books and preserve the library. This first library was an **efficacious** experiment that became the **paragon** of future libraries.

In the twentieth century, school and
(30) public libraries became centers that fostered America's penchant for reading and writing, and libraries had to keep up with this surge by providing access to newspapers, pamphlets, textbooks, and
(35) other reference materials. As immigrants from Europe entered the **contiguous** United States, libraries also became centers for English and adult education,

thus shifting their focus from paper texts
(40) to other forms of information. Another significant shift in the library system occurred with the invention of the mobile library: This project ensured that those in rural areas and under-resourced locations
(45) could have access to reading material. War also significantly effected the library's role in the twentieth century; the library joined the rebuilding effort after World War II by creating Victory Books, designed
(50) to boost soldiers' morale. As military veterans arrived in academic settings, academic libraries grew exponentially during the 1950s and 1960s.

In the twenty-first century, with
(55) advances in technology, the delivery of information has expanded beyond bound books. Even though the **salient** feature of libraries is still access to books, the focus of the modern library includes digital
(60) collections and ebooks in addition to physical texts. Many modern libraries also offer complimentary Wi-Fi access, and in some libraries they are the only source of free Internet access to their communities.
(65) In providing this free service, libraries demonstrate not only their attempt to stay current with technology, but also their continued goal of serving their patrons.

Although the first library and the modern
(70) library may seem radically different, they have some important commonalities. Both libraries were designed to be centers of community life, and they still fulfill that purpose. In addition, early
(75) and contemporary libraries both allow information to be **disseminated** to the larger community, regardless of the form that the information takes. Finally, libraries

throughout the years have **enhanced**
(80) their surrounding communities. This is
evidenced by the improvement in the lives
of the individuals living in the communities.

1. The main purpose of the passage is to
   A) detail the evolution of the library.
   B) describe the "Articles of Agreement."
   C) explore how books became
      accessible to all people.
   D) compare the first library to libraries
      in later centuries.

2. Why did Benjamin Franklin and the
   Junto begin the first library?
   A) They did not want to invest their
      own money in expensive books.
   B) They preferred to share books with one
      another rather than buy individual books.
   C) They wanted books to be available
      to people beyond the wealthy and
      the clergy.
   D) They wanted access to books that
      were unrelated to their studies.

3. As it is used in line 16, "motley"
   most nearly means
   A) consisting of several parts.
   B) showing great variety.
   C) originating from one location.
   D) existing in multiple volumes.

4. As it is used in line 28, "paragon"
   most nearly means
   A) a basis for comparison.
   B) a way to measure quality.
   C) an idea that is easily duplicated.
   D) a model of excellence.

5. According to lines 35–40, what effect did
   immigration have on the library system?
   A) It forced libraries to provide access
      to other reference materials.
   B) It led libraries to focus on education
      and information outside of paper texts.
   C) It encouraged libraries to become
      mobile to reach under-resourced areas.
   D) It led to an increase in the number of
      academic libraries.

6. Based on the information in the second
   paragraph (lines 29–53) it can reasonably be
   inferred that twentieth century libraries were
   A) responding to patrons' changing needs.
   B) making Americans better readers
      and writers.
   C) helping soldiers recover from the war.
   D) becoming more popular than earlier
      libraries.

7. As it is used in line 57, "salient"
   most nearly means
   A) traditional.
   B) unimportant.
   C) unique.
   D) prominent.

8. The author's main purpose in the third
   paragraph (lines 54–68) is to
   A) show the digital texts that twenty-first
      century libraries have in their
      collections.
   B) describe how twenty-first century
      libraries have expanded their focus
      beyond physical texts.
   C) provide examples of how twenty-first
      century patrons use computers in
      the library.
   D) investigate why twenty-first century
      libraries offer free Internet access.

9. According to the passage, what is one
   characteristic that the first library has in
   common with the contemporary library?
   A) They require annual contributions
      from their patrons.
   B) They have responded to patrons'
      changing needs.
   C) They share information with the
      community.
   D) They supply more than just
      physical texts.

10. Which choice provides the best evidence
    for the answer to the previous question?
    A) Lines 19–26 ("The first. . . library")
    B) Lines 35–40 ("As. . . information")
    C) Lines 57–61 ("Even though. . . texts")
    D) Lines 74–78 ("In addition. . . takes")

Vocabulary for Comprehension
Part 2

*Read these passages, which contain words in **boldface** that appear in Units 10–12. Then choose the best answer to each question based on what is stated or implied in the passage(s). You may refer to the passages as often as necessary.*

Questions 1–10 are based on the following passages.

Passage 1

Although graduate students comprised 14 percent of higher education students in 2015, they accounted for 40 percent of the $1.19 trillion in student debt in the
(5) United States. In addition, the number of students owing at least $100,000 in loan debt has quintupled. In 2006, around 500,000 graduate students owed at least $100,000 in loan debt. In 2014, another
(10) 1.82 million graduate students owed at least $100,000. The average amount that graduate students owed was $57,600. Those earning a master's degree owed between $50,000 and $60,000, while law
(15) degree recipients owed an average of $141,000, and medical degree recipients owed an average of $162,000. This is undoubtedly a **provocative** issue because there are tremendous consequences for
(20) having such an indebted population.
　　When students apply for loans, they expect to secure a lucrative job upon graduation. Yet receiving employment is not **contingent** upon completing
(25) graduate school. While some students are **fortuitous** enough to pay off their debts, many discover they are unable to do so. Many **perceptive** theorists have delivered **incisive** critiques of the federal lending
(30) system that allows graduate students to borrow unlimited funds. They argue that graduate student loan debt is not just an education problem. Repayment of student

loans affects how quickly people can save
(35) for a down payment on a home and their mortgage eligibility. So, is accumulating six-figure debt worth it in the long run?

Passage 2

At the beginning of the twentieth century, attending graduate school was
(40) seen as a **winsome** goal for many. Today, graduate degrees have replaced undergraduate degrees as the minimum requirement for employment in some fields. To be competitive in today's job
(45) market, students need the résumé boost of a graduate degree to distinguish themselves from the competition. Graduate-degree holders also tend to receive promotions at a higher rate, as
(50) long as they can perform the required duties of their position with **equanimity**. In addition, graduate degrees offer a sense of prestige, and many candidates for professional degrees (JDs and MBAs)
(55) have the possibility of being recruited by firms and corporations on their respective campuses; opportunities not available to students not attending those schools.
　　Another benefit of a graduate degree is
(60) receiving a **munificent** boost in salary as compared to students with undergraduate degrees: in 2012, the monthly median income of an employee with a graduate degree was $1,772 more than an
(65) employee with a bachelor's degree. That figure amounts to $21,264 over the course of a year. Some fields are more lucrative than others for graduate-degree holders:

an employee with a graduate degree in
(70) chemistry can command $40,000 more
per year than one with an undergraduate
degree. Though some are dubious about
whether graduate school is worth the
price, many others are grateful for the
(75) opportunity to **satiate** their aspirations
with additional schooling.

1. What is the main idea of Passage 1?
  A) Student debt is a problem for borrowers,
  the government, and the economy.
  B) Law and medical school degrees cost
  more than master's degree programs.
  C) Graduate degree holders rarely secure
  jobs that help pay off student loans.
  D) Graduate degree recipients are
  ineligible to receive mortgages.

2. As it is used in line 18, "provocative"
  most nearly means
  A) negative.
  B) unpleasant.
  C) vexing.
  D) important.

3. As it is used in line 28, "perceptive"
  most nearly means
  A) skilled at decision-making.
  B) capable of keen understanding.
  C) unlikely to change opinions.
  D) prone to controversial statements.

4. The purpose of Passage 2 is to
  A) explain why graduate school attendance
  has skyrocketed in the twenty-first century.
  B) analyze the rate at which graduate
  degree holders receive promotions.
  C) provide evidence for the financial
  benefits of receiving a graduate degree.
  D) highlight the various advantages of
  receiving a graduate degree.

5. As it is used in line 40, "winsome"
  most nearly means
  A) pleasing.
  B) difficult.
  C) unattainable.
  D) distinctive.

6. As it is used in line 51, "equanimity"
  means the same as
  A) pride.
  B) diligence.
  C) competence.
  D) composure.

7. The authors of Passage 1 and Passage 2
  would most likely agree that
  A) graduate school is unnecessary for
  many twenty-first century students.
  B) graduate school indebtedness is a
  problem that has been overlooked.
  C) graduate school is valuable for students
  who can secure profitable employment.
  D) graduate degrees are necessary to
  compete in today's job market.

8. Which statement best describes the overall
  relationship between Passage 1 and
  Passage 2?
  A) Passage 1 provides facts and
  Passage 2 presents opinions.
  B) Passage 1 is informative and
  Passage 2 is narrative.
  C) Passage 1 has a practical stance and
  Passage 2 has a positive stance.
  D) Passage 1 is more general and
  Passage 2 is more specific.

9. In Passage 1, the author asserts that
  graduate school is often not worth the cost.
  In Passage 2, the author believes that
  A) many students benefit from receiving
  additional education in graduate school.
  B) graduate degrees have replaced
  undergraduate degrees for all
  entry-level jobs.
  C) graduate students should study
  chemistry and other lucrative fields.
  D) more students should have attended
  graduate school in the past.

10. Which choice provides the best evidence
  for the answer to the previous question?
  A) Lines 38–40 ("At the . . . many")
  B) Lines 41–44 ("Today . . fields")
  C) Lines 67–72 ("Some fields . . . degree")
  D) Lines 72–76 ("Though … schooling")

Synonyms

*From the word bank below, choose the word that has the same or nearly the same meaning as the **boldface** word in each sentence and write it on the line. You will not use all of the words.*

bedlam	dun	imperious	recondite
contiguous	florid	implicit	redundant
cupidity	foist	munificent	sanctimonious
discursive	gist	politic	specious

1. Since the acronym *ATM* stands for *automated teller machine*, it would be **superfluous** to say "ATM machine." _____

2. The **unspoken** message of the tragic folk ballad is that life can be cruel and unfair. _____

3. If you don't understand the basics of ice hockey, a game between two powerful teams can seem like pure **chaos**. _____

4. It is a myth that the French queen Marie Antoinette responded to the peasants' hunger with the **arrogant** remark "Then let them eat cake." _____

5. Mexican artist Frida Kahlo celebrated the **flamboyant** visual style of her country in both her artwork and her personal appearance. _____

6. If you look on a map, you will see that the parcel of land that is for sale and the southern edge of the state park are **abutting**. _____

7. It would not be **judicious** to change the city's parking regulations without consulting with business leaders first. _____

8. Every night, I watch the 11 o'clock sports news to get the **substance** of what happened to the teams I follow. _____

9. The investigation unearthed new details about the **avarice** that had crept up into the highest levels of the state's government. _____

10. I hope I won't have to **hound** you for the money you promised to contribute toward our class gift to the school. _____

11. To someone like me, who had never played badminton doubles before, the scoring rules can seem absurdly **arcane**. _____

12. In Arthur Miller's play *The Crucible*, the actions of the **self-righteous** judges who unjustly condemn their neighbors to death during the Salem witch trials are both tragic and chilling. _____

Two-Word Completions

Select the pair of words that best completes the meaning of each of the following sentences.

1. In a series of _____ attacks, chock-full of the most withering political _____, the famous orator Demosthenes fulminated against King Philip of Macedon's nefarious efforts to curtail Greek rights and liberties.
   a. searing . . . invective
   b. motley . . . annotations
   c. scintillating . . . heresies
   d. gratuitous . . . clangor

2. Florida Fats and the other _____ of McDuffy's Billiard Emporium seem to come from every walk of life. One is unlikely to find such a(n) _____ crew under any other roof in town.
   a. reprobates . . . contiguous
   b. paragons . . . fortuitous
   c. caricatures . . . abstemious
   d. denizens . . . motley

3. "The flamboyant plumage of the male of the species has always struck me as overly _____," the ornithologist observed. "In contrast, the female looks so drab and _____ in her somber browns and grays."
   a. salient . . . gauche
   b. debonair . . . censurable
   c. ostentatious . . . dowdy
   d. prosaic . . . scintillating

4. The whole purpose of _____ dozens of fliers, press releases, advertisements, and other media was to put a quick and sudden stop to the _____ rumors about our candidate, but the tales persisted.
   a. procrastinating . . . provocative
   b. disseminating . . . pernicious
   c. accruing . . . gratuitous
   d. absolving . . . palpable

5. "We must take immediate steps to counteract this highly dangerous development," the new President told his advisors, "for the longer we _____, the more _____ its effects will be."
   a. disseminate . . . deleterious
   b. accrue . . . inimical
   c. procrastinate . . . pernicious
   d. corroborate . . . prosaic

6. Most of the adults seemed to find Kal's Kiddie Karnival a bit of a bore, but their children were _____, and the youngsters' appetites for the kind of fare that Kal served up were not _____ when the show was over.
   a. seared . . . absolved
   b. enhanced . . . accrued
   c. inculcated . . . extenuated
   d. enthralled . . . satiated

7. Office workers usually lead relatively _____ lives between nine and five. For that reason, many a "desk jockey" finds a weekly trip to the gym a(n) _____ way to keep fit.
   a. sedentary . . . efficacious
   b. prosaic . . . pernicious
   c. covert . . . gratuitous
   d. ostentatious . . . provocative

Denotation and Connotation

The **denotation** of a word is its literal meaning, the one found in the dictionary. A denotation is neutral, free from any emotional associations. A **connotation** is the emotional association a reader makes to a word. A word can evoke positive or negative connotations.

Consider these synonyms for the neutral word *sear*:

grill   broil   burn   scorch

For a chef, *grill* and *broil* are methods of preparing food; the words have neutral or even positive connotations. A chef would find the words *burn* and *scorch* to have very negative connotations, however—no cook wants to burn or scorch food.

Look at these examples of words that are similar in denotation but have different connotations.

NEUTRAL	POSITIVE	NEGATIVE
pleasant	debonair	slick
representation	cartoon	caricature
unadorned	simple	dowdy

Expressing the Connotation

Read each sentence. Select the word in parentheses that expresses the connotation (positive, negative, or neutral) given at the beginning of the sentence.

positive
1. To show his appreciation to those who taught him to read, Mr. Halstead made a (**generous, munificent**) donation to the school's library.

negative
2. The audience, appalled at the speaker's (**invective, criticism**), left the room in droves.

neutral
3. Though the scientist conducted (**incisive, cutting-edge**) research, no one believed the new drug would curtail the flu epidemic.

neutral
4. Kelly is not one who likes to (**procrastinate, wait**) when she has a deadline to meet.

negative
5. We did not want Sheila in our study group because of her (**tyrannical, imperious**) attitude toward others.

negative
6. Some snake bites have a (**deleterious, lethal**) effect on humans.

positive
7. Everyone at the concert hall was (**pleased, enthralled**) with the maestro's interpretation of Bach.

positive
8. The chief executive officer answered the shareholder's question with a (**politic, shrewd**) response.

Classical Roots

equa, equi, ega, iqui—equal

This root appears in **equanimity** (page 146). The literal meaning is "equal-mindedness." The word now means "composure; evenness of mind or temper." Some other words based on the same root are listed below.

egalitarian	equate	equilibrium	iniquitous
equable	equidistant	inequity	unequivocal

From the list of words above, choose the one that corresponds to each of the brief definitions below. Write the word in the blank space in the illustrative sentence below the definition. Use an online or print dictionary if necessary.

1. wicked, very unjust, vicious

The former dictator was tried for _____ deeds.

2. to regard or treat as equivalent; to make equal, equalize

It's a mistake to _____ politeness with kindness.

3. clear, plain, absolute, certain

There was no mistaking his _____ refusal to compromise.

4. asserting or promoting social, political, or economic equality; advocating the removal of inequalities among people

Most utopian societies are envisioned as _____.

5. balance (*"equal balance"*)

It's not easy to maintain one's _____ in a difficult situation.

6. uniform, marked by lack of noticeable or extreme variation; steady

Los Angeles is famous for its _____ climate.

7. equally separated from a given point or location

The two suburbs are _____ from St. Louis.

8. an act or situation of injustice and unfairness

A society based on _____ is ripe for revolution.

Read the following passage, taking note of the **boldface** words and their contexts. These words are among those you will be studying in Unit 13. It may help you to complete the exercises in this Unit if you refer to the way the words are used below.

Ansel Adams
<Essay>

Jeffrey Pine, Sentinel Dome, Yosemite National Park, California © 1940 by Ansel Adams

For someone celebrated today as one of America's greatest photographers, Ansel Adams had an **inauspicious** start in life. He was just four years old when much of his native city, San Francisco, was destroyed by the earthquake and fire of 1906. That day, a strong aftershock pushed young Ansel into a brick wall with such force that it broke his nose, which remained crooked for the rest of his life. One year later, the loss of the family fortune in a financial panic left his mother **disconsolate** and distant from her son. Hindered by dyslexia as a student, Adams

barely kept his head above water in school. As a teen, his shyness and social awkwardness resulted in a relatively solitary adolescence.

Fortunately, Adams found great joy and inspiration in music and nature. A self-taught pianist, he set aside regular schooling to follow his passion for music. The discipline and structure that his musical studies demanded **buttressed** his otherwise restless youth. But it was nature itself which became his **incontrovertible** muse. Adams fell in love with the Sierra Nevada mountains on his first visit, in 1916. He returned to the Yosemite Valley, the jewel of this mountain range along California's eastern border, every year of his life. On that first trip, Adams's father gave his son a camera, a gift that would **abet** a life devoted to nature and to art.

Three years later, the seventeen-year-old Adams joined the Sierra Club, a new organization dedicated to preserving natural resources and nature's unique treasures. This proved to be an **opportune** decision, as the group's leaders wished to **foment** a strong conservation movement and needed Adams's assistance. Part of their plan was to have a photographer document the Sierra Club's adventure outings, and members **broached** the idea to the boy who seemed always to have a camera in tow. The delighted young photographer agreed, and soon Adams became a **connoisseur** of the Sierra landscape— Yosemite in particular—while honing his skills as a visual artist. Adams and the Sierra Club were good for each other: The photographer's **prolific** output not only lured new supporters to the environmental cause, but Adams himself found a platform for his artistic vision—celebrating the glories of nature.

The competent pianist evolved into a gifted photographer. Ansel Adams's keen eye spurred him on to master the technical aspects of his new love. He arrived each year at Yosemite **encumbered** with unwieldy photographic gear, notebooks, and maps. He was willing to toil **herculean** hours if the effort helped improve his skills. Yet, despite a rigorous workload, he would allow himself the occasional harmless **carousal** with his ever-widening circle of friends and colleagues.

Adams was a driven man. He traveled the country photographing, lecturing, and writing. As an enthusiastic promoter of photography as a fine art, he helped establish the nation's first museum department of photography at the Museum of Modern Art in New York. And he remained a committed activist for preserving the wilderness. His dedication to the National Park system and vigorous support of the major environmental causes never abated.

While some critics noted an "absence of humanity" in Ansel Adams's landscape photographs— for his photographs celebrated nature, not mankind—his **rejoinder** was that his work continued the tradition of Thomas Cole, Frederic Church, Albert Bierstadt, and other nineteenth-century Romantic painters who sought to imbue the

Ansel Adams, 1961

splendors of nature with an emotional and inspirational majesty. Everyone benefited from such a vision: At a time of indifference to, if not **blatant** disregard for, the nation's natural resources, seeing the places Adams captured so beautifully in photographs motivated Americans to preserve them for all time.

Thanks to Ansel Adams, those who might never visit the glorious Yosemite National Park can still experience the drama of its beauty. The enduring appreciation for Adams's photos is largely due to his insistence upon high-quality images **collated** in what might be called "coffee-table books." This idea let him straddle the worlds of fine art photography, environmental education, and popular culture. Through money earned by the national parks and environmental groups from selling calendars, books, and other items featuring his exquisite photographs, even in death Adams has continued to benefit the rugged land he loved and championed.

Audio

For iWords and audio passages, go to SadlierConnect.com.

Definitions

Note the spelling, pronunciation, part(s) of speech, and definition(s) of each of the following words. Then write the appropriate form of the word in the blank space in the illustrative sentence(s) following.

1. abet
(ə bet')

(*v.*) to encourage, assist, aid, support (especially in something wrong or unworthy)

To allow a man in his condition to get behind the wheel of a car is to _____ a potential crime.

2. blatant
(blā' tənt)

(*adj.*) noisy in a coarse, offensive way; obvious or conspicuous, especially in an unfavorable sense

Your comments showed a _____ disregard for my feelings.

3. buttress
(bə' trəs)

(*v.*) to support, prop up, strengthen; (*n.*) a supporting structure

He has read so widely that he can produce facts to _____ any argument he advances.

I had to add _____ on either side of my rickety shed to keep it from collapsing.

4. carousal
(kə raủ' zəl)

(*n.*) noisy revelry or merrymaking (often with a suggestion of heavy drinking)

Vikings are notorious for having enjoyed a _____ after each of their battles.

5. encumber
(in kəm' bər)

(*v.*) to weigh down or burden (with difficulties, cares, debt, etc.); to fill up, block up, hinder

I feared that joining another club would _____ me with too many obligations.

6. grisly
(griz' lē)

(*adj.*) frightful, horrible, ghastly

Katherine Anne *Porter's Pale Horse, Pale Rider* reveals the _____ effects of the influenza virus during the epidemic that followed World War I.

7. inauspicious
(in ô spish' əs)

(*adj.*) unfavorable, unlucky, suggesting bad luck for the future

Our road trip got off to an _____ start when we ran out of gas within five miles of home.

8. incontrovertible
(in kän trə vər' tə bəl)

(*adj.*) unquestionable, beyond dispute

The document was remarkable for its tact yet also _____ in its facts.

9. nonplussed
(nän pləst')

(*adj.*, *part.*) puzzled, not knowing what to do, at a loss
She thought she was prepared for all contingencies, but she was _____ by the turn of events.

10. prolific
(pro lif' ik)

(*adj.*) abundantly productive; abundant, profuse
Haydn was a more _____ composer than Mozart, in part because he lived much longer.

Using Context

*For each item, determine whether the **boldface** word from pages 190–191 makes sense in the context of the sentence. Circle the item numbers next to the six sentences in which the words are used correctly.*

1. I decided to head home from the wedding reception when it was clearly turning into a **carousal** that would last all night.

2. Unlike Agatha Christie, this **prolific** author has written only three mysteries to date.

3. Your story is so full of **incontrovertible** facts that I dare not repeat the tale for fear that others would laugh at it.

4. The loud **buttress** coming from the street festival on the next block made it difficult to sleep.

5. I am determined to work hard to become a doctor one day, and I will make sure nothing will **abet** me from achieving my goal.

6. I have no intention of seeing the latest war story film, so you can spare me the **grisly** details of what was shown on screen.

7. The first question on the test stumped me, and I was worried about this **inauspicious** start, but fortunately, I was able to get through the rest of the exam with ease.

8. The politician was clearly not well prepared for the press conference, since he seemed **nonplussed** at every question that was posed to him.

9. I did not want to **encumber** my mother with more work, so I cleaned up any mess I made along the way as I prepared dinner.

10. I have always been taught to respect my elders, so it pains me to see them show such **blatant** contempt toward their teachers.

Choosing the Right Word

*Select the **boldface** word that better completes each sentence. You might refer to the passage on pages 188–189 to see how most of these words are used in context. Note that the choices might be related forms of the Unit words.*

1. Very few poems by Emily Dickinson were published during her lifetime, but she was nevertheless a (**nonplussed, prolific**) poet, writing more than 1,700 poems.

2. Although police identified the perpetrator using fingerprints, DNA, *and* video footage, he (**inauspiciously, blatantly**) denied that he had committed the crime.

3. I truly felt that reality could never be as horrible as the (**incontrovertible, grisly**) phantoms that were disturbing my dreams.

4. I know that she is wealthy and comes from a prominent family, but does that status excuse her (**blatant, nonplussed**) disregard of good manners?

5. You will never be able to complete this challenging hike if you (**encumber, abet**) yourself with so much "essential equipment."

6. Dr. Slavin's original diagnosis, although questioned by several colleagues, was strongly (**buttressed, encumbered**) by the results of the laboratory tests.

7. What we need is not opinions or "educated guesses" but (**inauspicious, incontrovertible**) proof that can stand up under the closest examination.

8. Well-meaning but misguided friends (**abetted, encumbered**) his plans to run away to Hollywood and "become a movie star."

9. I like a good time as much as anyone, but I don't think that the celebration of our nation's birthday should become a rowdy (**carousal, buttress**).

10. I was so (**grisly, nonplussed**) when my acting partner forgot her lines and stared blankly at the audience that I, too, had trouble remembering my dialogue.

11. The opening of our show took place most (**inauspiciously, incontrovertibly**) in the midst of a transit strike and a record-breaking snowstorm.

12. I wasn't so much surprised at not getting the job as I was (**encumbered, nonplussed**) by the strange explanation that I was "overqualified."

Completing the Sentence

Choose the word from the word bank that best completes each of the following sentences. Write the correct word or form of the word in the space provided.

abet	**buttress**	**encumber**	**inauspicious**	**nonplussed**
blatant	**carousal**	**grisly**	**incontrovertible**	**prolific**

1. I will not in any way _____ their plans to play a cruel and humiliating trick on an unoffending person.

2. He is such a(n) _____ writer that his books occupy almost an entire shelf in the school library.

3. The New Year's Eve party started off quietly enough, but it soon became a full-fledged _____.

4. The big game had a truly _____ start for us when our star quarterback fumbled and lost the ball on the first play.

5. The testimony of three different witnesses, all confirming the same basic facts, made the guilt of the accused _____.

6. I don't think you can really accuse the producers of _____ favoritism simply because they chose a friend for the title role.

7. She is so _____ with family obligations that she rarely has a free moment for herself.

8. The mangled bodies of the victims told their own _____ story of what had happened.

9. I was utterly _____ when I realized that football practice and the rehearsal for the class show were at the same time.

10. The towering walls of many medieval cathedrals are prevented from falling down by huge "flying _____" on the outsides of the buildings.

Definitions

Note the spelling, pronunciation, part(s) of speech, and definition(s) of each of the following words. Then write the appropriate form of the word in the blank space in the illustrative sentence(s) following.

1. aver
(ə vər′)

(*v.*) to affirm, declare confidently
I will _____ your fitness to do the work to any prospective employer who inquires.

2. broach
(brōch)

(*v.*) to bring up or begin to talk about (a subject); to announce, introduce; to break the surface of the water; to turn sideways to the wind and waves; to pierce (a keg or cask) in order to draw off liquid; (*n.*) a spit for roasting; a tool for tapping casks
She opted not to _____ the subject of the moldy smell in the bedroom for fear of insulting her hosts.

3. collate
(kō′ lāt)

(*v.*) to compare critically in order to note differences, similarities, etc.; to arrange in order for some specific purpose
We decided to _____ the recipes according to how complicated they are.

4. connoisseur
(kän ə sər′)

(*n.*) an expert; one who is well qualified to pass critical judgments, especially in one of the fine arts
She was a _____ of both music and film.

5. disconsolate
(dis kän′ sə lət)

(*adj.*) deeply unhappy or dejected; without hope, beyond consolation
Macbeth hardly seems _____ when his wife dies; instead, he bluntly says he has no time to grieve.

6. foment
(fō ment′)

(*v.*) to promote trouble or rebellion; to apply warm liquids to, warm
Toward the end of the film, the peasant leader attempts to _____ a storming of the scientist's castle.

7. herculean
(hər kyü lē′ ən)

(*adj.*) (*capital H*) relating to Hercules; (*lowercase h*) characterized by great strength; very hard to do in the sense of requiring unusual strength
We saw that getting the huge desk up the stairs would require a _____ effort.

8. impassive
(im pas′ iv)

(*adj.*) showing no feeling or emotion; inanimate; motionless
Since nervous laughter is the sign of an inexperienced actor, I tried to adopt an _____ expression on stage.

9. opportune
(äp ər tün′)

(*adj.*) suitable or convenient for a particular purpose; occurring at an appropriate time

If you intend to give that dog a bath, you had better pick an _____ moment, and then pounce!

10. rejoinder
(ri join′ dər)

(*n.*) a reply to a reply, especially from the defendant in a legal suit

When he explained where he had been and what he had done, her _____ was sharp and critical.

Using Context

*For each item, determine whether the **boldface** word from pages 194–195 makes sense in the context of the sentence. Circle the item numbers next to the six sentences in which the words are used correctly.*

1. Since I had been absent the day before, I tried to **collate** my friend's notes from our classes only to find that I could not make out her chicken-scratch handwriting.

2. When I saw that both my parents were in unusually good moods, I knew this was an **opportune** moment to ask for permission to go to the concert with my friends.

3. We were all having such a lovely time at dinner that I did not want to ruin the fun, so I decided to not yet **broach** the topic of my upcoming move to another state.

4. I can tell you are lying when you **aver** eye contact with me and instead stare down at the floor.

5. I would hardly call him a **connoisseur** of French cooking when he refused to eat anything but croissants when he was in Paris.

6. When I see someone litter, I try to **foment** the anger that rises up in me and simply clean up after them rather than causing a scene in public.

7. The principal did not appreciate the boy's sarcastic **rejoinder** when asked why he wasn't in class.

8. As excited as she was to tell her family about being accepted to her first choice college, she tried to keep her face **impassive** until everyone was present to hear her news.

9. My feet were so tired after a day spent walking around the city that even climbing a flight of stairs seemed like a task that would require **herculean** effort.

10. You must work on refining your **disconsolate** manners before we attend the state dinner.

Choosing the Right Word

*Select the **boldface** word that better completes each sentence. You might refer to the passage on pages 188–189 to see how most of these words are used in context. Note that the choices might be related forms of the Unit words.*

1. With tireless patience, the wily detective (**fomented, collated**) bits and pieces of evidence until he gained an insight into how the crime had been committed.

2. The speaker's inept replies to questions from the floor were met with a barrage of indignant (**broaches, rejoinders**).

3. Isn't it ridiculous to say that the disorder was (**averred, fomented**) by outsiders when we all know that it resulted from bad conditions inside the institution?

4. Cleaning up the old beach house seemed an almost impossible task, but she attacked it with (**herculean, disconsolate**) energy.

5. I still cannot figure out how to get my printer to (**collate, broach**) pages automatically when I want to make multiple copies of a document.

6. If you are going to wait for an occasion that seems (**opportune, impassive**) in *every* respect, then in all probability you will have to wait forever.

7. Her many blue ribbons prove she is a (**connoisseur, herculean**) of baking.

8. When they offered to help him, he proudly (**averred, collated**) that he could handle the situation on his own.

9. What could be more (**herculean, disconsolate**) than the long drive home on a rainy night after we had lost the championship game by one point!

10. His parents are such sensitive people that I'm not at all sure how I should (**broach, foment**) the news of his injury to them.

11. Psychologists tell us that people who seem to be unusually (**impassive, opportune**) are often the ones most likely to lose control of their emotions in times of stress.

12. I don't know anything about quiches and soufflés, but I'm a true (**rejoinder, connoisseur**) when it comes to pizza.

Completing the Sentence

Choose the word from the word bank that best completes each of the following sentences. Write the correct word or form of the word in the space provided.

aver	**collate**	**disconsolate**	**herculean**	**opportune**
broach	**connoisseur**	**foment**	**impassive**	**rejoinder**

1. Aren't you exaggerating when you suggest that the job of stock clerk calls for someone with _____ strength?

2. Although she remained outwardly _____ during the trial, I could sense the emotional turmoil beneath the surface.

3. Now that you mention it, I don't think that "Says you!" was a particularly effective _____ to her trenchant and insightful criticisms of your proposal.

4. I know you are really disappointed at not getting that job, but don't allow yourself to feel so _____ that you won't have the energy to look for another.

5. Although we have had our disagreements, I will _____ now that he has always been scrupulously honest in his dealings with me.

6. One need not be a(n) _____ of modern dance to recognize that Martha is exceptionally talented in that field.

7. If the pages aren't _____ properly, they'll be out of proper sequence when our class magazine is bound.

8. When I saw the worried expression on the face of my employer, I realized that it wasn't a(n) _____ time to ask for a raise.

9. "When I first _____ this topic two years ago," I observed, "my ideas were met with indifference and some skepticism."

10. It would be impossible to _____ ethnic discord in a school where students of different backgrounds understand and respect one another.

Synonyms

*Choose the word or form of the word from this Unit that is the same or most nearly the same in meaning as the **boldface** word or expression in the phrase. Write that word on the line. Use a dictionary if necessary.*

1. an all-night **jamboree**   _____
2. **incite** a rebellion   _____
3. carefully **rearranged** files   _____
4. a **colossal** challenge   _____
5. a **productive** artist   _____
6. gave a conciliatory **answer**   _____
7. **introduce** the idea of running for office   _____
8. **indisputable** evidence   _____
9. **endorse** her sleazy scheme   _____
10. was **heartbroken** after the tragedy   _____
11. **horrendous** evidence of the wreck   _____
12. **hampered** with cares and troubles   _____
13. **baffled** by the answer   _____
14. **profess** his undying love   _____
15. her **unemotional** response to the tragedy   _____

Antonyms

*Choose the word or form of the word from this Unit that is most nearly opposite in meaning to the **boldface** word or expression in the phrase. Write that word on the line. Use a dictionary if necessary.*

1. an **inconsequential** threat   _____
2. a true **amateur** when it comes to modern art   _____
3. a **propitious** time to request a vacation   _____
4. a theory **weakened** by the results   _____
5. arrived at an **inconvenient** time   _____

Writing: Words in Action

Write a fund-raising letter explaining why the fine arts museum you work for wants to present an extensive new exhibition of Ansel Adams's works. Provide at least three reasons that Adams deserves a major exhibition. Use at least two details from the passage (pages 188–189) and three or more words from this Unit.

Vocabulary in Context

*Some of the words you have studied in this Unit appear in **boldface** type. Read the passage below, and then circle the letter of the correct answer for each word as it is used in context.*

A recent lavishly illustrated book on America's national parks **averred** in its subtitle that these sanctuaries were this country's "best idea." Yellowstone, whose protection President Ulysses Grant signed into law in March 1872, was the world's first national park. In 1916, after energetic support from conservationists like Theodore Roosevelt, President Woodrow Wilson inaugurated the National Park Service. The goal was to conserve the parks "by such means as will leave them unimpaired for the enjoyment of future generations."

In a happy stroke of fortune, the creation of America's national parks coincided with the growth of the nation's railroads. Rail lines like the Northern Pacific were quick to recognize that visitors to Yellowstone were unlikely to remain **impassive** after encounters with such spectacular landscapes. In colorful posters, the railroad guaranteed that tourists would return home amazed. The Northern Pacific even arranged a visit by landscape artist Thomas Moran. His painting *The Grand Canyon of Yellowstone* helped to persuade Congress to pass the bill establishing the national park.

Numerous other railroads forged **opportune** alliances with the parks springing up over the western states. For these enterprises, tourism was anything but a **grisly** prospect. On the contrary, it was an **incontrovertible** harbinger of growth, promise, and profit. The Great Northern Railway lobbied for the creation of Glacier National Park, the Southern Pacific for Yosemite, and the Santa Fe for the Grand Canyon. The railroads were so successful at lobbying for new parks that **nonplussed** environmentalists of the time became supporters of the railroads they had once seen as environmentally destructive.

---

1. To **aver** is to
- **a.** deny
- **b.** broach
- **c.** suggest
- **d.** assert

2. A person who is **impassive** may be described as
- **a.** passionate
- **b.** biased
- **c.** unemotional
- **d.** deliberate

3. An **opportune** alliance is
- **a.** convenient
- **b.** exploitative
- **c.** vengeful
- **d.** untoward

4. Something **grisly** would inspire
- **a.** appreciation
- **b.** horror
- **c.** curiosity
- **d.** mockery

5. The word **incontrovertible** most nearly means
- **a.** dubious
- **b.** rebellious
- **c.** unforgivable
- **d.** indisputable

6. If you are **nonplussed**, you are
- **a.** indifferent
- **b.** flabbergasted
- **c.** insulted
- **d.** ashamed

Read the following passage, taking note of the **boldface** words and their contexts. These words are among those you will be studying in Unit 14. It may help you to complete the exercises in this Unit if you refer to the way the words are used below.

Revolutionary Women
<Historical Nonfiction>

During the American Revolution, myriad colonial-era women, stirred by patriotic fervor, were not **amenable** to continuing their customary roles in the home. Instead, from the **inception** of the conflict, they influenced the trajectory of the war. The following is an account of a handful of these notable women.

For Mercy Otis Warren of Massachusetts, the pen was mightier than the sword; in the early 1770s, as tensions between England and the colonies escalated, Warren put her writing aptitude to work for the Patriots. One of

Mercy Otis Warren, circa 1763

her plays, *The Adulateur* (1772) **berated** Massachusetts's royal governor, while two others, *The Defeat* (1773) and *The Group* (1775), attacked Loyalists—colonists loyal to England. Warren's plays were reprinted in newspapers and converted many people living in the colonies to the Patriot cause.

Dicey Langston, only fifteen years old and a girl, seemed an improbable spy; yet for months this **precocious** South Carolinian outwitted the Loyalist troops encamped around her family's plantation. Langston surreptitiously relayed vital information to Patriot militias encamped in the countryside, and one night she traveled twenty miles on a **tortuous** country path and crossed a **turgid** stream to warn the militia of a Loyalist attack. Their attack thwarted, the Loyalists finally determined that Langston was a spy and **sadistically** attempted to shoot her father, but Langston shielded him with her body and **supplicated** with the soldiers to shoot her first. The soldiers, impressed with her bravery, let both Langstons live.

Not every woman of the Revolution was a Patriot. Flora MacDonald was born in Scotland and achieved notoriety by saving the life of "Bonnie Prince Charlie," a Scottish royal who aspired to the throne of England. MacDonald retained her **obdurate** support for the monarchy even after emigrating to North Carolina with her husband in 1774. She helped raise a Loyalist unit to fight the Patriots, but at the Battle of Moores Creek Bridge, the Loyalists lost. The **carnage** was horrific, and MacDonald's husband was imprisoned, so MacDonald, with her resources **depleted**, moved to Canada.

Some women of the Revolution, such as Catherine Schuyler, were saboteurs who

Mrs. Schuyler Burning Her Wheat Fields on the Approach of the British, by EG Leutze, 1852

deprived the invading army of supplies. Schuyler ignited the wheat fields on her land in upstate New York in 1777, when a voracious British army was approaching from Canada. Schuyler elected not to feed this **extraneous** force, but deciding to burn the wheat must have been difficult, for there was no **surfeit** of food in the colonies.

Women were excluded from the army, but a number of women masqueraded as men to serve in the Continental Army. The identity of one, a woman from Maine, is unknown, although she served until war's end; but another, Ann Bailey of Massachusetts, was found out after just three weeks. Bailey was fined and imprisoned for her deception, her record stating: "Discharged. Being a woman dressed in men's cloths." (sic) Sally St. Clair enlisted with her boyfriend and died during a British siege in Georgia. One of the best-known cases of a woman serving in the army is that of Deborah Sampson, who as "Robert Shurtliff" fought courageously and met all the **criteria** of a good soldier for eighteen months. A doctor treating her for an **infirmity** discovered her secret, but Sampson received an honorable discharge and even a pension for her service. Later she **expatiated** on her experiences during a lecture tour of her native New England.

Line engraving depicting Deborah Sampson as a soldier in the Continental army

Audio

For iWords and audio passages, go to SadlierConnect.com.

Definitions

Note the spelling, pronunciation, part(s) of speech, and definition(s) of each of the following words. Then write the appropriate form of the word in the blank space in the illustrative sentence(s) following.

1. carnage
(kär′ nəj)

(*n.*) large-scale slaughter or loss of life
Until television began to broadcast footage of war, the _____ of battle was rarely made real to far-off civilian populations.

2. criterion
(pl., **criteria**)
(krī tir′ ē ən)

(*n.*) a rule, test; a standard for judgment or evaluation
She was disturbed to discover that the _____ for the award was based on style, not substance.

3. deplete
(di plēt′)

(*v.*) to use up as a result of spending or consumption; to diminish greatly
Dwelling on all that could go wrong with your project will _____ your energy and courage.

4. extraneous
(ek strā′ nē əs)

(*adj.*) coming from the outside, foreign; present but not essential, irrelevant
One handy way to dodge a difficult question is to earnestly begin talking about something _____ to it.

5. inception
(in sep′ shən)

(*n.*) the beginning, start, earliest stage of some process, institution, etc.
He has worked here steadily since the firm's _____ and knows every facet of the job.

6. obdurate
(äb′ dyü rət)

(*adj.*) stubborn, unyielding
Vincent van Gogh was _____ in painting whatever he wished, even when no one would buy his work.

7. precocious
(pri kō′ shəs)

(*adj.*) showing unusually early development (especially in talents and mental capacity)
She showed a _____ talent for science.

8. sadistic
(sə dis′ tik)

(*adj.*) delighting in cruelty, excessively cruel
The Geneva Convention of 1949 outlawed torture and _____ treatment of prisoners of war.

9. **supplicate**
(səp′ lə kāt)

(v.) to beg earnestly and humbly
He chose to _____ for mercy not on his own account, but so that his wife would not suffer.

10. **tortuous**
(tôr′ chü əs)

(adj.) winding, twisted, crooked; highly involved, complex; devious
The cameras had to be portable in order to follow the athletes up the narrow and _____ path to the summit.

Using Context

*For each item, determine whether the **boldface** word from pages 202–203 makes sense in the context of the sentence. Circle the item numbers next to the six sentences in which the words are used correctly.*

1. My brother was happy with the amount of money he had earned that summer, but unfortunately he had to **deplete** most of his savings when his car needed extensive repairs.

2. The draft of the novel is still in its **obdurate** stage, so there is still time to make any changes before it goes to the printer.

3. The **tortuous** route we took on the road trip made for an efficient journey, but it didn't allow for much sightseeing.

4. When deciding which applicant to hire, the manager said it would come down to one **criterion**: who has the most experience.

5. After hours of arguing over where they would eat that night, he chose to **supplicate** and let his sister decide.

6. I normally prefer novels that stick to the story, but one of my favorite authors often includes **extraneous** details that, while not necessary, make the fictional world more real to me.

7. She showed a **precocious** talent for music before she could even read, but as she got older she preferred to focus her time on other hobbies.

8. My eyes welled up reading about the **carnage** caused by the earthquake, and I immediately started researching what I could do to help the families who lost their loved ones.

9. His **sadistic** laughter at the humiliation of his supposed friends revealed what a bully he really was.

10. As much as I love summer, I am always sad at the **inception** of the school year when I must say good-bye to my teachers and some of my friends.

Choosing the Right Word

*Select the **boldface** word that better completes each sentence. You might refer to the passage on pages 200–201 to see how most of these words are used in context. Note that the choices might be related forms of the Unit words.*

1. Given the kinds of tools the ancient Egyptians had to work with, the construction of the pyramids was an extraordinarily (**precocious, sadistic**) feat of engineering.

2. The prolonged drought has so (**depleted, supplicated**) the supplies in our reservoir that we may have to consider rationing water.

3. Passengers who are stranded on airplanes and forced to sit on the tarmac for hours may begin to think of airlines as (**extraneous, sadistic**) agencies.

4. The sales manager said she would apply only one (**criterion, carnage**) when assessing my plan for an advertising campaign: "Will it sell more mouthwash?"

5. Some journalists find researching materials in a library a (**tortuous, precocious**) task, preferring to sit and let their computers do the work.

6. Although she is not given to physical maltreatment, I think there is a truly (**precocious, sadistic**) element in her willingness to belittle others in public.

7. In the poems and prayers of many ancient cultures, human beings (**deplete, supplicate**) their deities for mercy and aid.

8. Since its (**carnage, inception**), the electric guitar has been a symbol of innovation, energy, and rebellion.

9. What disturbs the coach is not that Tom called the wrong play but that he refuses (**obdurately, precociously**) to admit that he made a mistake.

10. She tried to justify the lies she had told us, but I was unable to follow her (**obdurate, tortuous**) explanation.

11. At the very (**inception, criterion**) of my career, I set the goals and adopted the basic strategies that were to guide me through many years of outstanding success.

12. The (**inception, carnage**) caused each year by careless driving has become a major national scandal.

Completing the Sentence

Choose the word from the word bank that best completes each of the following sentences. Write the correct word or form of the word in the space provided.

carnage	deplete	inception	precocious	supplicate
criterion	extraneous	obdurate	sadistic	tortuous

1. Any child who can read at the age of three must be considered remarkably _____.

2. Her instructions told me exactly what I wanted to know, without a single _____ detail.

3. At the very _____ of his administration, the new president announced a list of the objectives he hoped to accomplish.

4. The stream followed a(n) _____ course as it twisted through the broken countryside.

5. Although I ask no special consideration for myself, I am not too proud to _____ on behalf of my children.

6. In spite of all our efforts to appeal to whatever human sympathies the kidnappers might have, they remained _____.

7. Although he announces piously how much it hurts him to punish people, I think he takes a(n) _____ pleasure in it.

8. Usefulness is not the only _____ for including words in this book, but it is the primary one.

9. My last date turned out to be such an expensive affair that my funds were sadly _____ for the rest of the month.

10. It is difficult to imagine the _____ that would result from an all-out war fought with nuclear weapons.

Definitions

Note the spelling, pronunciation, part(s) of speech, and definition(s) of each of the following words. Then write the appropriate form of the word in the blank space in the illustrative sentence(s) following.

1. amenable
(ə mē′ nə bəl)

(*adj.*) willing to follow advice or authority, tractable, submissive; responsive; liable to be held responsible

They will be _____ to your instructions as long as what you say makes sense.

2. berate
(bi rāt′)

(*v.*) to scold sharply

He removed the dog from obedience school when he discovered that the instructors had _____ it too harshly.

3. credulous
(krej′ ə ləs)

(*adj.*) too ready to believe, easily deceived

Though he was no dolt, his _____ nature and desire to believe the best of people made him quite easy to deceive.

4. expatiate
(ek spā′ shē āt)

(*v.*) to expand on, write or talk at length or in detail; to move about freely

We would like you to _____ on the interesting matters you only touched upon earlier today.

5. infirmity
(in fərm′ ə tē)

(*n.*) a weakness or ailment (physical, mental, moral, etc.)

Was his "deafness" an _____ of old age or a lack of interest in the conversation?

6. jejune
(ji jün′)

(*adj.*) lacking in nutritive value; lacking in interest or substance; immature, juvenile

My favorite teacher turned history from a _____ study of the distant past into a relevant topic of discussion.

7. potpourri
(pō pü rē′)

(*n.*) a collection of diverse or miscellaneous items; a general mixture; petals mixed with spices for scent

The furniture was a _____ of hand-me-downs from my father's parents and my stepmother's aunt.

8. sententious
(sen ten′ shəs)

(*adj.*) self-righteous, characterized by moralizing; given to use of maxims or adages; saying much in few words, pithy

The _____ advice, though wise, was too general to help their particular situation.

9. **surfeit**
(sər′ fət)

(*n.*) an excess or overindulgence, as in eating or drinking, causing disgust; (*v.*) to feed or supply with anything to excess

A _____ of food, drink, and clowning puts Shakespeare's Falstaff in disgrace with the King.

10. **turgid**
(tər′ jid)

(*adj.*) swollen, bloated, filled to excess; overdecorated or excessive language

The heavy rains turned the fields swampy and the river _____.

Using Context

*For each item, determine whether the **boldface** word from pages 206–207 makes sense in the context of the sentence. Circle the item numbers next to the six sentences in which the words are used correctly.*

1. The restaurant manager was alarmed to find that she had a **surfeit** of silverware on opening day and had to run out to buy some more.

2. Because she looks young and naïve, many salespeople assume that she has a **credulous** nature and try to upsell her on their products, but she always sees through such deceptions.

3. I don't feel like it's truly fall until I can **expatiate** the scent of a baking apple pie permeating the house.

4. While the office manager is quite easygoing, we all know that he will **berate** anyone who shows up even a minute late.

5. I heard my mother's **turgid** footsteps and knew she was in a hurry to get somewhere.

6. She claims that her poor memory is an unfortunate **infirmity**, but I think she just doesn't listen to most people in the first place.

7. "I don't understand how you can stand such **jejune** nonsense," said my English professor as he looked at my latest video game.

8. Your **sententious** attitude only serves to show disrespect to both your peers and members of authority and does not, as you say, display an independent spirit.

9. The international friends have regular potluck dinner parties where the food served is a **potpourri** of delicious delicacies from around the world.

10. The children were rowdy and defiant when their parents were around, but the babysitter found the children to be quite **amenable** to her rules when their parents left.

Choosing the Right Word

*Select the **boldface** word that better completes each sentence. You might refer to the passage on pages 200–201 to see how most of these words are used in context. Note that the choices might be related forms of the Unit words.*

1. Although *Gone with the Wind* won a Pulitzer Prize, critics often (**berate, expatiate**) the novel for its stereotypical portrayals of African Americans.

2. Vic is so (**sententious, credulous**) that he actually believed me when I said that I had invented an automatic composition-writing machine.

3. In her efforts to impress moral principles on the children, she made use of (**turgid, sententious**) formulas, such as "To be good, do good."

4. You cannot dismiss everything he says as (**amenable, jejune**) simply because he is young and lacks experience of the world.

5. I have had my (**surfeit, infirmity**) of excuses and evasions; now I want action.

6. Although he (**expatiates, berates**) fluently on the need for a new community action program, I have yet to see him do anything to bring it about.

7. Our dean is a strict disciplinarian, but I have always found her (**amenable, turgid**) to reasonable requests.

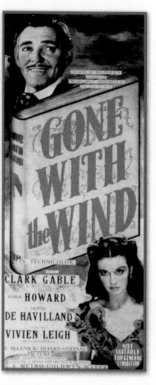

8. Few things are more tragic than to see a great mind fall victim to a serious (**surfeit, infirmity**).

9. Instead of constantly (**berating, expatiating**) the children, why don't you try to explain quietly and clearly how you expect them to behave?

10. A well-known actor submitted his poems to a publisher, who deemed the verses (**credulous, jejune**) and tedious.

11. Her (**credulous, turgid**) conversation, with its exaggerated adjectives and far-fetched figures of speech, made me realize once and for all the virtues of plain speaking.

12. I think the class show will be much more effective if it has a constant theme running through it, instead of being just a (**potpourri, surfeit**) of songs, dances, and sketches.

Completing the Sentence

Choose the word from the word bank that best completes each of the following sentences. Write the correct word or form of the word in the space provided.

amenable	credulous	infirmity	potpourri	surfeit
berate	expatiate	jejune	sententious	turgid

1. "How do you expect your mind to grow when you feed it solely on the _____ pap that comes out of the television?" I asked pointedly.

2. When I asked him why he wasn't going to the prom, he answered in his usual _____ style, "No dough, no dance!"

3. It's painful to have to listen to her _____ on her own virtues when I'm dying to give some fascinating details about my own life and accomplishments.

4. The more _____ you are, the easier it will be for swindlers and con artists to hoodwink you.

5. The simple and austere prose of the Gettysburg Address stands in stark contrast to the _____ and overblown rhetoric of a great many other nineteenth-century orations.

6. You deserve to be severely _____ for your misbehavior during such a solemn ceremony.

7. When my stubborn younger brother proved so _____ to my request, I began to suspect that he had some special reason for wanting to please me.

8. Wouldn't you agree that television has been _____ lately with sitcoms and reality shows?

9. One of the benefits I gained from my summer job in the new hospital was learning to be patient with people suffering from various types of _____.

10. Our reading program this term is a delightful _____ of stories, essays, poetry, and drama from many different periods.

Synonyms

*Choose the word or form of the word from this Unit that is the same or most nearly the same in meaning as the **boldface** word or expression in the phrase. Write that word on the line. Use a dictionary if necessary.*

1. a **guideline** by which to judge the entries _____
2. **elaborate** on his favorite subject _____
3. gave a **fiendish** chuckle _____
4. a **gifted** youngster _____
5. the horrendous **bloodbath** from the war _____
6. feeling the **afflictions** of aging _____
7. **entreat** the captain on behalf of her son _____
8. a **meandering**, complicated plot _____
9. was present at the product **launch** _____
10. an **unsophisticated** view of history _____
11. a **mélange** of spices _____
12. not **acquiescent** to that idea _____
13. a **didactic** way of addressing the group _____
14. too **naïve** to perceive trickery _____
15. the **overblown** rhetoric of the politician _____

Antonyms

*Choose the word or form of the word from this Unit that is most nearly opposite in meaning to the **boldface** word or expression in the phrase. Write that word on the line. Use a dictionary if necessary.*

1. **complimented** for his actions _____
2. **flexible** at the negotiating table _____
3. **pertinent** details in the instructions _____
4. had a **dearth** of food for the holiday party _____
5. **replenish** our natural resources _____

Writing: Words in Action

Write an editorial—pro or con—from the perspective of a colonial woman about the actions of the revolutionary women mentioned in the passage. Use examples from your reading (refer to pages 200–201), personal experiences, and prior knowledge to support your opinion. Use three or more words from this Unit.

Vocabulary in Context

*Some of the words you have studied in this Unit appear in **boldface** type. Read the passage below, and then circle the letter of the correct answer for each word as it is used in context.*

Born in Albany, New York, in 1757, Elizabeth Schuyler was the offspring of two prominent colonial families. Her father, Philip Schuyler, was a Revolutionary War general, and her mother, Catherine Van Rensselaer, came from one of New York's wealthiest families. Albany was home to a **potpourri** of cultivated, aristocratic families, and Elizabeth enjoyed a childhood of stimulating company and class privilege. She met Alexander Hamilton, then General Washington's chief aide, in the winter of 1779 and married him a few months later.

Alexander, of course, would soon embark on a distinguished career as a founding father of the republic, serving as a Congressman, Secretary of the Treasury, a member of Washington's Cabinet, coauthor of the *Federalist Papers*, and principal author of Washington's *Farewell Address*. What is perhaps less well known is that Elizabeth assisted him every step of the way. She helped Alexander with his writing, critiqued his ideas, and drafted correspondence to foreign heads of state, all while managing a household with eight children.

In 1804, a **credulous** Alexander accepted a duel with Aaron Burr over disputed insults, an "affair of honor." When Alexander died from the resulting wound, his family's bank account had been **depleted**, mainly on the purchase of a new Manhattan estate. Facing what could have could have been a **jejune** life of poverty, Elizabeth instead dedicated her remaining years to charity work and the preservation of her husband's historical record. As the federalism espoused by Alexander gradually fell out of favor, Elizabeth became an **obdurate** defender of his legacy. In response to praise about her efforts on behalf of orphans, Elizabeth gave a humbly **sententious** reply: Her Maker had given her a duty "and the skill and inclination to perform it."

---

1. A **potpourri** of families is
   a. diverse
   b. sophisticated
   c. upper class
   d. deeply rooted

2. If you are **credulous**, you are
   a. believable
   b. honorable
   c. indebted
   d. gullible

3. To **deplete** a bank account is to
   a. fund it
   b. close it
   c. use up the money
   d. withdraw some money

4. A **jejune** life lacks
   a. privilege
   b. interest
   c. obstacles
   d. normalcy

5. The word **obdurate** most nearly means
   a. unpleasant
   b. hardened
   c. open
   d. stubborn

6. A **sententious** reply is
   a. self-important
   b. well reasoned
   c. pithy
   d. terse

*Read the following passage, taking note of the **boldface** words and their contexts. These words are among those you will be studying in Unit 15. It may help you to complete the exercises in this Unit if you refer to the way the words are used below.*

New Tribe Discovered in Amazon
<Newspaper Article>

by Humberto Ronaldo Fonseca
PORTO VELHO, Brazil

Brazilian officials have released photographs of an extremely isolated tribe living deep in the Amazon rainforest in western Brazil. The images show a community of approximately 150 people with a proud and fearless **demeanor**. The photos also indicate that the tribe has metal goods, such as a machete knife and a pan, and **sartorial** tools such as needles and thimbles. It is likely these items were acquired through inter-tribal trading of goods or resources, experts say. They believe the people shown in the photographs are descendants of tribes that retreated into the jungle a century ago. Christine Morris, of the travel-adventure magazine *Exploring*, took the photographs. Tribal advocates see the release of such photos as a tool to **thwart** illegal logging. Many Brazilian tribes use the jungle as a **bulwark** against contact with the modern world.

Little **definitive** information is known about the day-to-day ways of this and other indigenous people, according to Amazon Today (AT). The group is expert on **enigmatic** tribes so isolated that their members only recently came in contact with outsiders, although many are aware of airplanes from overflights. AT's Web site counters notions of indigenous tribes as primitive survivors. "Everyone has neighbors, even when they're some distance away, and they'll know who their neighbors are. No man is an island," says the group's Web site. Amazon Today is **adamant** that the tribes "are not backward or 'Stone Age'; they just live differently."

Anthropologists, propelled by **presentiment**, have attempted to study the disappearing tribes. Many tribes, like the one just photographed, move easily throughout a vast area and adapt to new locations due to the region's consistent climate, which means plants and animals are alike throughout. The common environment accounts for a similarity in customs and lifestyles among Amazonian tribes, according to Maria Teresa Santiago, the head of outreach at Amazon Today.

The nomadic tribes move from place to place, often in boats made of hollowed tree trunks that they propel with handmade paddles, experts say. The people survive by hunting; by gathering wild fruits, nuts and honey; by fishing with woven baskets; and by cultivating small gardens. When the soil is depleted, they move on. Usually, the men hunt and fish while the women tend crops. Children assist the adults and learn how to thrive in their environment, as almost all of the food, clothing, and medicines for the tribes come from jungle resources. The **onus** for passing down knowledge of the jungle's medicinal assets rests with medicine men. As long as isolated tribes have access to natural resources and territory, they have told researchers they "live well," according to a 2007 study by Amazon Today. Many of these tribes made deliberate decisions to remain apart from outsiders after the so-called rubber boom, during which indigenous people were exploited for their land and labor for rubber plantations. Although Western demand meant a **profligate** lifestyle for some Europeans who owned plantations, the owners failed to **remit** profits to local tribes.

Contact, whether **impromptu** or carefully planned, comes with problems, particularly disease. Many indigenous peoples lack the

requisite immunities to diseases brought in from the outside world. During the past 100 years, from the time records were kept, 50 percent of a tribe's members died within a year of contact. Today, Brazilian officials say they have long known of so-called uncontacted or isolated tribes in the area where the latest tribe was photographed. When outsiders leave metal pots, tools, and machetes behind in areas frequented by these tribes, the indigenous people take the objects, often without revealing themselves. Since the late 1980s, out of **deference** to their way of life, Brazilian officials have monitored the tribes and **curtailed** efforts to contact them. This policy **mollified** an international **brouhaha** over the tribes' dismal survival rates after contact.

Amazon Rain Forest

Brazil

A road winds through a logged area in the Brazilian rain forest.

Audio

For iWords and audio passages, go to SadlierConnect.com.

Definitions

Note the spelling, pronunciation, part(s) of speech, and definition(s) of each of the following words. Then write the appropriate form of the word in the blank space in the illustrative sentence(s) following.

1. brouhaha
(brü' hä hä)

(*n.*) a confused hodgepodge of sounds, hubbub; an uproar or commotion that goes far beyond what is justified

After the _____ had finally subsided, we asked the group to give us a written list of all their complaints.

2. choleric
(käl' ər ik)

(*adj.*) easily made angry, bad-tempered

His _____ temperament and erratic behavior made him an ineffective ruler.

3. curtail
(kər tāl')

(*v.*) to cut short, bring to a halt, or end sooner than expected; to reduce

It is time yet again to _____ the flow of unsolicited nonsense that somehow reaches me as email.

4. demeanor
(di mē' nər)

(*n.*) the way a person behaves, overall impression made by comportment, manner, etc.; facial appearance, mien

Charles Dickens's Mr. Pickwick has such a cheerful and sympathetic _____ that few can resist him.

5. impromptu
(im prämp' tü)

(*adj., adv.*) without preparation, offhand, suddenly or hastily done; (*n.*) an extemporaneous composition or remark; a minimal piece suggestive of improvisation

His _____ speech allowed him to express not only what he was thinking but also what he was feeling.

An _____ by Schubert may not stun you at first, but you'll find hours later that you haven't forgotten it.

6. mawkish
(mô' kish)

(*adj.*) excessively and objectionably sentimental; having a mildly sickening flavor

Jimmy Stewart's portrayal of his character in *It's a Wonderful Life* was poignant without being _____.

7. presentiment
(pre zen' tə ment)

(*n.*) a vague sense of approaching misfortune

Ironically, by denying their _____, they made their worst fears come true.

8. remit
(ri mit')

(*v.*) to send or hand in (as money); to cancel (as a penalty or punishment), forgive; to lessen, diminish; postpone, defer

They would _____ a certain sum each year to a local charity.

9. sartorial
(sär tôr′ ē əl)

(*adj.*) of or pertaining to a tailor or his work; having to do with clothes or dress (especially men's)

Paging through historical picture books is a fascinating study in _____ standards through the centuries.

10. thwart
(thwôrt)

(*v.*) to oppose successfully; to prevent, frustrate

Our dog's friendliness would _____ the sternest efforts of the most expensive guard-dog trainer.

Using Context

*For each item, determine whether the **boldface** word from pages 214–215 makes sense in the context of the sentence. Circle the item numbers next to the six sentences in which the words are used correctly.*

1. His lack of **sartorial** sense is obvious in his mismatched outfit and clunky shoes.

2. I warned that I would **curtail** the meeting and make the final decision on my own if we veered off into unrelated topics.

3. Her **presentiment** at hearing that her brother had arrived for a surprise visit was clearly shown in the wide smile on her face.

4. "I must **remit** that you pay for the damage done to my car window," said the neighbor to the parents of the boy whose baseball had crashed through the glass minutes earlier.

5. Many people wanted her as a tutor because of her patience and **choleric** manner when explaining concepts that students were struggling with.

6. He carefully made an **impromptu** plan for how he would propose, timing the schedule of events down to the minute and planning the exact number of flowers to buy.

7. I hoped that the birthday card to my friend did not seem overly **mawkish**, but I wanted to express my sincerest gratitude for everything she has done for me.

8. As I watched the rain falling outside, I reminded myself that nothing would **thwart** my goal of going for a run every day this week.

9. Before she even opened her mouth to say hello, I could tell by her pleasant **demeanor** that we would become fast friends.

10. The **brouhaha** caused by the new store opening in town showed that this was still a divisive issue for the residents.

Choosing the Right Word

*Select the **boldface** word that better completes each sentence. You might refer to the passage on pages 212–213 to see how most of these words are used in context. Note that the choices might be related forms of the Unit words.*

1. I am a great admirer of Charles Dickens, but even I must admit that the death of Little Nell in *The Old Curiosity Shop* is too (**sartorial, mawkish**) to be truly effective.

2. The recent (**presentiment, brouhaha**) over the choice of a host for our local beauty pageant seemed to me nothing more than a "tempest in a teapot."

3. The special privileges extended to the senior class have not been entirely withdrawn, but they have been sharply (**thwarted, curtailed**) for the rest of the term.

4. His aggressive and suspicious (**presentiment, demeanor**) led the detectives to suspect that he was more involved with the crime than he alleged.

5. When we received bad news from home, we had to (**remit, curtail**) our vacation and return a few days earlier than planned.

6. He delivered his speech poorly, but since he was the best-dressed man on the dais that afternoon, he enjoyed a (**sartorial, mawkish**) if not an oratorical triumph.

7. When you have a feeling that something is about to happen, you may unconsciously act in a way that will help the (**brouhaha, presentiment**) to come true.

8. Far from being (**impromptu, sartorial**), all those jokes and wisecracks you hear on talk shows are usually prepared by professional writers and are carefully rehearsed.

9. Her constant blustering and (**impromptu, choleric**) behavior may be no more than an unconscious attempt to conceal her lack of self-confidence.

10. After tallying the bills and invoices, the young newlyweds began the odious task of (**remitting, curtailing**) payments to the wedding planner, florist, and photographer.

11. We all admired her (**demeanor, presentiment**), which was dignified without any suggestion of superiority or stuffiness.

12. Their efforts to win the game by a last-minute trick play were (**thwarted, remitted**) when our alert safety intercepted the deep pass.

Completing the Sentence

Choose the word from the word bank that best completes each of the following sentences. Write the correct word or form of the word in the space provided.

brouhaha	curtail	impromptu	presentiment	sartorial
choleric	demeanor	mawkish	remit	thwart

1. By talking so much about your _____ that "we're going to have an accident," you are making me nervous and preventing me from driving properly.

2. The candidate seems much more human and appealing when she delivers a(n) _____ speech than when she reads a prepared text.

3. Attached to every bill for the merchandise was a brief notice asking the customer to _____ payment promptly.

4. At first, I was glad to see my old classmate again, but he embarrassed me with his _____ talk about "those wonderful, golden school days."

5. We heard that the South High fans were planning to "kidnap" our mascot before the game, and we were determined to _____ them.

6. When the chairperson saw that the speakers were becoming more heated without offering any new facts or ideas to clarify the situation, she decided to _____ the discussion period.

7. In his black jacket, light gray slacks, and tailored sport shirt, he was a model of _____ elegance.

8. I think that the phrase "having a short fuse" aptly describes my new boss's _____ and curmudgeonly disposition.

9. I was surprised that so trivial an incident should have provided such a fearful _____ in the popular press.

10. Throughout the trial she maintained a(n) _____ of quiet dignity and confidence that made a favorable impression on the jury.

Definitions

Note the spelling, pronunciation, part(s) of speech, and definition(s) of each of the following words. Then write the appropriate form of the word in the blank space in the illustrative sentence(s) following.

---

1. adamant
(ad′ ə mənt)

(*adj.*) firm in purpose or opinion, unyielding, obdurate, implacable, inflexible; (*n.*) an extremely hard substance

The government was _____ in its refusal to negotiate with terrorists.

When writers referred to _____ centuries ago, they sometimes meant diamonds or magnetized iron.

---

2. bulwark
(bəl′ wərk)

(*n.*) a strong defense or protection, a solid wall-like structure for defense; (*v.*) to provide such defense or protection

The only evidence of a once thriving civilization is this _____ against the ocean tides.

The singer's staff had to _____ him against fans who wanted to get near him.

---

3. cloy
(kloi)

(*v.*) to spoil or destroy an appetite by too much indulgence, especially in sweet or rich things; to glut, satiate, surfeit

A steady diet of videos began to _____, and I was glad to begin a book.

---

4. deference
(def′ ər əns)

(*n.*) courteous yielding to the wishes and ideas of another person; great respect marked by submission, as to a superior

Some moderate _____ is due the boss, but too much can seem to conceal other motives.

---

5. definitive
(də fin′ ə tiv)

(*adj.*) conclusive, final, the limit of what can be done

She is working on what she hopes will be the _____ biography of Emily Dickinson.

---

6. enigmatic
(en ig mat′ ik)

(*adj.*) puzzling, perplexing, inexplicable, not easily understood

He was staring me straight in the eye, neither pleased nor displeased, his expression _____.

---

7. mollify
(mäl′ ə fī)

(*v.*) to soften; to calm, allay (as an emotion); reduce in intensity

The senator hoped to _____ her angry public, but nothing she said was likely to get her reelected.

---

8. onus
(ō′ nəs)

(*n.*) something that is heavy or burdensome (especially an unwelcome responsibility); a stigma; blame

The _____ is on us to meet the deadline.

---

9. **profligate**
(präf′ lə gət)

(*adj.*) given over to dissipation and self-indulgence, immoral; recklessly extravagant; (*n.*) a person given to wild spending

He was the family's _____ son, the charming one from whom nothing was expected.

She was a _____, and no matter how much money she earned, she always spent more than she had.

10. **requisite**
(rek′ wə zit)

(*adj.*) needed, necessary, regarded as essential or indispensable

If you have the _____ coordination and an ear for music, I'll pay for your first year of dance instruction.

Using Context

*For each item, determine whether the **boldface** word from pages 218–219 makes sense in the context of the sentence. Circle the item numbers next to the six sentences in which the words are used correctly.*

1. The **deference** that the toddler shows to his parents proves that they have not effectively been able to set boundaries.

2. High heels seem almost a **requisite** part of women's fashion these days, but since I can barely walk in them I choose to break the rules by wearing flats.

3. I am sorry that you're having trouble in math class, but I must remain **adamant** in my decision to not let you copy my homework.

4. As I'm not a doctor, I cannot give a **definitive** diagnosis, but I would assess your lack of motivation and desire to watch television all day as laziness.

5. Your **profligate** reaction to my promotion makes me think you are simply jealous of me.

6. Her explanation of the events was so **enigmatic** that I suspected she was hiding something.

7. After being left out in the sun all day, the potato salad started to **cloy**, so I tossed it in the trash to prevent people from eating it.

8. He thinks he can **mollify** my anger by showering me with gifts and compliments, but he has yet to give me the one thing that will truly make me feel better: an apology.

9. Pharmacists must work meticulously, for the **onus** is on them to make sure people get the correct dosage of medications.

10. The **bulwark** between the two teams is no longer just a friendly rivalry but has devolved into a hostile need for each team to beat the other.

Choosing the Right Word

Select the **boldface** word that better completes each sentence. You might refer to the passage on pages 212–213 to see how most of these words are used in context. Note that the choices might be related forms of the Unit words.

1. Expressing his mystification at the Soviet Union, Churchill referred to it as a "riddle wrapped in a mystery inside an (**enigma, onus**)."

2. There are so many aspects to Shakespeare that there will never be a truly (**definitive, enigmatic**) study of his work.

3. I came to realize that the demure little woman who never raised her voice had a will of pure (**adamant, deference**).

4. Scholastic proficiency, emotional stability, and a genuine interest in young people are (**profligate, requisite**) qualities for a good teacher.

5. The scientific method stands as a(n) (**bulwark, onus**) against the tides of irrationality and superstition.

6. After years of (**profligate, enigmatic**) living, he experienced a profound change of heart and devoted the rest of his life to serving humanity.

7. Her bitter anger was eventually (**mollified, cloyed**) by our skillful appeals to her vanity.

8. Our coach is (**adamant, requisite**) that we not drink sugary sports drinks before a game and insists that we hydrate only with water.

9. I am surprised that he now shows such exaggerated (**deference, adamant**) to people whose "aristocratic" pretensions he has always regarded with contempt.

10. Her unvarying sweetness, like a diet composed entirely of desserts, does begin to (**cloy, mollify**) after a while.

11. Though my sister has many close friends, she is a(n) (**bulwark, enigma**) who is reluctant to share her private thoughts and feelings.

12. Let us place the (**deference, onus**) for the defeat where it belongs—on each and every one of us!

Completing the Sentence

Choose the word from the word bank that best completes each of the following sentences. Write the correct word or form of the word in the space provided.

adamant	cloy	definitive	mollify	profligate
bulwark	deference	enigmatic	onus	requisite

1. How can you watch those silly reruns of old family shows day after day without being _____ by their gooey sentimentality?

2. In _____ to the wishes of the widow, the funeral services will be brief, and no eulogy will be delivered.

3. He was so _____ with his inheritance that he consumed in a few years the fortune it had taken his parents a lifetime to accumulate.

4. I see no point in your applying for that job when it is perfectly clear that you lack the _____ qualifications.

5. Although we must have armed forces to protect the country, the most important _____ of national security is the devotion of the people to our democratic institutions.

6. She was willing to compromise on many issues, but elimination of the ridiculous requirements for those jobs was the one point on which she was absolutely _____.

7. The circumstances surrounding the death are so _____ that the police are not even sure that a crime was committed.

8. Somehow, whenever more money is needed for our club activities, the _____ of raising it always seems to fall on me.

9. We are still looking for a(n) _____ answer to the question of whether or not our prisons can rehabilitate as well as punish.

10. By getting the students to apologize for their thoughtless discourtesy, we _____ the anger of the elderly elevator operator.

Synonyms

*Choose the word or form of the word from this Unit that is the same or most nearly the same in meaning as the **boldface** word or expression in the phrase. Write that word on the line. Use a dictionary if necessary.*

1. a heavy **burden** to bear _____

2. a **maudlin** love story _____

3. sweet snacks **slaked** her appetite for dinner _____

4. challenge his **tailoring** standards _____

5. **pacify** the unruly villagers _____

6. a solemn and mournful **bearing** _____

7. would **pay** the fine _____

8. the **hullabaloo** outside the door _____

9. **obstruct** a complicated plot _____

10. a clearly expressed yet **mystifying** statement _____

11. felt protected inside the **fortress** _____

12. his **crotchety** reaction to any interruption _____

13. accused of having **improvident** habits _____

14. received an **omen** _____

15. show **respect** for the office of the presidency _____

Antonyms

*Choose the word or form of the word from this Unit that is most nearly opposite in meaning to the **boldface** word or expression in the phrase. Write that word on the line. Use a dictionary if necessary.*

1. **extend** our time together _____

2. is **flexible** about her decision _____

3. gave a **tentative** answer _____

4. **superfluous** skills for the job _____

5. a **prepared** statement for the press _____

Writing: Words in Action

What responsibility do nations have to respect indigenous people's way of life and protect the areas where they live? In a brief essay, support your opinion with details from your reading (refer to pages 212–213), studies, and prior knowledge. Write at least three paragraphs, and use three or more words from this Unit.

Vocabulary in Context

*Some of the words you have studied in this Unit appear in **boldface** type. Read the passage below, and then circle the letter of the correct answer for each word as it is used in context.*

Almost thirty years ago, an **enigmatic** group of people walked out of the Amazon forest and into the dusty streets of San José de Guaviare, Colombia. Nobody knew who they were, and nobody could ask them, since the newcomers spoke a language that no one understood. Finally, municipal authorities found a translator, an indigenous boy who had been raised by a colonist family and thus spoke Spanish. Newspapers around the world soon carried the story: the Nukak Makú, perhaps America's last uncontacted nomadic tribe, had abandoned their forest home and entered the twentieth century.

The problem, explained the Nukak, was not of their own making. Even in that remote region of southern Colombia, a frontier was steadily advancing into the Nukak's forest habitat. Colonists, missionaries, and oil exploration companies moved ever deeper into the Amazon, displacing game, felling trees, and contaminating rivers. When the newcomers showed no regard for the ways their invasion would **curtail** others' way of life, the Nukak had little choice but to try their luck in the nearest town.

Inevitably, the transition has been difficult for the Nukak—and for their new neighbors, the citizens of San José. A recurring issue is food. As a displaced people, the Nukak receive monthly rations of rice, eggs, and sugar, a diet that can **cloy** if one is used to eating meat, fish, fruit, and nuts. When their rations run out, the Nukak, who have no concept of private property, help themselves to whatever they find growing in nearby farms. Government officials serve as mediators, working to **mollify** the aggrieved farmers, but it would only take one **choleric** individual to shatter the town's fragile peace. Through it all, the Nukak maintain their friendly spirit and famously gentle treatment of children, a trait that some unkind observers have deemed **mawkish**.

---

1. An **enigmatic** group of people is

  a. tragic   **c.** poverty-stricken
  b. lost   **d.** puzzling

2. The word **curtail** most nearly means

  a. bring to a halt   **c.** undermine
  b. extend   **d.** expose

3. A diet can **cloy** if it

  a. undernourishes   **c.** is bland
  b. has new flavors   **d.** spoils the appetite

4. To **mollify** is to

  a. confront   **c.** yield
  b. calm   **d.** criticize

5. A **choleric** individual is

  a. diseased   **c.** easily angered
  b. selfish   **d.** misunderstood

6. The word **mawkish** most nearly means

  a. overly sentimental   **c.** inappropriate
  b. awkward   **d.** unduly lenient

Vocabulary for Comprehension
Part 1

*Read this passage, which contains words in **boldface** that appear in Units 13–15. Then choose the best answer to each question based on what is stated or implied in the passage. You may refer to the passage as often as necessary.*

Questions 1–10 are based on the following passage.

There is a passage in Act II of Samuel Beckett's *Waiting for Godot* in which the leading characters, Vladimir and Estragon, try to make the time go a little

(5) faster by calling each other names. They are both inventive, and several aimless arguments have left them with unresolved animosity to work off. They are **amenable** to the contest, and the exchange of

(10) **blatant**, **impromptu** insults quickly escalates. Just as they are beginning to enjoy themselves, Estragon pauses for a moment to think—and then, with an air of finality, calls Vladimir a critic. Vladimir is

(15) silenced. He does not waste time trying to think of a reply because there is no reply. The contest is over. There is no greater insult than to call someone a critic.

The line gets a big laugh—especially

(20) from any theater people in the audience. Estragon is obviously not an actor or any other kind of theater person, but as a character in a play, he is as entitled as anyone else to express his dislike for critics.

(25) Theater people look askance at critics. They regard critics as parasites, and nobody except critics would dispute the fundamental accuracy of the observation: It is easy to imagine a world with theaters and

(30) no critics, but a world with critics and no theaters would be absurd.

The investment of time, effort, money, talent, and hope that goes into a new play is colossal and **tortuous**, and the

(35) producers who conjure up the means to pay the bills and keep the dream afloat are—as everyone who has seen *The Producers* can testify—heroes who would

sacrifice everything for their art. It is

(40) fiendishly difficult to write a good play, and it is even more fiendishly difficult to tell a good play from a bad play—until the curtain rises and the play is performed. The sets, the costumes, the wigs, the

(45) lights, the months of rehearsal, the gallons of blood, sweat, and tears that the actors pour into the quest for reality and reliable laughs—all these elements come together as the curtain rises. They constitute the

(50) real drama that revolves around the success or failure of the play, the drama played out by a cast of real people whose livelihood is governed by the promise of full houses and the threat of empty seats.

(55) After all that work, should a critic have, or wish to use, the power to close a play with 700 **jejune** words hurriedly cobbled together for his or her newspaper in time for the deadline? These **sententious**

(60) **connoisseurs** reliably fail to recognize greatness and insult what they cannot understand. Critics greeted Harold Pinter's *The Birthday Party* with "bewildered hysteria," and one critic, after seeing John

(65) Osborne's *Look Back in Anger*, expressed shock and disbelief that a colonel's daughter should have to live in such a shabby little apartment. Perhaps Estragon saw trouble ahead when he made his

(70) little joke. Various **choleric** critics thought their evening had been wasted after the London opening of *Waiting for Godot* and described the play **definitively** as a failure. In 1999 a later generation of

(75) critics took part in a British Royal National Theater poll that voted *Waiting for Godot* "the most significant English language play of the twentieth century."

1. The main purpose of the passage is to
   A) reconcile the conflicting interests of critics and theater people.
   B) question the right of theater people to complain about critics.
   C) question the role and function of the theater critic.
   D) end critical injustice toward theater people.

2. As it is used in line 10, the word "blatant" most nearly means
   A) flagrant.
   B) impassive.
   C) unbridled.
   D) dour.

3. It may reasonably be inferred from the second paragraph (lines 19–31) that the author
   A) is a theater critic.
   B) is a theater person.
   C) has a low opinion of critics.
   D) never goes to the theater.

4. Which choice provides the best evidence for the answer to the previous question?
   A) Lines 19–20 ("The line . . . audience")
   B) Lines 21–24 ("Estragon is . . . critics")
   C) Line 25 ("Theater . . . critics")
   D) Lines 26–31 ("They regard . . . absurd")

5. From the description of how a play would be received when the curtain rises (lines 39–54), the author suggests that
   A) the critics will decide whether the show is good or bad.
   B) the critics will influence the audience's response to the play.
   C) the audience will decide whether the show is good or bad.
   D) the audience's feelings will become irrelevant.

6. According to the third paragraph (lines 32–54), the real drama of an opening night
   A) is driven by fear of what tomorrow's newspaper will say.
   B) is in never knowing if the play is good or bad.
   C) involves real people whose jobs depend on the success of the play.
   D) occurs when the curtain rises.

7. As it is used in line 57, the word "jejune" most nearly means
   A) unkind.
   B) complaining.
   C) juvenile.
   D) banal.

8. As it is used in line 59, the word "sententious" most nearly means
   A) thoughtless.
   B) self-righteous.
   C) snobbish.
   D) succinct.

9. What is the author suggesting about the plays named in the last paragraph?
   A) The author recognizes their greatness immediately.
   B) The author admires them even if nobody else does.
   C) Theater people enjoy performing them.
   D) They are masterpieces that critics did not like.

10. Which word best describes the tone of the passage?
    A) Fair-minded
    B) Plaintive
    C) Persuasive
    D) Satirical

Vocabulary for Comprehension
Part 2

*Read this passage, which contains words in **boldface** that appear in Units 13–15. Then choose the best answer to each question based on what is stated or implied in the passage. You may refer to the passage as often as necessary.*

Questions 1–10 are based on the following passage.

Speech is fundamental to the way we define ourselves as human, but the origins of speech are impossible to trace with any useful degree of scientific
(5) accuracy. Spoken words leave no physical evidence, and there are no fossilized sentences waiting to be discovered.

It is impossible to imagine the development of human communities
(10) without spoken language—and equally impossible to imagine the creation of cities without written language. Writing is an invention, as the wheel and the printing press are inventions. Unlike spoken
(15) words, written language has left **prolific** physical evidence of its widespread use—as a way of making lists and creating inventories, for example. It has reduced the **onus** of memory, reached far
(20) beyond its capacity, and has given shape to thought. The flow of written language generated—and continues to generate—an accurate and detailed record of the daily lives, accomplishments, and
(25) aspirations of the citizens and creators of the first cities in the ancient world.

Writing and cities were both invented in Sumer, Southern Mesopotamia (modern-day western Iraq), between 3500 and
(30) 3000 BCE. The cities were built—a **herculean** task—in Sumer's fertile interior, and contractors needed a reliable means of ordering a constant supply of materials to be imported through ports hundreds of
(35) miles away in the Persian Gulf and the Mediterranean. They also needed records of their transactions. **Encumbered** with tracking the details of their transactions,

it was **incontrovertible** that contractors
(40) would need a way to record their dealings. Sumerian cuneiform was created to fulfill these requirements with no **extraneous** elements. Cuneiform took its name from the small, portable wedges (Latin: *cuneus*)
(45) of soft clay that provided the surfaces on which the writer worked with a sharpened reed to form designs, known as *glyphs, hieroglyphs*, and *pictographs*. At its **inception**, glyphs often conveyed literal
(50) elements applicable to the lists of commodities. It was an **inauspicious** start, but cuneiform rapidly developed in fluency and subtlety as glyphs came to symbolize ideas and syllables.

(55) Around 3200 BCE the introduction of phonograms—glyphs representing the sounds of a spoken language—released the full genius of Sumerian cuneiform. Until this moment it had been a communication
(60) device that was applicable to every language, but now the phonic element could be taken from *any* spoken language, and that gave Sumerian cuneiform the potential to *transform* into the written form
(65) any spoken language. Phoenician traders made Sumerian cuneiform their own and disseminated it throughout the Mediterranean. The Egyptians created a language so totally and uniquely
(70) Egyptian that it is still regarded by some commentators as the original form. The Greeks equipped it with an immensely powerful nonpictographic alphabet that consisted of an unprecedented range of
(75) consonants and vowels. This alphabet provided the **requisite** materials that built the epics of Homer; the plays of Sophocles, Euripides and Aeschylus; the histories of Herodotus and Xenophon; and the

(80)   philosophy of Plato. It was also the model
       for the Romans alphabet we use today.
           The development of writing allowed
       history and literature to be recorded. The
       story of Sumerian cuneiform—of how the
(85)   shopping lists of builders became the
       classical foundation of western civilization—
       is perhaps the greatest epic of all.

1. The primary purpose of the passage is to
   A) describe the characteristics of
       Sumerian cuneiform.
   B) trace the origins and development
       of early written language.
   C) demonstrate the principle that great
       things often have humble beginnings.
   D) show how Greek became the most
       important language of the ancient world.

2. As it is used in line 15, the word
   "prolific" most nearly means
   A) important.
   B) sparse.
   C) abundant.
   D) comprehensible.

3. In the first and second paragraphs (lines
   1–26), the author's discussion about
   speech and written language is intended to
   A) demonstrate the superiority of writing
       over spoken language.
   B) show that speech is natural and
       writing is artificial.
   C) compare and contrast the functions
       of speech and writing.
   D) emphasize that only humans can use
       language.

4. Which of the following summarizes the
   central idea of the second paragraph
   (lines 8–26)?
   A) Human communities are unimaginable
       without language.
   B) Writing was a way of increasing
       the power of memory.
   C) Evidence of early written language
       is plentiful.
   D) Writing played an essential part in
       recording the growth of cities.

5. Which choice provides the best evidence
   for the answer to the previous question?
   A) Lines 12–14 ("Writing is. . . inventions")
   B) Lines 14–18 ("Unlike . . example")
   C) Lines 18–21 ("It has . . . thought")
   D) Lines 21–26 ("The flow . . . world")

6. In the third paragraph (lines 27–54),
   the author focuses on the
   A) creation and development of cities.
   B) technique of writing in cuneiform.
   C) origins of Sumerian cuneiform.
   D) introduction of phonograms

7. As it is used in line 31, the word
   "herculean" most nearly means
   A) superhuman.
   B) inhuman.
   C) impossible.
   D) historic.

8. As it is used in line 51, the word
   "inauspicious" most clearly means
   A) impressive.
   B) unpromising.
   C) historically significant.
   D) vaguely promising.

9. The purpose of the fourth paragraph
   (lines 55–81) is to
   A) show how Sumerian cuneiform
       became the most important language
       in the ancient world.
   B) trace the way Sumerian cuneiform
       evolved into a variety of different
       languages.
   C) describe how the Romans created
       the alphabet we use today.
   D) stress the vital part played by
       phonograms in the development of
       Mediterranean languages.

10. The organizational structure of the passage
   is best described as
   A) cause and effect.
   B) comparison and contrast.
   C) chronological order.
   D) generalization and examples.

Synonyms

*From the word bank below, choose the word that has the same or nearly the same meaning as the **boldface** word in each sentence and write it on the line. You will not use all of the words.*

amenable	carousal	encumber	infirmity
aver	cloy	foment	opportune
berate	collate	impromptu	potpourri
broach	definitive	inception	requisite

1. When my friend lost his wallet this morning, I knew it was not an **appropriate** time to ask him for a donation to the charity.

   _____

2. His **spontaneous** speech was much more heartfelt than anything he could have prepared ahead of time.

   _____

3. She claimed she could not clean up due to her injured knee, but I suspected she was faking the **malady** to get out of helping.

   _____

4. Some bullies may not start fights themselves, but they will try to **instigate** trouble between good friends to cause a rift.

   _____

5. Even though the manager knew that he was experienced and qualified, he still had to complete the **obligatory** seminars.

   _____

6. After many sleepless hours of hearing the **jamboree** next door, I finally decided to call the front desk to complain about the noise.

   _____

7. When I asked for a letter of recommendation, my teacher assured me that he would **affirm** my standing as a model student.

   _____

8. My grandparents' display cabinet is a **hodgepodge** of statues, plaques, trophies, and a few vases and ornate bottles.

   _____

9. The principal did not want to **reprimand** anyone but would do so if any student was caught playing on a phone during the assembly.

   _____

10. Though I have yet to find an **exhaustive** book on the topic of my final paper, I expect to find all the necessary information online.

    _____

11. "I hate to **overload** you with so much housework, but we have unexpected company visiting tomorrow," my mother said to me.

    _____

12. The teacher's retirement party was bittersweet, for she had been with the charter school since its **outset**, and the building would not feel the same without her.

    _____

Two-Word Completions

Select the pair of words that best completes the meaning of each of the following sentences.

1. Friends hoped that the tearful _____ of the mother would soften the king's heart toward the young reprobates, but the dour old man _____ refused to yield to her entreaties.
   - **a.** demeanor . . . mawkishly
   - **b.** presentiments . . . obdurately
   - **c.** deference . . . disconsolately
   - **d.** supplications . . . adamantly

2. Once our fossil-fuel reserves are exhausted, they are gone forever. For that reason, we should try to _____ our use of these precious resources so that they are not _____ too quickly.
   - **a.** mollify . . . buttressed
   - **b.** remit . . . expatiated
   - **c.** curtail . . . depleted
   - **d.** abet . . . nonplussed

3. His start in life had been _____, but with hard work and a good deal of luck, he became a widely respected _____ of fine antique furniture and rare books.
   - **a.** profligate . . . criterion
   - **b.** inauspicious . . . connoisseur
   - **c.** sartorial . . . rejoinder
   - **d.** tortuous . . . bulwark

4. Though one of her parents reacted to the unexpected news of her death with a(n) _____ display of emotion, the other received it with all the _____ restraint of a true stoic.
   - **a.** sadistic . . . deferential
   - **b.** blatant . . . impassive
   - **c.** enigmatic . . . credulous
   - **d.** mawkish . . . choleric

5. No matter how much protective consumer legislation we pass to _____ would-be swindlers and con artists, there probably will always be _____ people around for them to prey on.
   - **a.** thwart . . . credulous
   - **b.** buttress . . . adamant
   - **c.** curtail . . . precocious
   - **d.** abet . . . jejune

6. Mozart was a(n) _____ youngster who wrote his first opera at the age of eleven. Though he was never as _____ a composer of theater music as some of his contemporaries, his output of stage works was by no means negligible.
   - **a.** credulous . . . profligate
   - **b.** enigmatic . . . blatant
   - **c.** precocious . . . prolific
   - **c.** sententious . . . incontrovertible

7. During the battle, the _____ had been horrendous. Where the fighting had been the fiercest, the bodies were piled three deep. It took days to complete the _____ task of burying the dead.
   - **a.** onus . . . mawkish
   - **b.** carnage . . . grisly
   - **c.** brouhaha . . . herculean
   - **d.** surfeit . . . turgid

Idioms

In the essay "Ansel Adams" (see pages 188–189), the author states that Adams barely "kept his head above water" when he was in school. Of course, Adams was not literally drowning; the saying is an idiom that means "managing to survive in a difficult situation."

Idioms are short, witty expressions that should be interpreted figuratively. You often can only grasp their meanings in context. Although idioms can add color and verve to writing, they should be used sparingly. When idioms are overused, they become clichés—expressions so commonplace that they have become stale and meaningless.

Choosing the Right Idiom

Read each sentence. Use context clues to figure out the meaning of each idiom in **boldface***. Then write the letter of the definition for the idiom in the sentence.*

1. I would **give my right arm** to be able to get a job working at a radio station. _____

2. My parents told me that if I **play my cards right**, they will help me buy a car. _____

3. His name **rings a bell**, but I'm not sure I can remember what movie he is in. _____

4. Jack decided to **bury the hatchet** with his brother and attend his birthday party. _____

5. When someone stole her secret formula for a new lotion, and all her research **went down the drain**, Claire was furious. _____

6. I hate to **split hairs** with you, but the trip took fifty-five minutes, not an hour. _____

7. I have to **hand it to you**, Doug: Your speech motivated everyone to participate in the savings program. _____

8. Well, I sure had fun vacationing at the beach, but it's **back to the salt mines** when I get home. _____

9. Jon was **on cloud nine** when he learned he had just been awarded a full scholarship. _____

10. Tori, who **had her heart set on** seeing the Broadway show, cried when the tickets were sold out. _____

a. wanted to do something very much; desired deeply

b. in an ecstatic state

c. end a fight or make peace

d. sounds familiar

e. be willing to sacrifice something of great value

f. give credit or acknowledgment

g. argue about insignificant details

h. was wasted, lost, or destroyed

i. return to the routine of work

j. do the correct thing to achieve a desired result

Classical Roots

quer, ques, quis—to
seek, ask

The root *quis* appears in **requisite** (page 219), which means "essential, necessary." Some other words based on related roots are listed below.

disquisition	inquisition	perquisite	query
inquest	inquisitive	prerequisite	requisition

From the list of words above, choose the one that corresponds to each of the brief definitions below. Write the word in the blank space in the illustrative sentence below the definition. Use an online or print dictionary if necessary.

1. a demand or application made in an authoritative way; to demand or call for with authority
The department made a(n) _____ for ten additional trucks.

2. to ask, ask about, inquire into; to express doubts about; a question or inquiry
If you have a question about that newspaper article, _____ the editor.

3. a legal inquiry before a jury (*"asking into"*)
The family of the victim attended the coroner's _____.

4. an extra payment; anything received for work besides regular compensation (*"that which is sought"*)
She enjoyed the _____ of her office.

5. a long and formal speech or writing about a subject
The scientist prepared a scholarly _____ on her findings.

6. a severe investigation; an official inquiry conducted with little regard for human rights
The zealous reporter turned a simple interview into a(n) _____.

7. that which is necessary beforehand; a qualification (*as for enrolling in a course*)
Beginning Spanish is a(n) _____ for advanced Spanish.

8. eager for knowledge; given to inquiry or research, curious; nosy, prying
A good detective needs a(n) _____ mind.

Synonyms   *Select the two words or expressions that are most nearly the same in meaning.*

1. **a.** spontaneous   **b.** evanescent   **c.** sanctimonious   **d.** hypocritical
2. **a.** coalition   **b.** pause   **c.** disagreement   **d.** hiatus
3. **a.** scour   **b.** saturate   **c.** foist   **d.** permeate
4. **a.** treachery   **b.** amnesty   **c.** perfidy   **d.** cowardice
5. **a.** autonomy   **b.** independence   **c.** recognition   **d.** decadence
6. **a.** diverse   **b.** dowdy   **c.** motley   **d.** enthusiastic
7. **a.** overt   **b.** implicit   **c.** unstated   **d.** gratuitous
8. **a.** approbation   **b.** approval   **c.** indifference   **d.** onus
9. **a.** clever   **b.** deleterious   **c.** gauche   **d.** graceless
10. **a.** profitable   **b.** extravagant   **c.** punctilious   **d.** grandiose
11. **a.** charm   **b.** enthrall   **c.** prate   **d.** horrify
12. **a.** clangor   **b.** weariness   **c.** lassitude   **d.** eagerness
13. **a.** repress   **b.** elicit   **c.** foment   **d.** cause
14. **a.** learn   **b.** recapitulate   **c.** summarize   **d.** disabuse
15. **a.** witty   **b.** discordant   **c.** choleric   **d.** scintillating

Antonyms   *Select the two words or expressions that are most nearly opposite in meaning.*

16. **a.** dilatory   **b.** expensive   **c.** prompt   **d.** fractious
17. **a.** extricate   **b.** rearrange   **c.** collate   **d.** embroil
18. **a.** supplicate   **b.** produce   **c.** aver   **d.** disavow
19. **a.** novel   **b.** insular   **c.** provincial   **d.** hackneyed
20. **a.** subservient   **b.** remarkable   **c.** imperious   **d.** impassive
21. **a.** resilient   **b.** politic   **c.** imprudent   **d.** abundant
22. **a.** gossamer   **b.** simple   **c.** agreement   **d.** dissension
23. **a.** torpid   **b.** intellectual   **c.** grisly   **d.** energetic
24. **a.** sadistic   **b.** decisive   **c.** humane   **d.** infirmity
25. **a.** harsh   **b.** enigmatic   **c.** deliberate   **d.** inadvertent

Two-Word Completions

Select the pair of words that best completes the meaning of each of the following sentences.

26. To our disappointment and _____, the author made a host of _____ demands in return for appearing at the book fair.
 a. penury … insurgent
 b. consternation … petulant
 c. adulation … beneficent
 d. odium … jejune

27. The _____ manner of the hostess, who greeted us with warmth, left us unprepared for the _____ behavior of the waitstaff.
 a. affable … brusque
 b. crass … meritorious
 c. bizarre … culpable
 d. adamant … bovine

28. My dog knows she can _____ treats from me because I am _____ to her sad, imploring eyes.
 a. transcend … jaded
 b. remonstrate … surreptitious
 c. exhort … unwieldy
 d. wheedle … susceptible

29. Rather than _____, the response of the boisterous crowd in the theater grew more and more _____.
 a. abominate … anomalous
 b. ferment … ignoble
 c. infringe … heinous
 d. abate … bombastic

30. Since the _____ of this complex project, the stage crew has executed its responsibilities with masterful _____.
 a. presentiment … occult
 b. brouhaha … equanimity
 c. inception … aplomb
 d. avarice … criterion

31. In its effort to encourage citizens to _____ their water use, the state government has _____ information to communities in counties that are at risk for drought.
 a. absolve … concocted
 b. curtail … disseminated
 c. satiate … contrived
 d. deplete … accrued

32. The opposing team's _____ arguments with the referee ignited the _____ fans and motivated them to demand an apology from the visitors.
 a. definitive … amenable
 b. impromptu … irrevocable
 c. blatant … nonplussed
 d. provocative … intemperate

Supplying Words in Context

To complete each sentence, select the best word from among the choices given. Not all words in the word bank will be used. You may modify the word form as necessary.

amnesty	axiomatic	decadence	fetter
anathema	coalition	elicit	ingratiate
anomalous	contraband	equitable	mitigate
austere	debase	erudite	nominal

33. Speaking in such a disrespectful way would have been _____ to my grandparents.

34. The police dogs are specially trained to be able to detect _____.

35. If people pay their overdue fines by the end of the month, they will be given _____ regarding late fees.

36. Both sides involved in the recent controversy were pleased by the _____ nature of the settlement.

37. In an effort to _____ himself, he offered to do all of the chores.

38. In order to tackle so difficult an issue, I recommend we seek to form a _____ of interested groups that will work together.

acculturation	castigate	flout	propensity
aspersion	desecrate	impugn	sedulous
assuage	enjoin	novice	surmise
astute	filch	proclivity	vicarious

39. For a(n) _____ at the sport, she performed extremely well.

40. Your _____ observation indicates a great deal of experience in this academic field.

41. To _____ the rules in such an obvious manner could not help but draw attention.

42. As I had been warned repeatedly, for the teacher to _____ me was completely understandable.

43. Speaking soothingly, my father sought to _____ my sorrowful feelings when my best friend moved to Europe.

44. The process of _____ may involve a complete immersion in the new language and habits of living.

Word Associations

*Select the word or expression that best completes the meaning of the sentence or answers the question, with particular reference to the meaning of the word in **boldface** type.*

45. Which of the following is the best remedy for being **callow**?
a. vitamins
b. sun and surf
c. time and experience
d. dancing lessons

46. The usual reason for **expurgating** a book is to
a. make it more readable
b. get rid of objectionable material
c. reissue it as an e-book
d. translate it into a foreign language

47. The distinguishing symptom of a person suffering from **megalomania** is
a. delusions of grandeur
b. problem dandruff
c. high blood pressure
d. chronic depression

48. Which of the following would by definition be guilty of **peculation**?
a. a coward
b. a judge
c. a philanthropist
d. an embezzler

49. You would **buttress** an argument if you wanted to
a. avoid it
b. repudiate it
c. incite it
d. support it

50. A person who is the **epitome** of wit
a. is an ideal example of wittiness
b. employs wit in a strange way
c. uses it maliciously
d. is actually not very witty

51. If you receive a **noncommittal** reply to a request, you will probably be
a. deeply depressed
b. in a state of uncertainty
c. ready to fight
d. overjoyed

52. Which of the following reactions would best characterize someone suffering from **ennui**?
a. a grimace
b. a smile
c. a wink
d. a yawn

53. A person who has suffered an **egregious** defeat has lost
a. as a result of unfair tactics
b. by a close score
c. conspicuously
d. gloriously

54. Good advice to someone who is constantly being **dunned** is
a. Pay your bills!
b. Don't waste fuel!
c. Keep your eye on the ball!
d. Go home!

55. Taking **umbrage** would be a reasonable reaction when you are
a. rewarded
b. introduced to someone new
c. complimented
d. insulted

56. To describe an author as **prolific** is to refer to the
a. author's relations with critics
b. number of books the author produced
c. author's nationality
d. size of the author's bank account

Choosing the Right Meaning

Read each sentence carefully. Then select the item that best completes the statement below the sentence.

57. Nothing in the politician's record could lead anyone to **ascribe** to him such outlandish views.

The word **ascribe** most nearly means
a. reverberate   b. revive   c. attribute   d. expiate

58. The children's reaction to the strange man's behavior only served to further **disconcert** the other people in the park.

The word **disconcert** most nearly means
a. replace   b. upset   c. aggrandize   d. praise

59. The polar expedition's exploits have been **blazoned** on the pages of history, inspiring generations of geographers and adventurers.

The best definition for the word **blazoned** is
a. displayed   b. cajoled   c. absolved   d. ignored

60. The **acrimonious** nature of our first encounter has made our relationship extremely difficult ever since.

The word **acrimonious** most nearly means
a. weird   b. magnanimous   c. herculean   d. hostile

61. The administrator said he would **expedite** our application so we would not have to spend the afternoon waiting for the results.

The word **expedite** most nearly means
a. facilitate   b. augment   c. berate   d. delay

62. Taking the medication for the full course prescribed will serve best to **ameliorate** the condition.

The word **ameliorate** is best defined as
a. lament   b. improve   c. contrive   d. disavow

63. The author's wise **precepts** laid out a philosophy of life that would be fruitful to use as a model.

The word **precepts** most nearly means
a. innuendos   b. caveats   c. infractions   d. principles

64. Our school principal projected such an **aura** of competence that no one questioned her ability to make the right decisions on behalf of the school.

The word **aura** most nearly means
a. cause   b. atmosphere   c. expectation   d. fear

65. The planners recognize the need to **transmute** the economic system from an industrial base to a concentration on providing services.

The word **transmute** most nearly means
a. inveigh   b. converge   c. accrue   d. change

The following is a list of all the words taught in the Units of this book. The number after each entry indicates the page on which the word is defined.